THE HOPE OF ISRAEL

THE LITTMAN LIBRARY OF
JEWISH CIVILIZATION

'*Get wisdom, get understanding:
Forsake her not and she shall preserve thee*'

PROV. 4: 5

*The Littman Library of Jewish Civilization is a registered UK charity
Registered charity no. 1000784*

The Hope of Israel

◆

MENASSEH BEN ISRAEL

English translation by
MOSES WALL, 1652

◆

Edited, with an introduction and notes, by

HENRY MÉCHOULAN
and
GÉRARD NAHON

Introduction and notes translated from the French by
RICHENDA GEORGE

The Littman Library of Jewish Civilization
in association with Liverpool University Press

The Littman Library of Jewish Civilization
in association with Liverpool University Press
4 Cambridge Street, Liverpool L69 7ZU, UK

www.liverpooluniversitypress.co.uk/littman

Managing Editor: Connie Webber

Distributed in North America by
Oxford University Press Inc., 198 Madison Avenue,
New York, NY 10016, USA

First published 1987 by Oxford University Press on behalf
of the Littman Library of Jewish Civilization

First issued in paperback 2004

Catalogue records for this book are available from the
British Library and the Library of Congress

ISBN 978-1-904113-20-1

Printed in Great Britain by
CPI Group (UK) Ltd, Croydon, CR0 4YY

Foreword

O U R sole aim in this undertaking has been to allow critical study of this work. So that it may be set again in its historical context, we have defended it from the unjust censure of certain commentators. We have not sought to produce a work of literature, but we have tried to present a difficult text as clearly as possible.

Spes Israelis and *Esperança de Israel*, as will be seen, were written in great haste for specific reasons, and it is because this fact was not known that critics of the writing of this book have been somewhat unsubtle in their judgements.[1] It is true that numerous quotations are inaccurate, the titles of some works inexactly given, and very many proper names incorrect or wrongly spelt. We have made the necessary corrections in the text, indicating the author's mistakes in the notes. Menasseh ben Israel has, moreover, often quoted biblical texts from memory. We have given the references for these implicit quotations in the body of the text. We have avoided the use of square brackets as far as possible.

Biblical verses given in the Introduction and Notes are taken from the Authorized Version of the Bible, 1611, unless otherwise mentioned.

In the Index, authors of the Middle Ages are listed, according to custom, by their forenames. We have also given patronymics and surnames with useful references.

In identifying certain quotations and clarifying various points we have had generous help from Jean Aubin, R. D. Barnett, F.-F. Blok, Leo Fuks and Renata Fuks-Mansfeld, Yosef Kaplan, Pilar Léon Tello, Pierre Nautin, A. K. Offenberg, Wilhelmina Christina Pieterse, Flor Romero de Nohra, Marie-France Schmidt, François Secret, Haïm Vidal Sephiha, B. N. Teensma, and Georges Vajda. We thank them all most warmly, not forgetting L. T. S. Littman and V. D. Lipman.

Without Professors Chaim Perelman and André Robinet this book would not have seen the light of day. We are very happy to take this opportunity of thanking them.

[1] See, for example, the opinion of K. Magnus, who writes in her *Jewish Portraits*, London, 1905, p. 75, that the writing of the work is indigestible, with the scholarship dumped on it without the slightest care. The whole thing gives the impression of having been 'machine made' rather than by hand.

The correction of the manuscripts and proofs has been in the patient and capable hands of Evelyne Méchoulan; this book is very largely hers.

HENRY MÉCHOULAN

GÉRARD NAHON

Contents

Abbreviations

Bibl. aut. esp.	*Biblioteca des autores españoles*
Enc. Jud.	*Encyclopaedia Judaica*
Jew. Enc.	*The Jewish Encyclopaedia*
REJ	*Revue des Études Juives*

Editions and Translations

Spanish

Miqweh Israel. Esto es Esperança de Israel. Obra con suma curiosidad conpuesta por Menasseh ben Israel theologo, y philosopho Hebreo. Trata del admirable esparzimiento de los Diez Tribus, y su infalible reduccion con los de mas, a la patria: con muchos puntos, y historias curiosas, y declaracion de varias prophecias, por el Author rectamente interpretadas. Dirigido a los Señores Parnassim del K. K. de Talmud Tora. En Amsterdam. En la Imprension de Semuel ben Israel Soeiro, Año 5410.

Reprinted at Smyrna, 1659, by Jedidiah ibn Gabbai[1] and at Amsterdam in 1723.[2]

Origen de los Americanos, Miqweh Israel. Esto es Esperanza de Israel. Reimpresión a plana y renglón del libro de Menasseh ben Israel teólogo y filósofo hebreo, sobre el origen de los Americanos publicado en Amsterdam 5410 (1650) con un preámbulo, una noticia bibliográfica de las principales obras que sobre los orígenes, historia y conquistas de América y Asia se han impreso, y el retrato y al biografía del autor, por Santiago Pérez Junquera. Madrid, 1881.

Origen de los Americanos, esto es Esperanza de Israel, por Menasseh ben Israel. Prólogo de Ignacio Bauer ... Madrid, Compañía ibero-americana de publicaciones, s.d. [1929], reprinted in 1974 (Editorial Plata).

Latin

Miqweh Israel. Hoc est Spes Israelis. Authore Menasseh ben Israel Theologo & Philosopho Hebraeo, Amstellodami. Anno 1650.

---

[1] We have had no access to this edition. It is mentioned in Cecil Roth, *A Life of Menasseh ben Israel, Rabbi, Printer and Diplomat,* Philadelphia, 1934, p. 302, and in M. Kayserling, *Biblioteca Española-Portugueza-Judaica,* New York, 1971, p. 92.

[2] We have not been able to consult this edition mentioned by C. Roth, *A Life of Menasseh,* p. 302. Our colleague and friend, Jacob Barnai (Jerusalem), tells us that there is a copy in the Library of the Hebrew Union College in Cincinnati.

English

The Hope of Israel: written by Manasseh ben Israel . . . Newly extant, and printed in Amsterdam, and dedicated by the author to the High Court, the Parliament of England, and to the Councell of State. Translated into English, and published by authority. In this treatise is shewed the place wherein the Ten Tribes at this present are, proved partly by the strange relation of one Antony Montezinus, a Jew, of what befell him as he travelled over the mountains Cordillaere with divers other particulars about the restauration of the Jewes, and the time when, Printed at London by R. I. for Hannah Allen, at the Crown in Popes-head alley, 1650.

The Hope of Israel: written by Menasseh ben Israel, an Hebrew divine, and philosopher. Newly extant, and printed at Amsterdam, and dedicated by the author to the High Court the Parliament of England and the Councell of State. Whereunto are added some discourses upon the point of the conversion of the Jewes: by Moses Wall. The second edition corrected and amended. London printed by R. I. for Livewell Chapman at the Crown in Popes-head Alley, 1651.

The Hope of Israel, written by Menasseh ben Israel ... The 2d edn., corrected and amended. Whereunto are added, in this second edition, some discourses upon the point of the conversion of the Jewes. By Moses Wall. London, printed by R. I. for L. Chapman, 1652.

Accounts of the Ten Tribes of Israel being in America, originally published by R. Mannaseh ben Israel. With observations thereon, and extracts from sacred and profane, ancient and modern history, confirming the same and their return from thence about the time of the return of the Jewes, by Robert Ingram, Colchester Eng. 1792. Printed and sold by W. Keymer.

Reprinted in 1850.

Reprinted in Lucien Wolf, *Menasseh ben Israel's Mission to Oliver Cromwell*, London, 1901.

Dutch

De Hoop van Israel. Een Werek met groote naukeurigheyt beschreven: door Menasseh ben Israel Hebreeuws Godtgeleerde en Wijsbegeer. Waer in hy handelt van de wonderlijcke verstroyinge der Tien Stammen, en hare gewisse herstellinge met de twee stammen Juda en Benjamin in't Vaderlandt. Met meer als 90. Beschrijvers bevestight: met een verant woordingh voor de eedele Volcken der Jooden. Den 3. Druck van veel Letter-mistellingen gesuyvert. Vermeerdert met de Reysen van

Benjamin Ionasz. van Tudelens. t'Amsterdam, voor Jozua Rex Boeck-
binder, op de Cingel . . . in't Jaer 1666.
The Dutch translation is by Jan Bara.

Yiddish

Amsterdam, 1691,[3] 1712,[4] Frankfurt, 1712.[5]

Hebrew

Sefer Miqweh Israel . . . translation by Eliaquim b. Yaaqob, Amsterdam,
1698.

Reprinted: Amsterdam, 1703;[6] *s.l.*, 1797; Vienna, 1813;[7] Vilna, 1818;[8]
Vilna, 1836, ed. Naftali Hertz b. Abraham; Warsaw, 1841, ed. Azriel
Zelig Mordechai b. Zvi Hirsch; Lemberg, 1847 (Anonymous Introduc-
tion from Lvov); Königsberg, 1858; Lemberg, 1870; Warsaw, 1873, ed.
Naftali Hertz b. Abraham of Bohoz; Podgorze, 1901; Pieterkov, 1929.

French

Espérance d'Israel. Introduction, translation, and notes by Henry
Méchoulan and Gérard Nahon, Paris, 1979.

---

[3] This may be a Hebrew translation. We have not been able to obtain it. See M.
Steinschneider, *Catalogus Librorum Hebraeorum in Bibliotheca Bodleiana*, Berlin, 1852–60,
reprinted Hildesheim, 1964, col. 1697.
[4] We have been unable to consult this edition. See C. Roth, *A Life of Menasseh*, p. 302,
and M. Steinschneider, *Catalogus*, col. 1650.
[5,6,7,8] We have had no access to these editions. See C. Roth, *A Life of Menasseh*, p. 302.

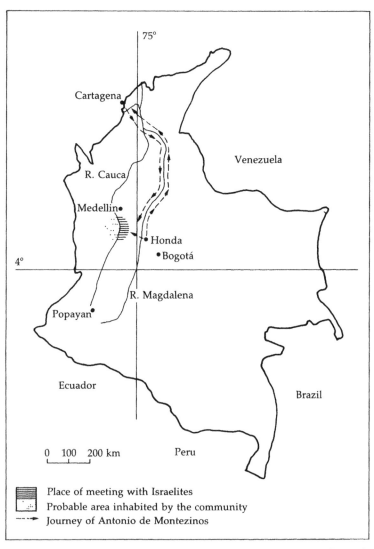

75°

Cartagena

Venezuela

R. Cauca

Medellin

4°

Honda

Bogotá

R. Magdalena

Popayan

Ecuador

Brazil

0   100   200 km   Peru

Place of meeting with Israelites
Probable area inhabited by the community
Journey of Antonio de Montezinos

Map of Colombia (taken from the *Atlas of Colombia* of the Instituto Geográfico
'Augustin Codazzi')

Introduction

WHEN *Spes Israelis* and *Esperança de Israel* were published in Amsterdam in 1650, the Republic of the United Provinces, after liberation from Spain, was enjoying a Golden Age. The interminable war waged by the people of the Netherlands against the power of Spain had just come to an end: by the Treaty of Münster of 30 January 1648, Philip IV had recognized *de jure* the independence of the area he had inherited from the House of Burgundy and Austria. Not only had the United Provinces succeeded in standing up to Spain, but in the economic field they had emerged among the leading European states.

Amsterdam had recently had the Scheldt closed. This enabled her to profit from the downfall of her rival Antwerp and attain the height of her power. By the brilliance and freedom of her intellectual and artistic life, the city could claim to be the capital of European thought.

Spain, standard-bearer of Roman Catholicism and considered by many Protestants to be a manifestation of the Antichrist, had been defeated; was it not the dawn of a new age? It was in that very year, 1650, that Rembrandt painted his *Vision of Daniel* based on verses of Scripture held by both Jews and Christians to be Messianic; perhaps in this way he wanted to sum up the 'Dutch Miracle', which he linked with the millenary expectations of the period.

This 'miracle' was in fact the achievement of a people who had, in the Middle Ages, won and defended their territory from the sea, who had developed such a flourishing cloth industry that Leiden supplied the whole of Europe, who had sent out their ships to all corners of the world. In this flat land were born the arts, sciences, skills, dreams, and values which have left such a mark on the West. Europe owes printing to Laurens Coster of Haarlem, in painting she is indebted to Hieronymus Bosch for his visions of high fantasy, and her humanists are still in debt to Erasmus of Rotterdam. But a war lasting eighty years was needed to make a model Republic out of a small group of provinces.

In the Netherlands it all began with the Reformation. The stakes at which, from 1523, the victims of the Inquisition perished did not have the effect desired by Spain. Confronted by the organization of the Calvinists and the advances they were making, Philip II sent the Duke of Alba to undertake a campaign of brutal repression. While the Southern provinces came to terms with the Spanish king, the Calvinist provinces in the North established the Union of Utrecht on 23 January 1579. The States General of these provinces actually set up the Republic in the very year that the 'Invincible' Armada was destroyed. In 1609 Philip III signed a twelve-year truce with the Provinces, thus *de facto* recognizing the Republic.

While the struggle with Spain was going on, the Republic was building up a flourishing economy and giving birth to a new system of political thought, based on the concept of a contract between the ranks of the establishment and the people.[1] A tiny state, the Republic of the United Provinces consisted of the provinces of Zeeland, Holland, Utrecht, Friesland, Groningen, Overijssel, and Gelderland, the region to the south of the Meuse and Drenthe won from Spain after 1579, in all a population of 2m. souls. The wealth of the country was indeed based on the sea; a very large share of world traffic was operated by her ships. Thanks to the *Oost Indische Compagnie* (1602) and the *West Indische Compagnie* (1621), her traders penetrated the Far East as well as the New World, setting up trading-posts and colonies in all parts, one of which was New Amsterdam, which became New York. At home, thanks to wise exploitation of the land and the waterways, the Dutch guaranteed the livelihood of their population, while famine and disasters were afflicting the other countries of Europe. Their industry, although still poorly developed—since they were not self-sufficient except in woollen goods—enabled the various social classes in the Republic to lead a comparatively decent and sometimes comfortable life.[2]

The long struggle for religious and political freedom, conflict

---

[1] We refer to histories of the United Provinces, especially to Jacques Basnage, *Annales des Provinces-Unies*, The Hague, 1726; Peter Geyl, *The Netherlands in the XVIIth Century, 1609-48*, London, 1961-4· Charles Wilson, *The Dutch Republic and the Civilization of the Seventeenth Century*, London, 1968; Yves Cazaux, *Naissance des Pays-Bas*, Paris, 1983; and K. O. Meinsma, *Spinoza et son cercle*, Paris, 1983, chs. 1 and 2.

[2] Among the many works on the economic expansion of the Netherlands in the seventeenth century, mention may be made of an article, although not recent, by André Sayous, 'Le rôle d'Amsterdam dans l'histoire du capitalisme commercial et financier', *Revue Historique*, 183, 1938, and Violet Barbour's *Capitalism in Amsterdam in the Seventeenth Century*, Baltimore, 1950. For daily life, Paul Zumthor, *La Vie quotidienne en Hollande au temps de Rembrandt*, Paris, 1960, and Roger Avermaete, *Rembrandt et son temps*, Paris, 1952, may be consulted.

between groups, and unending religious disputes allowed a *modus vivendi* between differing opinions to be arrived at in the United Provinces, an intellectual freedom new in Europe. This freedom had its expression in the world's first free press: the *Dutch Mercury*, the *Special News* of Leiden, the *Gazette* of Haarlem. . . .[3] It attracted the best minds from abroad into the Republic: Descartes spent the finest years of his life in Amsterdam.

The quintessence of the material, intellectual, and artistic richness of the United Provinces was to be found in Amsterdam. To what did this city owe her extraordinary prosperity? To the unique situation of her wonderfully sheltered port on the Zuyderzee, to her particularly well-developed domestic transport system with an ever improving network of canals, to the refuge offered by the city during the war of liberation to craftsmen and merchants from the Southern provinces, or to the doubling of the urban area between 1585 and 1595? What is certain is that this city of some 185,000 inhabitants generated amazing activity. In the mid seventeenth century her port made her the greatest trading centre in the world. Broad canals, excavated in concentric semicircles in such a way as to form building plots, encouraged merchants to put up houses and shops along their banks. This scheme was the idea of the architect and sculptor Hendrik de Keyser. A new system of fortifications (8km. of ramparts and curtain-walls) improved the inhabitants' security.

Between 1648 and 1652, Jacob van Campen presented Amsterdam with a new Town Hall, now the Royal Palace. Built on 13,659 piles, the administrative heart of Amsterdam is a perfect example of classical Dutch architecture, unrivalled in the capitals of Europe. These few lines testify to this:

The Magistrates of Amsterdam took possession of their newly-built Town Hall on 23 April 1654. It was formally inaugurated in the August of the same year. A black marble pillar was set up with an inscription which said that the foundations had been laid following a war carried on for eighty years against three kings of Spain: a war which had been brought to a glorious conclusion, guaranteeing the religion and freedom of the country, by the peace concluded at Münster . . . It is one of the wonders of Europe, truly worthy of a city which may be regarded as the principal warehouse of the riches of the Old and New Worlds.[4]

---

[3] On the pioneering role of the Dutch press, see Folke Dahl, *Amsterdam, earliest newspaper center of Western Europe: New contributions to the history of the first Dutch and French Corantos*, The Hague, 1939

[4] J. Jennet, *Histoire de la république des Provinces Unies des Païs-Bas . . .*, The Hague, 1704, vol. iv, year 1656, p. 83.

The city, the trading companies, and foreigners alike called on the services of the Bank of Amsterdam, founded in 1609. With the ruin of Antwerp, Amsterdam became the leading financial centre of the Western world.

Amsterdam was also a city of literature, the sciences, law, and, above all, the arts. During the spread of Calvinism, literacy made significant progress because everyone had to be able to read the Bible. It is impossible to mention all the Dutch writers of the seventeenth century, but the name of Hugo Grotius, the true founder of international law, must be recorded. In the artistic sphere, Rembrandt, then at the height of his creative powers, was painting biblical scenes and immortalizing the personalities of his city. Among them were many Jews, well known, like Doctor Ephraim Bueno, or unknown, such as the group of Portuguese Jews caught in front of the Old Synagogue in an etching. But the fame of the great master should not obscure the existence of a galaxy of other talents. Merchandise, learning, beauty, freedom, spirituality: such was Amsterdam.[5] A letter of 15 May 1631 from Descartes to Guez de Balzac captures the flavour:

... in this great city I find myself in there isn't a single man, except me, who is not busy trading. Everyone is so preoccupied making money that I could live my my whole life here without being noticed by anyone. I take a walk every day amidst the hubbub of a large population with as much freedom and tranquillity as you could in your country lanes; and my attitude to the men I see here is the same as it would be towards the trees which make up your forests or the animals which pasture there. Even the noise of their hectic activities disturbs my daydreams no more than that of some little stream would do. When I reflect sometimes on what is going on, I get the same pleasure from it as you would from seeing the peasants cultivating your land; for I see that all their work serves to beautify the place where I live and to ensure that I want for nothing. If it pleases you to see the fruit growing in your orchards and to be up to your eyes in its abundance, think how much greater a delight it is to see the ships arriving for us here, laden down with all the produce of the Indies and all that is rare in Europe. What other place could one find in the rest of the world where all the necessities of life and all the curiosities that could be desired are as easy to get as here? In what other country would we be able to enjoy such complete freedom, and sleep with so little worry, where troops are always ready to protect us, where poisoning, treachery and slander are practically unknown, and where the remnants of our forefathers' innocence linger on?[6]

[5] It is essential to consult *La Vie en Hollande au XVIIe siècle, tableaux, dessins, estampes, argenterie, monnaies, médailles et autres témoignages*. Exhibition organized by the Netherlands Institute, Paris, 1967.

[6] From René Descartes, *Œuvres et lettres*, Bibl. de la Pléiade, Paris, 1953, p. 942.

A city of trade, science and freedom, Amsterdam made it possible for a major centre of Judaism to emerge at the beginning of the seventeenth century. For, while Western Europe, from England in 1290 to France in 1394 and then Spain and Portugal between 1492 and 1496, had expelled the Jews, and while Louis XIII, by Letters Patent of 23 April 1615, was reaffirming the text of the 1394 expulsion and extending it to 'Jews who for several years have spread, in disguise, into many parts of this our kingdom', the States General of the United Provinces, in that same year, 1615, authorized Jews to practise their religion publicly.

The Amsterdam community had an importance in Jewish history out of all proportion to its membership, which at its height was less than 4,000 souls. There are those who speak of the 'Dutch Miracle' of the seventeenth century; some historians of Judaism use the term 'Miracle of Amsterdam' of the same period.[7] Indeed the use of the word 'miracle' would, up to a point, make it possible to dispense with further explanation; however it is desirable, even in broad outline, to review the history of the community, in order to emphasize its extraordinary character and exceptional influence. It is true to say that the birth of the Jewish community of Amsterdam—still poorly understood in spite of detailed research now in progress—is an important milestone in the eventful history of the Spanish and Portuguese Marranos.[8]

Although Marrano is the technical term used today by historians for Jews converted to Catholicism who preserved their old religion, the term was used pejoratively by the Spanish and Portuguese to describe New Christians whom they suspected of reverting to Jewish practices.[9] And while it is true that forced conversions of Jews took place in Christian countries and Islamic lands in other periods, those which followed the Spanish massacres of 1391 and those perpetrated at

---

[7] See Salo Wittmayer Baron, *A Social and Religious History of the Jews*, 2nd edn, *Late Middle Ages and Era of European Expansion 1200–1650*, vol. xv: Resettlement and Exploration, New York, London, Philadelphia, 1973, pp. 3–73, 379–411, and the review of it by Gérard Nahon in *REJ*, cxxxiv, 1975, fasc. 1–2, pp. 184–94. On Jewish history use may be made of the *Bibliographie sur le judaïsme et les Juifs et sur les relations entre Juifs et non-Juifs*, by Andrée Notre, under the editorship of Willy Bok, Brussels, 1971 (= Social Compass, 1971, 3), pp. 445–523.

[8] On the Marranos see Cecil Roth's classic work *A History of the Marranos*, 4th edn, with a new introduction by Herman P. Salomon, New York, 1974, a major article by I. S. Révah, 'Les Marranes', *REJ*, cxviii, 1959–60, pp. 29–77, and G. Nahon's updating 'Les Marranes espagnols et portugais et les communautés juives issues du marranisme dans l'historiographie récente (1960–75)', *REJ*, cxxxvi, 1977. fasc. 3–4, pp. 297–367.

[9] On the term 'Marrano' see Arturo Farinelli, *Marrano (storia de un vituperio)*, Geneva, 1925.

Lisbon in 1497 were the most cruel. These, in effect, were attacks on the liveliest, the best organized, the longest established, the most influential, and the most fruitful group of Jews in medieval Europe.[10] Spanish Jews had built up model communities which were political entities recognized by the kings;[11] they were the source of a Hebrew literature of unparalleled richness. Furthermore they had made a unique material, linguistic, and scientific contribution to Spanish civilization. After the expulsions from England and France in the thirteenth and fourteenth centuries, and the many partial expulsions from Germany, the Jews of Spain constituted the only important centre of Judaism in Western Europe.

On 4 June 1391 the Christians of Seville set upon the Jewish quarter, massacring many of the inhabitants and forcing the rest to be baptized. In the days which followed, killings and forced conversions increased in number in other parts of Spain. The converted Jews, who were put under the supervision of the bishops, had to observe their new religion, whether they wanted to or not. Twenty years later a mission, reinforced by acts of violence, was conducted by Vicente Ferrer and added to the number of those who had been converted in 1391: according to the Hebrew chronicler, Abraham ben Solomon of Torrutiel, these would have amounted to 200,000 souls.

By their numbers alone, the New Christians gave rise to feelings of rejection on the part of the Old Christians. In 1449 the converts were victims of cruelty in Toledo. A statute was promulgated in that city on 5 June of that year making them ineligible to hold certain public offices. This was the origin of the statutes of *limpieza de sangre*, of purity of blood.[12]

---

[10] As the great historian Americo Castro has well shown, it is impossible to understand the development of medieval Spain without considering the Jewish presence. See *Réalités de l'Espagne: Histoire et valeurs*, Paris, 1963.

On the history of the Jews in Spain, Yitzhak Baer's work, *A History of the Jews in Christian Spain*, Philadelphia, 1971, should be supplemented by numerous articles published in the Spanish journal *Sefarad*.

[11] It would be anachronistic to speak of a State within a State. On this question see Jacob Katz, 'A State within State, the History of an Antisemitic Slogan', *Proceedings of The Israeli Academy of Sciences and Humanities*, iv (3), Jerusalem, 1969, pp. 29–58, and G. Nahon's review in *REJ*, cxxix, 1970, pp. 324–6.

[12] On the famous statute of blood purity and its consequences see Albert A. Sicroff, *Les Controverses des statuts de pureté de sang en Espagne du XVᵉ au XVIIᵉᵐᵉ siècle*, Paris, 1960, and B. Netanyahu's clarification, 'Did the Toledans in 1449 rely on a real Royal Privilege?', *Proceedings of the American Academy for Jewish Research*, xliv, 1977, pp. 93–125. See also I. S. Révah, 'La controverse sur les statuts de pureté de sang . . .', *Bulletin Hispanique*, lxxiii, 3–4, Bordeaux, July–Dec. 1971, pp. 263–306; Henry Méchoulan, 'L'Altérité juive dans la

As discrimination against the New Christians worsened, the conviction grew that their Catholicism was purely a matter of form and that they were Judaizing with the assistance of declared Jews. Two consequences then ensued: the setting up, in 1480, of an Inquisition which very quickly led to thousands of arrests and sentences, some of which were to the stake, and the expulsion, by the decree of 31 March 1492, of Jews who had refused to be converted and were still living in Spain. Though most of these Jews took the path of exile to Italy, Turkey, the Holy Land, or Portugal, some ended up swelling the ranks of the converts. During the first years of the fifteenth century, the courts of the Inquisition hunted down Judaizing New Christians remorselessly, with the aim of eliminating crypto-Judaism from Spanish soil.

In 1580 Portugal was annexed to the kingdom of Spain. Portuguese converts in great numbers fled the Portuguese Inquisition, which was more savage than its predecessor, and settled in the big towns of Spain. These new Judaizing groups were quickly located by the Spanish Inquisition, which, to their cost, acted with renewed vigour.[13] The descendants of these converted Jews, still called *conversos*, posed a real social, economic, and political problem for Spain in the seventeenth and eighteenth centuries, a problem which also affected its overseas possessions in the Old and New Worlds.[14]

pensée espagnole, 1550–1650', *Studia Rosenthaliana*, viii, 1974, 1, pp. 31–58, and 2, pp. 171–202; and 'Nouveaux éléments dans la controverse des statuts de pureté de sang au xviiᵉ siècle', *Studia Rosenthaliana*, 1976, 2, pp. 142–50.

[13] Study of Inquisitorial proceedings has allowed historians like Isaac Baer, I. S. Révah, and Haïm Beinart to describe the Jewish practices and beliefs of a number of the accused. This very extensive documentation is challenged by a critical school represented by B. Netanyahu and E. Rivkin. For them the religious pretext was a means of bringing down a social class of merchants and confiscating their goods; the documents were purely and simply fabricated to that end. It must be emphasized, however, that the Holy Office also arrested poor individuals and that their maintenance sometimes caused provincial Inquisitions to run into deficit! See I. Baer, *A History* . . ., I. S. Révah, many works, and G. Nahon's comprehensive article, 'Les Séphardim, les Marranes, les Inquisitions péninsulaires et leurs archives dans les travaux récents de I. S. Révah', *REJ*, cxxxii, 1973, pp. 5–48. H. Beinart has written a great number of articles on the Marranos in addition to his major work, *Marranos on Trial by the Inquisition*, Tel Aviv, 1965 (in Hebrew). See the review by G. Nahon in *REJ*, cxxxix, 1970, pp. 286–99. B. Netanyahu, *The Marranos of Spain from the late XIVth Century to the early XVIth Century according to Contemporary Hebrew Sources*, 2nd edn, New York, 1973, may be consulted, also E. Rivkin, 'The Utilization of non-Jewish sources for the reconstruction of Jewish History', *Jewish Quarterly Review*, xlviii, 1957–8, pp. 183–203.

[14] Obviously reference must be made to Julio Caro Baroja's great book *Los Judíos en la España moderna y contemporánea*, Madrid, 1961, and to Yosef Hayyim Yerushalmi's thesis *From Spanish Court to Italian Ghetto: Isaac Cardoso. A study in Seventeenth Century*

The situation in Portugal was different. Relatively small in the Middle Ages, the Jewish community had not been scourged by the plague of massacres and conversions of 1391. It was reinforced in 1492 by Spanish immigrants who, having chosen exile in order to keep their faith, took up residence in Portugal, with the hard-won permission of the King, João II. He and his successor, Manoel 'the Fortunate', stepped up pressure on Jews to be baptized. When Manoel was making preparations to marry Isabella, a daughter of the Spanish royal house, she demanded the expulsion of the Jews as one of her wedding presents. The King complied and issued an edict on 5 December 1496 expelling the Jews from Portugal. The economic and fiscal benefits the kingdom was deriving from the Jews at a time of expansion were by no means negligible. The imperative of religious unification which had operated in Spain was an extraneous factor here. The authorities did not want the *actual* departure of the Jews: they saw this as a means of obtaining their conversion, voluntarily or by force. In the course of a Council of State held at Estremoz, the problem of the admissibility of the forced baptism of Jews was debated at length before it was accepted.[15] Now the Jews of Portugal were, for the most part, Spaniards who had preferred to leave their own country in 1492 rather than deny their faith. In order to remain Jews they were prepared to undergo the horrors of a new exile. Three ports had been assigned to those who had chosen to leave the kingdom. At the last minute they learnt that they must all embark at Lisbon. There they were imprisoned for several days without food and enjoined to accept baptism. In the face of refusal on the part of the majority, they were dragged by force into the churches, sprinkled with holy water, declared to be Christians and provided with godparents whose names they had to adopt from then on. In this fashion the Portuguese Jewish community in its entirety was swept into the embrace of the Church, although it cannot really be said that the Jews were expelled from Portugal.

These dramatic events at Lisbon were the source of a large number of converts but, in contrast with what happened in Spain, nothing was done to check up on the genuineness of their new faith. A law of 30 May 1497

Marranism, and Jewish Apologetics, New York, London, 1971. See also H. Méchoulan, *Le Sang de l'autre ou l'honneur de Dieu*, Paris, 1979.

[15] In April 1497, regardless of the protests of some advisers such as Don Fernando Coutinho, Bishop of Silves, the King ordered that boys and girls under the age of fourteen should be taken from their Jewish parents on Easter Sunday; allocated to various localities, they were to be brought up in the Catholic faith at the King's expense. The order was carried out without mercy, but very few Jews accepted baptism to keep their children.

placed the religious conduct of New Christians outside the jurisdiction of the magistrates and promised them equal treatment with Old Christians. As there was no Inquisition in Portugal, did these recent converts think they would lead an untroubled life? The King's policy, though not very scrupulous as to the means used or the results obtained, appeared to have purged Portugal of Judaism. In fact it had created a situation without precedent in Jewish history. Henceforth the New Christians—almost a tenth of the population of Portugal towards the end of the fifteenth century—were able to live by a merely superficial profession of the Christian faith. According to several historians, they knew how to profit from royal protection and the absence of the repression of an Inquisition to get an underground system of Jewish observance running smoothly, and to create a tenacious 'Marrano religion', which the Inquisition, finally set up in 1536, was never able to eradicate. From then on crypto-Judaism was to constitute a major problem, not only for Portugal but also for Spain where, as we have seen, it spread from 1580.

A secret form of Judaism, whose rites and articles of faith are revealed by the proceedings of the Inquisition and the evidence of former Marranos who escaped from the Peninsula, has come down over the centuries by the still poorly understood means of family tradition and through the meetings of Neo-Christian groups. It was characterized by the conviction that salvation is obtained not by the law of Christ but by that of Moses: it took the form of the recitation of prayers in Portuguese, particularly psalms, of the keeping of fasts, and of the celebration of festivals.[16] Other observances, notably dietary, were kept as far as was possible. On account of its secret life, led in suspicious and often hostile surroundings, the 'Judaism of the Marranos' deserves to be regarded as a specific religious phenomenon which has yet to be defined.[17]

The Portuguese Marranos were not content with standing firm in the face of the constraints imposed by the authorities, the Church, and the Inquisition: they were at the root of an amazing expansion of Judaism in

[16] The reference is to the Monday and Thursday fasts and that of Queen Esther. It is known that she, having concealed her faith and her people from King Ahasuerus, was particularly dear to the Marranos. The festivals celebrated were those of the Sabbath, *Kippur* known as 'Great Day', *Sukkot* known as 'Feast of Tabernacles', and Passover.

[17] João Lúcio de Azevedo's classic work, *História dos Cristãos Novos Portugueses*, Lisbon, 1921, is always useful; it may be supplemented by I. S. Révah's comprehensive article, 'Les Marranes portugais et l'Inquisition au XVIᵉ siècle', in the collection published under the editorship of Richard D. Barnett, *The Sephardi Heritage*, London, 1971, pp. 479–526, and António José Saraiva's critical book, *Inquisição e Cristãos Novos*, Oporto, 1969.

the West. Although there was no mass flight of Portuguese Jews in 1497 into countries of asylum, there was a tide of emigration which lasted from the sixteenth to the eighteenth century. This fluctuating movement was a function of the Portuguese monarchy's changing policy on New Christians leaving the kingdom, of the degree of intensity of Inquisitorial repression at any time, and of the individual or family's means and financial situation. Several countries offered a more or less secure shelter to these refugees: the Portuguese and Spanish Empires, Occidental and Oriental Jewish communities (Italy, and above all, the Ottoman Empire), and areas outside the sway of the Catholic Church (the United Provinces and England in the seventeenth century).

New Christians took part in the Spanish and Portuguese colonization of the East and West Indies, lured no doubt, as were Old Christians, by the prospect of profit, but also perhaps motivated by the wish to escape from an oppressive situation and build themselves a new life far away.

Though they sometimes carved out a materially comfortable existence for themselves, they did not, however, find the tranquillity they had counted on. Courts of the Holy Office were quickly set up in the colonies: as early as 1563 an *auto-da-fé* was held in Goa and, in 1571, Philip II established a Court of the Inquisition in Mexico. The necessity for crypto-Judaism spread even to the New World. To be really sure of refuge, it was essential to reach a truly Jewish community: Salonica, Constantinople, or Jerusalem. Portuguese Synagogues were founded in these places as early as the sixteenth century. For many Marranos the journey to the Ottoman Empire was interrupted, for a while or for ever, in Italy, in the communities of Rome, Ancona, Ferrara, Pisa, or Livorno. In Venice the Portuguese Marranos who had reverted to Judaism took a considerable part in the maritime trade of the city of Saint Mark. The Portuguese community of Venice, the core of sixteenth Sephardic dispersal in the West, provided other communities with leaders, rabbis, systems of internal regulation, and a printed literature unparalleled for diversity and quality. The Portuguese Marranos also reached the Northern Netherlands, the Dutch colonies in America, and England and her possessions. They were responsible for the creation of the first genuine Jewish communities of the New World, those of Recife in Brazil, and of Surinam in Dutch Guiana, before 1650. Subsequently all American Jewish communities, among them Curaçao, Jamaica, and New Amsterdam, were to be founded by individuals and families descended from Peninsular Marranism.[18]

[18] Jacob R. Marcus, *The Colonial American Jew 1492–1776*, Detroit, 1970.

Just as the Spanish and Portuguese stock invigorated Jewish communities abroad with a constant supply of new people, Jews settled outside the Peninsula contributed to the maintenance of crypto-Judaism in Spain, Portugal, and the colonies. In spite of the danger, individuals would return to conclude business deals, see their relatives, even to teach Judaism in the 'land of idolatry'.[19] Thus one Francisco Rodrigues d'Olivença from Amsterdam was to be found in Lisbon on 12 March 1618.[20] He had some pages of a Jewish prayer ritual printed in Amsterdam hidden in his hat.[21]

The power of dreams over the Marranos of Portugal must also be taken into account. To the hope of Messianic Redemption was added a more tangible expectation of leaving their country for a Jewish community which would be the fount of all material and spiritual good. At the beginning of the seventeenth century, it seems, the Portuguese Jewish community of Amsterdam played an important part in the plans of the Peninsular Marranos: it expressed and incarnated the Hope of Israel.

In the sixteenth century Antwerp had sheltered a good number of New Christians, who obtained residence permits, contributed to the city's prosperity, and devoted themselves to the clandestine practice of Judaism.[22] Did the progressive diminution of the Neo-Christian groups in Antwerp lead in turn to the emergence of the Jewish community of Amsterdam? Did Judaizing Portuguese individuals and families gradually abandon Antwerp towards the end of the sixteenth century to settle in Amsterdam? This plausible theory must not prevent consideration of the traditional version of its origins lovingly handed down by the Amsterdam Jewish community itself.

One of these accounts tells how, in 1593, Manuel López Pereira and his sister, María Núñez, set sail from Portugal with their uncle, Miguel López, and some other New Christians. Their ship was sailing towards Northern Europe when it was attacked and captured by some English-

---

[19] This expression, in the Amsterdam community archives, denotes the Iberian Peninsula. For a Jew who belonged to this community, going back to the 'land of idolatry', for whatever reason, led on return to a serious penalty and required an act of contrition.

[20] The presence of this individual in Amsterdam is attested by a document issued by the notary Pieter Ruttens and dated 5 Jan. 1617. See E. M. Koen, 'Notarial Records Relating to the Portuguese Jews in Amsterdam up to 1639', in *Studia Rosenthaliana*, xi, 1977, p. 81, no. 1085.

[21] I. S. Révah, 'Fragments retrouvés de quelques éditions amstellodamoises de la version espagnole du rituel juif', in *Studia Rosenthaliana*, ii, 1968, no. 1, pp. 108–10.

[22] On Antwerp there is Ephraïm Schmidt's book, *L'Histoire des Juifs à Anvers (Antwerpen)*, n.p. [Antwerp], n.d. [1969].

men. The Portuguese were taken as prisoners to London, where a gentleman, captivated by the beauty of María Núñez, asked for her hand in marriage. When Queen Elizabeth was informed of the matter, she invited the young girl to see London in her coach, and ordered the release of the captives. María Núñez refused the dazzling offers of her noble suitor and, with her companions, brought the interrupted journey to an end at Amsterdam. Five years later she married one of the Portuguese who had shared in the adventure, according to some Duarte Saraiva, to others Emmanuel Lopes Homem of Oporto. This was the first marriage celebrated in Amsterdam according to Jewish rites.

Another tradition maintains that in the same year, 1593—in fact more probably in 1601—some New Christians landed at Emden in Friesland. After some picturesque encounters, they made contact with the German rabbi, Moses Uri ha-Levi. He advised them to make for Amsterdam, and agreed to follow them there, to introduce them into the Jewish fold, and to be their rabbi. His son, Aaron, who had learnt the art of printing and the Spanish language in Italy, would act as their intepreter. Religious services were held in Moses Uri ha-Levi's own house in the Jonckerstraat. On 15 September 1603 a solemn service, that of *Kippur*, the Atonement, was interrupted by a police raid: the Amsterdam magistrates had been informed that an illegal meeting of Spanish Catholics was being held. Jacob Tirado, alias James Lopes da Costa, the spokesman for the Portuguese, explained in Latin that he and his companions were Jews who had fled the Spanish Inquisition. Without actually authorizing the practice of Judaism, the Burgomasters of Amsterdam had respect for Jacob Tirado's good faith. Thus the Portuguese Jewish community of Amsterdam was officially born.[23]

The establishment of a Jewish community was something entirely new for the city, which in the Middle Ages did not seem to have any Jews among its population. Perusal of the notarial archives of Amsterdam

---

[23] See Uri ben Aaron ha-Levi, *Narracão da vinda dos Judeus Espanhoes a Amsterdam*, Amsterdam, 1711; J. S. da Silva Rosa, *Geschiedenis der Portugeesche Joden te Amsterdam 1593–1925*, Amsterdam, 1925; J. D'Ancona, 'De komst der Marranen in Noord-Nederland: De Portugese gemeenten te Amsterdam tot de vereniging (1639)', in H. Brugmans and A. Frank, eds., *Geschiedenis der Joden in Nederland*, i. Amsterdam, 1940, pp. 211 ff. Generally speaking, recent research in the archives of the Torre do Tombo (Inquisition Collection) of Lisbon would confirm these traditions. See H. P. Salomon, *Os primeiros portugueses de Amesterdão. Documentos do Arquivo nacional da Torre do Tombo 1595–1606*. Introdução, leitura, notas e cartas genealógicas, Braga, 1983. For sources for the history of Jews in the Netherlands see R. G. Fuks-Mansfeld, 'Sources for the History of the Jews in the Netherlands', in *Fourth Congress of Jewish Studies, Abstracts of papers. Medieval and Modern Jewish History*, Jerusalem, 1965, pp. 23–4.

shows that at the beginning of the seventeenth century there were a fair number of Portuguese merchants, who were Jews, living in Amsterdam, and that they maintained close contact with their relatives and friends in the Iberian Peninsula and in France. Historians are painstakingly reconstructing the lives of the 'founding fathers' of the community. These men played a part in the economic expansion of the United Provinces, notably from the foundation, in 1602, of the East Indies Company, in which they were shareholders. They were Manuel Carvalho, Melchior Mendes, Diego Dias Querido, Manuel Thomas . . . They made persistent approaches to the authorities for the right to have a publicly recognized synagogue and a community cemetery. In the event it was outside the jurisdiction of Amsterdam, at Alkmaar on 10 May 1604, that Philip de Jood, otherwise Moses Uri ha-Levi, the rabbi already mentioned, obtained from the authorities the right for Jews to live according to their religion, providing they obeyed the Burgomasters in all matters. On 10 November 1605 at Haarlem, the Portuguese merchants, Melchior and Francisco Mendes, achieved the granting of a charter stating that their 'Nation' could elect *parnassim* and *mamonim*.[24]

In Amsterdam itself things were moving less quickly. In 1607 the community acquired a cemetery at Groote for the burial of its dead, but it already had a religious and charitable organization and, most notably, its first brotherhood, the *hevrah bikkur holim*, dedicated to visiting the sick. This community took the name *Beth Ya'acob*, the House of Jacob. As early as 1608 a second Jewish community, *Neveh Shalom*, the Dwelling Place of Peace, came into being. In 1612 some prayer books for use by Jews were printed in Spanish by Isaac Franco. However in the same year, the Burgomasters, learning that a synagogue had just been built, forbade, on pain of demolition, the celebration of Jewish services there. Indeed the Calvinist clergy took a very unfavourable view of Judaism being officially practised in Amsterdam. A commission made up of two Burgomasters, Adriaan and Reinier van Pauw, and of the jurist, Hugo Grotius, was set up to give advice on the problem of the legal admission of Jews into the city. Grotius proposed compelling them to attend Christian sermons, and forbidding them to marry or have sexual relations with Christians, to employ Christians as domestic servants, or to engage in retail trade and certain professions. Strangely enough, he wanted every Jew in Amsterdam solemnly to swear on oath that he believed 'in a God, creator and ruler of all . . . that Moses and the

---

[24] Hebrew terms traditionally used, especially the former, for the leaders of the Jewish community.

prophets revealed the truth through divine inspiration and that there is another life after death in which the good will receive their reward and the evil their punishment'.[25] In 1615 the States General of the United Provinces, less severe than Grotius, authorized the Jews to practise their religion publicly, on condition that they did not contract marriages with Christians or make any attacks on Christianity. Without waiting for this decision, the Jews of Amsterdam had bought the land which is still today their cemetery, at Ouderkerk, south of the city on the Amstel. Their dead have rested there since the time beneath stelae sometimes, unusually for a Jewish cemetery, decorated with figurative sculptures.[26] In 1619 the Amsterdam City Council finally allowed the Jews to live in the city according to their own law.

In these conditions, immigration from the Iberian Peninsula, France, and the southern Netherlands increased. This, as well as internal disagreements, explains the secession in 1619 of part of the *Neveh Shalom* community: a third Jewish community in Amsterdam, *Beth Yisrael*, the House of Israel, was born. For the next twenty years, the Jews of Amsterdam were to be divided into three communities. Some were great merchants, manufacturers, doctors, or diplomats, while others came to swell the ranks of the poor wretches who were assisted by the communities and the charitable brotherhoods.[27] They brought the area round the Joodenbreestraat to life, and appeared in Rembrandt's drawings and paintings. They jealously preserved their forefathers' language, Spanish or Portuguese. Portuguese was the official language of the 'Nation', as its archives testify. Spanish, on the other hand, was almost always preferred for sacred or secular literature: it was in this language that Menasseh ben Israel published his *Hope of Israel*.[28]

Amsterdam was a symbol of religious freedom for the New Christians of the Iberian Peninsula and France. It was the very haven of mercy they dreamed of reaching, so that they might find again the living Judaism they had lost. Not only was the 'Portuguese Nation' of Amsterdam at the

[25] Hugo de Groot, *Remonstrantie nopende de ordre dije in de landen van Hollandt ende Westvrieslandt dijent gestelt op de Joden*, published by J. Meijer, Amsterdam, 1949, p. 116.

[26] L. Alvares-Vega, *The Beth Haim of Ouderkerk aan de Amstel: Images of a Portuguese Jewish cemetery in Holland*, Assen-Amsterdam, 1975.

[27] On the economic life of the Amsterdam Jews, failing recent detailed studies of particular value, Herbert I. Bloom's book, *The Economic Activities of the Jews of Amsterdam in the Seventeenth and Eighteenth Centuries*, Willamsport (Pa.), 1937, is still indispensable.

[28] On the role of the Spanish language, described by C. Roth as 'semi-sacred', see his article, 'The role of Spanish in the Marrano Diaspora', in *Studies in Book and Booklore. Essays in Jewish Bibliography and Allied Subjects*, n.p., 1972.

centre of a web of family ties which bound together the Sephardic and Neo-Christian diaspora, but it kept hope alive in the Peninsula and its possessions. Its existence and development totally transformed the life of the Marranos.

A visit to the three synagogues on the Houtgracht was not to be missed by foreign travellers with a taste for the exotic. On 26 July 1636 Charles Ogier, a Secretary at the French Embassy, went to the synagogue of *Beth Yaʿacob*, which was known as 'the Jews' Great Church', and described it with care and at length. He also visited *Neveh Shalom* as, in 1638, did Queen Marie de Medici.

In 1639, after lengthy negotiations, the leaders of the three communities decided to create one unified community, *Talmud Torah*, Teaching of the Law. The Jews of Amsterdam were embarking on the classic period of their history, when there was a veritable resurgence of the medieval Jewish communities of Spain and Portugal, which had vanished a century and a half earlier. They stamped their official documents with a seal bearing the device of a phoenix, symbolizing, according to tradition, their rebirth from the ashes of the Inquisition[29] The crowning event of this period was the solemn inauguration, in 1675, of the great synagogue, a jewel of seventeenth-century Dutch architecture.[30]

As seen through its *ascamot*, or community rules, the *Nação Espanhola e Portuguesa* appears a very well organized body. It was governed by a council, the *maʿamad*, made up of six *parnassim* or wardens, and a *gabbai* or treasurer. This leadership regulated internal taxation, appointed religious officers, including school masters and rabbis, took care that good morals and opinions were upheld, and in the last resort pronounced the *herem* or 'excommunication'.[31] In the articles of the *ascamot*

[29] See Stephen Birmingham, *The Grandees: America's Sephardic Élite*, New York–London, 1971, p. 67.

[30] Ernest Namenyi, 'L'Esnoga d'Amsterdam (1675–1950)', in *Revue de la pensée juive*, ii, no. 5, 1950, pp. 74–85.

[31] The Hebrew term means anathema. It was used to indicate the most serious penalty imposed on a member of the community by the rabbinical court, from which came the somewhat inappropriate use of the translation 'excommunication'. See Maurice Aron, *Histoire de l'excommunication juive*, Nîmes, 1882. In the Portuguese community of Amsterdam, the sentence was often pronounced by the *maʿamad*; it was graduated from exclusion for a few days with a fine to final exclusion from the group. See Joseph Nehama, *Dictionnaire du judéo-espagnol*, Madrid, 1977, p. 255, entry 'jérem'. On the matter at Amsterdam and the rabbinical aspect of Spinoza's 'excommunication', see Charles Touati's clarification in the *Annuaire de l'École Pratique des Hautes Études* (5ᵉ *section, sciences religieuses*), vol. lxxx–lxxxi, fasc. iii, Reviews of Conferences 1971–2 and 72–3, pp. 222–3, also H. Méchoulan, 'Le hérem à Amsterdam et ʾl'excommunication' de Spinoza', in

of 1639 referring to rabbis, may be found the appointments and salaries of Isaac Aboab, Menasseh ben Israel, Saul Levi Morteira, and David Pardo.[32]

In about 1650 the 'Nation' comprised about 400 families, some 2,000 souls, the majority of whom had been born in Portugal. Until 1657 they constitued a foreign group, by statute. One 29 June of that year, the Council of State granted citizenship to the chief merchants. In fact the States General already considered the Jews to be their nationals, and gave them protection when abroad. Better still the States sought a declaration from Louis XIII, which was granted at Saint Germain-en-Laye on 30 March 1637, under the terms of which Portuguese merchants from the United Provinces were not to be harried in France for professing Judaism.[33] In Amsterdam itself their religion was fully recognized: on 22 May 1642, Frederick Henry, Stadtholder of the United Provinces, accompanied by Queen Henrietta Maria, wife of Charles I of England, was received in the synagogue.[34] Jewish worship was so noticeable outside the synagogue that on 5 October 1645 the Pastor Wachtendorp complained that the streets and bridges were decorated with branches, in honour of the Jewish Feast of Tabernacles.[35] Another piece of evidence of the religious freedom enjoyed by the Jews of Amsterdam is the publication, in 1644 by Immanuel Benveniste, of an unexpurgated edition of the Talmud.

The success of these men, who were at the root of the fantastic expansion of the Jewish community of Amsterdam, cannot be over-emphasized. Although they had lived as Catholics for several gener-

Cahiers Spinoza iii, Paris, 1979–80 and Y. Kaplan, 'The Social function of the *herem* in the Portuguese Jewish community of Amsterdam in the seventeenth century' in *Dutch Jewish History*, Jerusalem, 1984, pp. 111–155.

[32] The principal regulations, in their original language, may be found in Joaquim Mendes dos Remedios's book, *Os Judeus Portugueses em Amsterdam*, Coimbra, 1911, and in A. Wiznitzer, 'The Merger Agreement and Regulations of Congregation Talmud Tora of Amsterdam 1638–9', in *Historia Judaica*, xx, 1958, pp. 109–32.

[33] The text appears in G. Nahon's article, 'Les rapports des communautés judéo-portugaises de France avec celle d'Amsterdam au XVIIᵉ siècle', in *Studia Rosenthaliana*, x, 1976, fasc. 1, pp. 163–4.

[34] We refer, in a general way, to the chronicle written in the eighteenth century by David Franco Mendes, *Memorias do estabelecimento e progresso dos Judeos Portuguezes e Espanhoes nesta famosa citade de Amsterdam*, edited with introduction and notes by Leo Fuks and Renata G. Fuks-Mansfeld, with a philological commentary by B. N. Teensma, in *Studia Rosenthaliana*, ix, no. 2, 1975; on this visit see below and H. Méchoulan's article, mentioned below, n. 37.

[35] Quoted by S. W. Baron, *A Social and Religious History of the Jews*, vol. xv, New York–London–Philadelphia, 1973, p. 32.

ations, they managed to create a zealous Jewish community, complete with the traditional structures, a community which would soon be a model for those of the Old and New Worlds alike. But these Marranos' transformation into authentic Jews only happened with the assistance of rabbis from outside. In addition to Moses Uri ha-Levi, whom we have already mentioned, their first rabbis were David Pardo, who came from the powerful Spanish Jewish centre of Salonica, and the Moroccan, Jacob Uziel, who was born in Fez, a major Jewish stronghold in North Africa. Even at the end of the seventeenth century the 'Nation' was to offer a rabbinical chair to a man from Oran, Jacob ben Aaron Sasportas. As for the actual organization of the community, it was based on that of Venice: the regulations of the 'Nation', the statutes of the brotherhoods and, no doubt, even the teaching methods all came from the Portuguese community of Venice, whose structures went back to the sixteenth century. The very name of the community, when unified in 1639, was copied from that of Venice, which was the first to be called *Talmud Torah*. Moreover in 1615 the powerful charitable brotherhood with international links, the *Santa Companhia de dotar orfãs e donzelas pobres*, the Holy Company for the Endowment of Poor Orphans and Young Girls, explicitly recognized its debt to Venice.[36]

It may also be noted that not all the Jews of the 'Nation' came straight from Spain or Portugal. Many were from Italy or North Africa. The full authority of the *parnassim* was needed to maintain the Portuguese identity of such a heterogeneous population. On the other hand, this variety of origins made its contribution towards the acceptance of Jewish Amsterdam as the metropolis of the Sephardic diaspora. Even the Holy Land was, in some respects, a dependency of Amsterdam, the Holy Land for which the reverence of these people, who had been living for so long in a land of idolatry, knew no bounds and where Jacob Tirado, the

---

[36] 'In the Name of God May He Be Blessed. At Amsterdam, 14 *Adar* first which is 12 Feb. 1615.

'The Company of Portuguese established with divine favour to marry orphans and poor girls of the Portuguese and Castilian Nation, living from Saint-Jean-de-Luz on the one side to Danzig on the other, as well as those of France, Flanders, England, and Germany . . . Set up by the rabbi, Rabbi Joseph Pardo, *in imitation of the Brotherhood of the Orphans of* Talmud Torah *in Venice*, and at the request of Jacob Coronel of Hamburg, to the greater praise of God, may He be Blessed.' Translation of the original Portuguese text published by I. S. Révah in his article, 'Le premier règlement de la "Santa Companhia de dotar orfans e donzelas pobres"', in *Boletim internacional de bibliografia luso-brasileira*, iv, 1963, pp. 650–91. See also Wilhelmina C. Pieterse, *350 jaar dotar: Gedenkschrift samengesteld door . . . ter gelegenheid van het 350-jarig bestaan in opdracht van de vereniging, Santa Companhia de Dotar Orphas e Donzellas te Amsterdam*, n.p. [Amsterdam], 1965.

founder of the first community, was to end his days. Indeed emissaries seeking money were received favourably by the 'Nation' from Jerusalem, Safed, and Tiberias, and the community gave allowances to poor Portuguese living in Jerusalem, whose names were entered annually in their registers.[37]

The intellectual life of the 'Nation' was dominated by one absolute imperative: to teach Judaism anew to immigrants who had, in whole or in part, lost it. As a result, there was an extraordinary blossoming of writing in the vernacular, Spanish or Portuguese, which set out the principles and rites of Judaism, answered the questions of the crypto-Jews whose links with tradition had been abruptly broken, and was intended to counteract the effects of Calvinist proselytism. This was encouraged by the general air of freedom in Holland; but works of anti-Christian propaganda could not be printed. Such works were, however, necessary to deal with the objections of Marranos who had received a solid education in the Catholic colleges of the Peninsula. A large number were written and many copies made which were circulated secretly.[38] The distribution of this literature was only made possible by the material prosperity of a good many members of the community, who bore the cost of printing it and bought a considerable part of the many Jewish printers' output. This literature came to maturity and produced its major works in the second half of the seventeenth century. But even before 1650 the intellectual life of Amsterdam's Jews was apparent in two areas: a model system of teaching, and the emergence of an already considerable literature.

In a country where education was widespread, where 'the Latin school' disseminated knowledge in all areas, and where 3,000 printers were soon to satisfy a great demand for books, the Jews set up their own system of education at an early date. On 20 May 1616, members of the *Beth Ya'acob* and *Neveh Shalom* communities founded a teaching brotherhood, which they called *Talmud Torah*, Teaching of the Law, the name which was later taken by the unified 'Nation'. In it the Hebrew

---

[37] For documents preserved in the Municipal Archives of Amsterdam, profitable use may be made of W. C. Pieterse's excellent inventory, *Inventaris van de Archieven der Portugees Israëlietische Gemeente te Amsterdam 1614–1870*, Amsterdam, 1964. For the Holy Land, for example, in the Municipal Archives of Amsterdam, see a list of 1646 (P.A. 334.19, fo. 213).

[38] This branch of Amsterdam Jewish literature is still represented today by manuscripts preserved in major libraries and particularly in the two great Jewish libraries of Amsterdam: the Portuguese community's *Ets Haïm Montezinos* and the *Rosenthaliana* of Amsterdam University. See L. Fuks and R. G. Fuks-Mansfeld's excellent catalogues (n. 64, below).

Bible, the Talmud, and all the disciplines of Judaism were certainly taught. In 1637 its directors considered that it was no longer meeting all needs and decided to set up a university, which they called *Ets Haim*, the Tree of Life. This was endowed with sufficient financial means and charged with supplying higher education; bursaries were to be given annually to students who merited them. Under the name of *Ets Haim* College, the establishment developed to the point where, in the second half of the seventeenth century, a Polish Jewish minister, Shabbetai Bass, would describe its graduated methods in glowing terms, and offer it as a model to Jewish communities in Poland. The courses given in classes were designed to provide training in the sacred texts, Hebrew grammar, and the writing of Hebrew poetry.[39] Comfortably-off students also studied the art of writing and the secular sciences at home with tutors.

Was the excellence of this teaching due to the influence of the Jesuit institutions which some of the founders of *Ets Haim* College had attended, or to the influence of the Dutch Latin school system, or to the opportunity to put new methods into practice in a community where there were no ossified educational traditions? These three possibilities should not detract from the merits of the rabbis, who had come from all quarters with a wealth of experience. This college was soon provided with a library, the nucleus of the distinguished *Ets Haim Montezinos* Library, still highly regarded by all.

The Jews, the 'People of the Book', established a flourishing printing-house in Amsterdam, which, in the seventeenth century, must have dominated the international market in Hebrew books. Indeed the great activity of the Jewish printers may be explained by the high educational level of members of the community, and the heavy demand for books explaining and extolling Judaism, in Hebrew as well as in Spanish and Portuguese, from the 'Nation' itself and from the communities with which it was in touch. These presses benefited not only from the considerable freedom in Amsterdam, but also from the decline of the Venetian printing houses. Among these Jewish printers, in addition to the rabbi, Menasseh ben Israel, who founded and ran his printing house from 1626 to 1643, Elias Aboab of Hamburg, and Joseph and Samuel, Menasseh's sons who continued his work, must be included Daniel de

---

[39] Shabbetai Bass, *Sifte Yeshenim* [The Lips of Sleepers], Amsterdam, 1680, Introduction. There is a translation into French by L. Hirschel, in *Spinoza, troisième centenaire de la mort du philosophe* (Catalogue of the Exhibition at the Netherlands Institute), Paris, 1977, p. 74.

Fonseca, the printer in 1627 of the Salonican rabbi Meir Aldabi's work, *Paths of Faith*, and the Venetian, Immanuel Benveniste, who printed the Babylonian Talmud between 1644 and 1648. They were responsible for Spanish versions of the Bible and the Jewish prayer ritual, in this way codifying oral biblical and liturgical traditions. It was in the second half of the seventeenth century that Joseph Athias was to set up a printing house which would be in production for fifty-six years, up to 1714. So Amsterdam was the main source of Hebrew and Jewish books for the people of Europe, both Jews and Christians.

It would not do, even in a brief review of the Jewish writers of Amsterdam in the first half of the seventeenth century, to omit those who did not have the good fortune to be published. Some works, by no means the least worthy, were only published later, and used to circulate in manuscript form in Amsterdam and in the diaspora. The printed books which have survived are only a pale reflection of the intense literary activity of the community.[40] It must be stressed that most of the writers had been born in the Peninsula. Alongside the rabbis was a galaxy of men of letters, mainly poets. Their verses, disseminated in many copies, were recited at literary meetings. They were sometimes added to volumes published by other authors in their honour, and printed in limited editions of which nothing now remains. The 'Nation' itself took note of the prodigious literary flowering in its midst. Also, in about 1684, its supreme poet, Miguel Levi de Barrios, wrote a *Relación de los poetas y escritores españoles de la Nación Judayca Amstelodama*, a miscellany of verse and prose, which brought to life again writers snatched in this way from oblivion.[41] It is not possible here to review the whole history of this literature, but some of its most illustrious figures may be mentioned. The New Christian, Fernão Álvares Melo, born at Fronteira in Portugal, who reverted to Judaism under the name of David Abenatar Melo, devoted himself to sacred poetry and produced a Spanish translation in verse of the Psalms of David.[42] In the same category, Moses Belmonte, born in Amsterdam, added to the *Targum*

---

[40] We recollect the old but still useful work by J. Amador de los Rios, *Études historiques, politiques et littéraires sur les Juifs d'Espagne*, Paris, 1861.

[41] See M. Kayserling, 'Une histoire de la littérature juive de Daniel Levi de Barrios', in *REJ* xviii, 1889, pp. 277–89, and W. C. Pieterse's thesis, *Daniel Levi de Barrios al geschiedschrijver van de Portugees Israëlietische gemeente te Amsterdam in zijn 'Triunpho del govierno popular'*, Amsterdam, 1968.

[42] *Los CL psalmos de David en lengua española, en varias rimas...*, Frankfurt, 1626. We now have available H. P. Salomon's important work, *Portrait of a New Christian, Fernão Alvares Melo*, Paris, 1982.

version of the Song of Songs a Spanish translation of the poet's works.[43] Religious morality was to be brilliantly represented by the work of Abraham Pereyra.[44] Sacred drama was notable for two masterpieces: one in Portuguese, the other in Hebrew.[45] The writer of the former, Paulo de Pina, was born in Lisbon but left it with the intention of becoming a monk at Rome. After much travelling in Europe and various spiritual experiences, he embraced Judaism, under the name of Rehuel Jessurun, and at Pentecost 1624 staged his *Diálogo dos Montes* in the Beth Ya'acob synagogue.[46] The author of the latter, Moses Zacuto, wrote the first Hebrew tragedy, entitled *Yesod Olam*, The Foundation of the World, in Amsterdam in about 1640.[47]

Secular poetry was equally appreciated, and some women became famous in this field. Doña Isabel Henriques, for example, had her moment of glory in the poetry circles of Madrid, then she too made her way to Amsterdam, where she allowed her muse full play, especially in verses dedicated to the rabbi Isaac Aboab.

While the eighteenth century outpouring of historical writing was yet to come, the writing of autobiography occupied a prominent position among the various disciplines favoured by the Jewish writers of Amsterdam. Abraham Farrar of Oporto, who was proud to describe himself as 'Judeo do desterro de Portugal' at the beginning of his *Declaração das seiscentas e treze Encommendanças*,[48] found that Manuel Cardoso de Macedo, the son of an Old Christian merchant from the Azores, struck a chord in his account of an eventful life, which remained in manuscript form until 1976.[49]

---

[43] Printed in Amsterdam, at Immanuel Benveniste's, in 1644; new ed., Berlin, 1874. The Hebrew term *targum*, translation, denotes the Aramaic version of the Bible.

[44] *La certeza del camino*, Amsterdam, 1666 (see the edition introduced and annotated by H. Méchoulan, to be published) and *Espejo de la vanidad del mundo*, Amsterdam, 1671.

[45] On Jewish theatre in Amsterdam see Henry V. Besso, *Dramatic Literature of the Sephardic Jews of Amsterdam in the XVIIth and XVIIIth centuries*, Nogent-le-Rotrou, 1947 (=*Bulletin Hispanique*, nos. 39 and 41).

[46] Amsterdam, 1767. In this piece personifications of Mount Sinai, Hor ha-Har, Mount Nebo, Mount Gerizim, Mount Carmel, and the Mount of Olives sing of the glory of the people of Israel. See Rehuel Jessurun, *Diálogo dos Montes*, ed., with an English verse translation, by Philip Polack, London, 1975.

[47] Berlin, 1874; Livorno, 1874. This piece was inspired by Proverbs 10: 25, 'As the whirlwind passeth, so is the wicked no more: but the righteous is an everlasting foundation.' It shows the patriarch Abraham persecuted by King Nimrod, for having destroyed his father's idols, and praising the Lord, who had revealed Himself to him. On this writer see J. Melkman, 'Moshe Zaccuto's play "Yesod 'Olam"', in *Studia Rosenthaliana*, i, 1967, no. 2, pp. 1–26.   [48] Amsterdam, 1627.

[49] This person tells of his adventurous life in England and Portugal, his sufferings in

Was the 'Jewish Nation of Amsterdam', which had been officially admitted to the city and was soundly organized and governed by wise and cultured merchants, now settled, becoming even a middle-class community? Did it find all its aspirations fulfilled on the peaceful banks of the Amstel? To what extend did it see itself as the 'Dutch Jerusalem' as have many historians?[50] Or, on the contrary, should reading *Esperança de Israel* provoke the idea that the Jews of Amsterdam considered their prosperous life in that city to be a miraculous prelude to the coming of the Messiah? Is our rabbi not taking an opportunity to stress the primacy of the divine promise over the present bliss of a settlement, which was indeed peaceful and successful but also dulled by the delights of Amsterdam?

MENASSEH BEN ISRAEL: A NEW LOOK AT HIS LIFE AND WORK 1604–1657

Spinoza's work is celebrated the world over and his thought still looked to for answers to present-day questions. He is thus paid the supreme accolade of being freed from the confines of purely academic respect, but Menasseh ben Israel, the learned and prolific rabbi who very probably taught the young Baruch,[1] had languished in unmerited obscurity. In the mid-seventeenth century, moreover, the master was at least as well known as his disciple. The greatest scholars and princes wrote to Menasseh ben Israel, visited him, and asked him questions. No doubt the preoccupations of these scholars and princes were not exactly the same as ours. On the other hand, those of the very humble men—the rabbi's co-religionists who had experienced suffering and misfortune, men crushed by the weight of injustice and poverty—were, alas!, very close to ours. Ways of formulating them change, but the problems

---

the prisons of the Inquisition, which incarcerated him for Calvinism, his contacts with New Christians in Lisbon who convinced him of the truth of Judaism, his departure for Hamburg, and finally his establishment in Amsterdam where he served the Beth Israel and then Talmud Torah communities as *shamash* (beadle). He died in 1652. See the Portuguese text, Dutch translation, and study of this autobiography in B. N. Teensma's article, 'De Levengeschiedenis van Abraham Perengrino alias Manuel Cardoso de Macedo', in *Studia Rosenthaliana*, x, 1976, no. 1, pp. 1–36.

[50] C. Roth gives the title 'The Dutch Jerusalem' to the chapter devoted to Amsterdam in his *A History of the Marranos*, pp. 236–51. S. W. Baron also calls a long chapter of his book, mentioned above n. 7, 'Dutch Jerusalem'.

[1] There is no actual proof that this teaching took place but it is very seriously presumed to have done so. See C. Roth, *A Life of Menasseh . . .* , p. 71 and *Spinoza, troisième centenaire de la mort du philosophe*, p. 30.

remain the same. Menasseh ben Israel has his place in the history of those who refuse to give in to violence; he is one of those campaigners who take an optimistic view of history, a man, as Professor André Robinet has so rightly said,

whose wish contains essentially a double hope: first, a hope of better tomorrows, a return of reason and tolerance, but also an undefined look towards utopian millennia. For if under the present authorities there is rejection and torture, then the thought of a life which is totally unalterable is intolerable to life itself. For life means not tolerating an intolerance[2].

The life of Menasseh ben Israel must be presented against a background of death, torture, and *auto-da-fé*, a life inseparable from his work, which was almost always inspired by this interrelationship. As long as he lived, Menasseh ben Israel, even when safe himself, heard the continual cries of distress from his brothers, hunted down in the Iberian Peninsula or massacred in Poland.[3]

His biographers differ on the subject of his birthplace. Some, like Cecil Roth, assert that he was born in Madeira,[4] others suggest La Rochelle. However our rabbi twice wrote that he was 'from Lisbon by origin'.[5] Wherever it was, the place where the young Manoel Diaz Soeiro—the future Menasseh ben Israel—was born was well used to persecution. In fact his father was imprisoned and tortured by the Inquisition, as we learn from our rabbi at the end of his book, *De Termino Vitae*: 'My father, Joseph ben Israel of pious memory, was stripped of all his goods by the Spanish Inquisition because he was a Jew. He was previously subjected to torture, which seriously impaired his health. . . . '[6]

So the Soeiro family's wanderings were the immediate consequence of the Holy Office's intolerance. The Dutch were particularly aware of this, as these lines of Barlaeus make plain:

---

[2] Preface to *Philosophes ibériques et ibéro-américains en exil*, University of Toulouse publications–Le Mirail, 1977, p. 8.

[3] Menasseh ben Israel makes a point, in almost all his work, of drawing attention to the unhappy lot of his co-religionists. In addition to the *Hope of Israel*, sect. 30 ff., see especially *De Termino Vitae*, Amsterdam, 1639, book iii, and the *Gratulacão ao celsissimo principe de Orange* . . . , Amsterdam, 1642. See also the *Piedra Gloriosa* . . . , Amsterdam, 1655, section xxiii. On the Polish massacres see Nathan Nata Hannover, *Le fond de l'Abîme*, introduction, translation, and notes by J.-P. Osier, Paris, 1982.

[4] Roth, *A Life of Menasseh* . . . , p. 29.

[5] See a letter from Menasseh ben Israel published by Elkan Nathan Adler in *About Hebrew Manuscripts*, OUP, 1905, p. 74, and *Hope of Israel*, sect. 30.

[6] *De Termino Vitae*, p. 236.

The tyranny of the Inquisitor deals ruthlessly with all thy people, O Judah, both by extortion and by fire and the sword, and it is no use hiding. Security is not to be found on the banks of the Seine nor by the banks of the Tagus. However the city on the Amstel is more sensible: it recognizes and publicly protects thy temples within its boundaries. And, hearing psalms of Alleluia intoned, the daughter of Zion exclaims, 'Here indeed are the people and the city of God.'[7]

Menasseh never forgot Manoel's tribulations. Settled in Amsterdam, the 'Jerusalem of the North', he was still a refugee who had been welcomed by the Dutch, to whom he expressed his gratitude in these moving words: 'We were protected from Spanish tyranny, and for that neither I nor my co-religionists will ever be able to thank you enough.'[8] He described himself as 'Portuguese by birth but Batavian in spirit'[9] meaning to express, at the same time, his origins and his loyalty to his adoptive country, which gave him both security and tolerance.

This tolerance, however, had to be paid for by exemplary behaviour, as much in political matters as in religious. This is demonstrated, for example, in the second article of the famous regulations proposed by Grotius, mentioned earlier.[10] We know also that worship in the synagogues was the object of discreet surveillance, as this report on confessional and civic loyalty drawn up by J. Brun shows:

And if a Jew were ever found guilty of having blasphemed against the mysteries of Christianity, believe me it would not be put up with for long. I am even bold enough to say that I have been in their synagogues a hundred times and that I have hunted with scrupulous care through their liturgy and prayer books to see if I could find any passage discreditable to Jesus Christ . . . But I could never find anything of the kind. These are people who conduct themselves with great modesty in this country . . . They are, moreover, very much for the interests of the country and fervently wish it all prosperity. Would to God that all Christians in these Provinces, born and brought up here, were as patriotic and as loyal to their Sovereign.[11]

Menasseh ben Israel was particularly conscious of the need to maintain the high opinion the Dutch had of the Jewish community. That

---

[7] F.-F. Blok's article 'Quelques humanistes de la Jérusalem de l'Occident', in *Humanists and Humanism in Amsterdam*, Amsterdam, 1973, p. 126 and n. 61, may be consulted on this epigram.

[8] *Conciliador o de la conveniencia de los lugares de la S. Escriptura que repugnantes entre si parecen*, pt 2, Amsterdam, 1641, unpaginated *epistola dedicatoria*. See also the *Gratulacão* . . . already mentioned, which is at the end of *De la fragilidad humana*, Amsterdam, 1642.

[9] *Conciliador* . . . , pt 2, unpaginated *epistola dedicatoria*.

[10] See above Introduction: Amsterdam, pp. 13–14.

[11] *La véritable religion des Hollandais*, Amsterdam, 1675, p. 221.

is why, in his writing, he almost always takes care to emphasize that he does not wish to clash with anyone, nor does he want to disturb anyone's mind. However, as we shall see, these protestations do not prevent him from taking up religious and political positions which are both clear-cut and definite, sometimes setting up the liberal minority as a target for the hostility of the Calvinist clergy. When he puts the weight of his authority behind religious and political writings which cause controversy, a sense of fear comes through: Portuguese by birth, Batavian in spirit, he remains a Jew. This may indeed be seen in the dedicatory epistle of his *De Termino Vitae*: 'And I would not now have had the courage to face up to work fraught with all kinds of difficulties and even dangers for my family, being a Jew, if the great army of sages had not, up to a point, liberated me from fear.'[12]

Contrary to the opinion of Heinrich Graetz, shared to some extent by Cecil Roth, Menasseh ben Israel was not a somewhat innocent and stylish academic, whose sole concern would have been to please everybody. Nor was he, as L. Wolf and C. Gebhardt describe him, an eccentric individual of weak character,[13] nor yet 'a sort of Jewish Victor Cousin taken up with reconciling the Holy Books'.[14] Menasseh ben Israel's thought was no less militant for being prudent. Though he knew how to use the language expected of him by each of his interlocutors, our rabbi was never short of real objectives in his discourse. Courteous, intelligent, open—he was incontrovertibly one of the spiritual fathers of what we now call 'Judaeo-Christian friendship'—a skilful negotiator, he knew how to win sympathy with a candour which could, in certain circumstances, lead him into a state of sound, if irascible, indignation. He also knew when to keep quiet and use cunning. Huet, the Bishop of Avranches, wrote of him: 'Rabbi Manassé ben Israel was a Jew of the highest order . . . and I had long and frequent conversations with him on religious matters. . . . He was, moreover, a very good man of gentle spirit, easy-going, reasonable and free from many Jewish superstitions and the empty dreams of the Kabbalah.'[15] In fact we know that

---

[12] Unpaginated epistle. On this matter see H. Méchoulan. 'Le problème du latin chez Menasseh ben Israël et quelques implications religieuses et politiques à propos d'une lettre inédite à Beverovicius', in *Studia Rosenthaliana*, xiv, no. 2, Assen, 1980, pp. 1–6.

[13] See H. Graetz, *Histoire des Juifs*, Paris, 1898, vol. v, p. 163; C. Roth, *A Life of Menasseh* . . . , p. 39; L. Wolf, *Menasseh ben Israel's mission to Oliver Cromwell*, London, 1901, p. xxiii, and C. Gebhardt, *Die Schriften des Uriel da Costa*, Amsterdam, 1922, p. xxvi.

[14] Alphonse Séché, *Histoire de la Nation juive des origines à nos jours*, Paris, 1944, p. 253.

[15] *Huetiana ou pensées diverses de M. Huet, Evesque d'Avranches*, Paris, 1722, p. 225. J. N. Paquot writes in his Memoirs, 'The celebrated M. Huet, on his return from Sweden in

Menasseh ben Israel was a fervent admirer of the Kabbalah. He did not want to discuss these matters with Huet, and was able to present the image the Bishop of Avranches would wish to see. A fine orator, our rabbi was skilled at adapting his speech to suit his interlocutor, to such an extent, it is true, as Professor C. Perelman writes, that 'to adapt oneself to a listener, is above all to choose as premises for argument theses accepted by him'.[16]

Neither his contemporaries nor, later, the compilers of the great dictionaries, such as Bayle[17] and Moréri,[18] were sparing in their respect for him, indeed their admiration. Although Menasseh ben Israel did not leave us an original philosophical system or any totally new theological thought, he did, by his wide learning not confined merely to a knowledge of Jewish writers, and by his lively expectation of happiness and universal justice, force the Christian world to recognize that a Jewish thinker might also be a good man. Menasseh ben Israel, whom his friend Rembrandt immortalized in engravings, is without doubt, together with Spinoza, the most notable figure in Amsterdam's Jewish community. Our rabbi's thought illuminates, in a very particular way, the judgements which Spinoza was to make on Jews and Judaism in the *Tractatus Theologico-Politicus.*[19]

Menasseh ben Israel was born in 1604 and moved to Amsterdam with his parents. When the Soeiros[20] arrived in the city, they were a poor, bruised family and were cared for by the Jewish 'Nation'. Our author had a difficult childhood, and was to be marked for life by privations, which were hardly less severe when he later became a rabbi. He was given his education by the community, which very quickly found him to

---

1652, had several interviews with him [Menasseh], as much about Jewish ceremonies as about the Christian religion. The rabbi did not seem to him to be very far from a knowledge of the truth.' In *Mémoires pour servir à l'histoire littéraire des dix Provinces-Unies des Pays-Bas*, Leuven, 1763, bio-bibliographical note, p. 398.

16 *L'Empire rhétorique*, Paris, 1977, p. 37.

17 See the *Dictionnaire*, Paris, 1820, article on 'Barlaeus', in which it may be read that Menasseh ben Israel was 'one of the cleverest men there were among the Jews in the 17th century'.

18 *Dictionnaire*, Paris, 1759.

19 See in particular chapters III and XVII. On this matter H. Méchoulan, 'Quelques remarques sur le chapitre III du *Traité théologico-politique*', in *Revue internationale de Philosophie*, no. 119–20, 1977, pp. 198–216, may be consulted as well as 'Juifs, Hébreux et pharisiens dans le *Traité théologico-politique*', in Acts of the Colloquium *Spinoza nel 350° anniversario della nascita*, Urbino, 1982, pp. 439–60.

20 On Menasseh ben Israel's family, see H. P. Salomon, 'The Portuguese background of Menasseh ben Israel's parents as revealed through the Inquisitorial archives at Lisbon', in *Studia Rosenthaliana*, xvii, no. 2, July 1983, pp. 105–46.

be particularly gifted. Among his teachers, mention must be made of the very learned rabbi, Isaac Uziel. He was not to be disappointed by his young pupil, who at fourteen was taking courses designed for adults. Menasseh ben Israel himself, with frank satisfaction, lets us know how precocious he was, in the second part of his *Conciliador*...[21] And so we know that he was especially brilliant at rhetoric and eloquent in Portuguese. He also tells us that he compiled a Hebrew grammar at the age of seventeen. To his profound learning in the religious field was soon to be added a certain skill in Latin[22] and a knowledge of Greek, mathematics, astronomy, and medicine. As far as modern languages were concerned, he had Portuguese, Spanish, and Dutch, as well as a fair amount of French and English. David Franco Mendes actually states that he knew eight languages.[23]

On the death of his master in 1622, Menasseh ben Israel, in spite of his youth, was deemed worthy to take his place. This appointment was an honour from the moral point of view, but financially it was disastrous, since our rabbi had no other means beyond the small salary granted to him.[24] In 1623 he married a member of the illustrious Abrabanel family, who were proud to trace their origins back to King David, as may be seen in the Latin text, intended for a non-Jewish public, in which Menasseh ben Israel enlarges with satisfaction on this glorious ancestry (*Hope of Israel*, section 32). Menasseh, who was extremely proud of having children with such noble origins, suffered from not being able to keep his family in reasonable comfort. Nevertheless his material difficulties had no effect upon his manifold occupations, which went well beyond the usual limits of a rabbinical ministry. Acutely aware of all the persecution suffered by Marranos in Spain as well as in Portugal, Menasseh received new arrivals from the Peninsula, listened to their tales, and tried to lead those in doubt back to their ancestral faith. In his enthusiasm he sometimes confused New Christians with Catholics of old stock, who were scandalized and made a point, on returning to Spain, of denouncing him to the Holy Office. Although we can produce

---

[21] *Conciliador*..., pt 2, fo. 3v.   [22] On this subject see above, n. 12.

[23] In *Memorias do estabelecimento e progresso dos Judeos portuguezes e espanhoes nesta famosa citade de Amsterdam*, published in *Studia Rosenthaliana*, p. 22.

[24] In the articles of the *ascamot* (community rules) for 1639 concerning rabbis, it may be read that the rabbi Menasseh ben Israel, who was to preach each month on the Sabbath, would earn 150 florins; 'O *Haham* Menasse ben Israel, com obrigacao de *darsar* cada mes en Sabat e recebera 150 florins.' See above, Introduction: Amsterdam, n. 32. We note that at the same period, the great Saumaise [Salmasius] was getting 2,000 florins at the University of Leiden.

28   *Introduction*

no concrete evidence, this does not prevent us from speculating that he
was a member of an organization devoted to enabling Marranos to leave
the Peninsula.

Our rabbi's energy was far from exhausted by these activities. He was
also a bookseller,[25] founded a printing house, as we have seen, and in
1627 published the first Hebrew book in Amsterdam. His presses
operated until 1656, under Menasseh's own direction until 1643 when
his sons Joseph and Samuel took over the running of the enterprise.[26] In
1632 he brought out the first part of his *Conciliador* . . . which, according
to C. Joly, had a European audience[27] and about which Basnage wrote
in these terms:

He was not yet twenty-eight when he published the *Primera parte del Conciliador*
. . . In it he sought to reconcile apparent contradictions in the Scriptures,
through the commentaries of ancient and modern scholars and by his own
conjectures. This work, to be completed later, has made him a coryphaeus in his
nation. In fact no other rabbi has worked on this subject with such thorough
scholarship. . . . Grotius, the learned Grotius, consulted him about some
passages of Scripture which were causing him trouble, and received some useful
enlightenment on them: that is why Grotius encouraged him to go on publishing
his works and used also to point them out to scholars as being very useful for
Christians who want to know about Holy Scripture.[28]

Other leading figures, such as the Vossius family, Colvius, Ravius, and
Saumaise (Salmasius), also had recourse to Menasseh's insight.[29]

---

[25] On this activity see L. and R. Fuks, 'Menasseh ben Israel as a bookseller in the light
of new data', in *Quaerendo*, xi, no. 1, Amsterdam, 1981, pp. 34–45.

[26] See H. I. Bloom, *The Economic Activities of the Jews* . . . , pp. 46 ff.

[27] C. Joly met Menasseh ben Israel during a stay in Amsterdam and reported on the
encounter in these terms: 'There I saw Master Manassé ben Israel, a Doctor well known
among them [the Jews] for his writings. I got to know him through his book called
Conciliator which I had read in Paris. . . .' in *Voyage fait à Munster en Westphalie et autres lieux
voisins en 1646 et 1647*, Paris, 1670, p. 108. Denis Vossius was responsible for a Latin
translation of the first part of *Conciliador* . . . , which came out in Amsterdam in 1634 and
explains the book's wide distribution.

[28] *Histoire des Juifs depuis Jésus Christ jusqu'à présent*, The Hague, 1716, vol. ix, pp. 999
ff. This statement may be confirmed by the existence of Grotius's consultation with
Menasseh ben Israel (Amsterdam University Library, *Catalogue of manuscripts of the
Remonstrant Church*, vii, 1923, no. 40, pp. 94–6. Correspondence between Menasseh ben
Israel and Jean-Gérard Vossius may also be found there).

[29] Although the friendship between the Vossius family (J.-G., D., and I.) and
Menasseh ben Israel is well known, that with Saumaise [Salmasius] is not. This illustrious
humanist consulted Menasseh as we have shown (see H. Méchoulan, 'Lorsque Saumaise
consultait Menasseh ben Israel: Deux lettres inédites du rabbin d'Amsterdam à l'humaniste de Leyde', in *Studia Rosenthaliana*, xiii, no. 1, Jan. 1979, pp. 1–17). On Menasseh
ben Israel's relationship with members of the Republic of Letters, C. Roth, *A Life of*

Basnage's praise is not excessive if the difficulties encountered by the spiritual leaders of Amsterdam's Jewish community are borne in mind. These men had to receive refugees, Marranos hoping to rediscover the religion from which their ancestors had been forcibly converted. But they did not necessarily achieve their objectives, being, as they were, constrained by respect for the demands of strict orthodoxy. Every *émigré* is a kind of adventurer, who brings with him his own restlessness. The official and traditional Judaism presented to these New Christians from Spain and Portugal was not inevitably the religion which they had imagined or expected. Without doubt the best example of this gap between the dream and the reality of the rediscovered ancestral faith was Uriel da Costa.[30] He has left a moving account of his own intransigence and the difficulties he had in adapting to Judaism, while others, less eloquent or more cautious, must also have experienced hesitation followed by doubts, or analysis with a savour of either theism or atheism. These people will have found their best arguments in the searching questions which Reason puts to the Old Testament every time a contradiction is found in it. Unlike La Peyrère, not all their contemporaries had recourse to the Preadamites[31] in order to try to find a coherence which the sacred texts were often far from providing. It was with the aim of counteracting these attitudes, which were threatening both the religion and the security of the community, that our rabbi wrote the *Conciliador*, a work in four parts, completed in 1651. For the free-thinkers, 'lovers of novelty' as Menasseh ben Israel called them, missed no opportunity of pointing out the contradictions in the Old Testament, and of casting doubt on the unity of the writing of the Pentateuch.

None of these problems had escaped the notice of generations of rabbis, who had meticulously tried to explain them in their commentaries. Nevertheless Menasseh ben Israel deserves the credit for having

Menasseh . . . , chapter 7, may be consulted. Roth does not mention the cordial links which existed between our rabbi, Ravius, and Colvius. In fact Ravius, a celebrated Hebrew scholar, was more than a mere purchaser of the output of our rabbi's printing house. He was among Menasseh and Vossius's friends, as the end of a letter from Ravius to Isaac Vossius demonstrates; 'Omnes communes amicos et Rabbi Menassen [*sic*] salutabis', Royal Library of Leiden University, MS Br. F. II, ep. 801. We are grateful to Professor Blok for these details.

[30] On Uriel da Costa, the works of C. Gebhardt and the more recent ones of I. S. Révah may be consulted. See the translation and study of Uriel da Costa's *Exemplar Humanae Vitae* in J.-P. Osier, *D'Uriel da Costa à Spinoza*, Paris, 1983. This major work constitutes a veritable 'dossier' on the matter.

[31] *Praeadamitae sive exercitatio super versibus duodecimo, decimotertio & decimoquarto capitis quinti Epistolae D. Pauli ad Romanos quibus inducuntur primi homines ante Adamum conditi*, n.p., 1655.

put them together and for providing the reader with a reconciliation of all the apparently contradictory passages in Holy Scripture. Menasseh reminded doubters and unbelievers that God had deliberately made Scripture obscure, so that reading it would give rise to a wide range of commentaries, all compatible with faith. Also that the study of the sacred texts would never become rigid, and might be compared to an ever-flowing spring.[32] That those who were too bold or too hasty in their judgement should not forget that there are many approaches to Scripture: the historical way and the mystic way, which itself is made up of tropology, allegory, and analogy, and that each of these methods allows an infinite number of opinions.[33] Menasseh ben Israel would have subscribed totally to this analysis by Pierre Chaunu: 'Bible reading is a science. It requires a great deal of patience. The Jewish people, which has lived through the most distressing and tragic of human histories, owes the miracle of its survival to daily meditation on the Law and the Prophets, and to reflection on each letter of the Book from the beginning.'[34] It was precisely against this type of reading, against this kind of exegesis and its consequences that Spinoza protested in the *Tractatus Theologico-Politicus*, when he made the rule that 'knowledge of Scripture should come from Scripture alone'.[35] The philosopher was also opposed to this explanation of the survival of the Jewish people because, according to him, it was only because they were hated by other nations that the identity of the Jews was so indestructible.[36]

Three years after the publication of *Conciliador . . .*, Menasseh ben Israel brought out the *De Creatione Problemata*, dedicated to David de Wilhem.[37] In this work our rabbi takes up again a critical view put forward by Maimonides, 'Rabbi Moses of Egypt'. This criticism is aimed at Aristotle and endeavours to demonstrate his error in 'claiming that the whole universe, just as it is, has always been and will always be so . . .'.[38] For Maimonides, as for Menasseh ben Israel, the creation of

[32] *Conciliador . . .*, pt 2, fo. 3.   [33] Ibid.

[34] *La Violence de Dieu*, Paris, 1978, p. 52.   [35] See chapter VII.

[36] H. Méchoulan, 'Quelques remarques sur le chapitre III du *Traité théologico-politique*', in particular pp. 205–6.

[37] Amsterdam, 1635. On the links between Menasseh ben Israel and David de Wilhem, see H. Méchoulan, 'A propos de la visite de Frédéric-Henri . . . à la synagogue d'Amsterdam, une lettre inédite de Menasseh ben Israel à David de Wilhem suivie de la traduction française du discours de bienvenue', in *Lias*, Review of the Institute for Relations between the Countries of Western Europe in the seventeenth Century, at the Catholic University of Nijmegen, v, 1978, 1, pp. 82–6.

[38] Maimonides, *Guide for the Perplexed*, trans. M. Friedländer, London, 1885, vol. ii, ch. 13, 3rd proposition.

the world by God is an article of faith. Indeed to accept the theory of the eternity of the world, as Aristotle insists, leads inevitably 'to undermining religion at its foundation, to charging all miracles with being necessarily untrue, and to denying all that religion has made us hope or fear'.[39] Our rabbi must have had a precise object in using Maimonides's thought in this way. It may be wondered whether some heterodox thinkers, like Ribera and Prado, within the community, had predecessors who had contested the divine creation of the world. Juan de Prado indeed stated later, as I. S. Révah reports: 'The world was not created, but it has always been as it is now, and always will be.'[40] In defending Maimonides's thesis, Menasseh ben Israel could not but attract the sympathy of both Jews and Christians. At the beginning of the *De Creatione Problemata*, Barlaeus, a friend of our rabbi's, wrote a famous sonnet which sets out a universal piety and recognizes Jewish truths which are acceptable to Christians; Barlaeus concludes by mentioning their friendship, which was unimpaired by confessional differences.[41] After the *Conciliador* ... , the *De Creatione Problemata* confirmed Menasseh ben Israel's desire to demonstrate the common foundations of Judaism and Christianity. He pursued this line further by publishing, in 1636, a work as important as the *Conciliador*, the *De la resurrección de los muertos*. The object of this book was to combat the heterodoxy which was threatening to disrupt the spiritual unity of the Amsterdam community. It was written at the time when the Uriel da Costa affair was shaking the fabric of Jewish society in Amsterdam. Uriel da Costa's spiritual revolt which, we must recall, denied, among other thinks, the immortality of the soul and consequently the idea of

---

[39] Ibid.
[40] 'Aux origines de la rupture spinozienne: Nouveaux documents sur l'incroyance dans la communauté judéo-portugaise d'Amsterdam à l'époque de l'excommunication de Spinoza' in *REJ*, iii (cxxiii), fasc. 3 and 4, July–Dec. 1964, p. 378.
[41] The last part of this sonnet may be translated:

> Even though your religion differs from mine
> We live as friends to serve God.
> May your wisdom and mine
> Be valued everywhere according to their worth!
> Such, Menasseh, is the object of my friendship.
> Believe me, it is very straightforward.
> As long as I live, I will remain a Christian,
> And you live for ever as a Jew.

On the stir created by this sonnet , see Bayle's *Dictionnaire*, article on Barlaeus, and F. F. Blok's study already mentioned. We are indebted to this writer for a very important piece of work on links between Barlaeus and the Jews: 'Caspar Barlaeus en de Joden: De Geschiedenis van een Epigram' in *Nederlands Archief voor Kerkgeschiedenis*, 1976–7.

rewards and punishments after death, arose at a particularly difficult time for the community's leaders. Outwardly they had to make their orthodoxy absolutely clear, while inwardly bending to the realities of the religious situation, for fear of seeing the resurgence of Judaism stemming from Iberian Marranism disintegrate. Uriel da Costa's 'Sadducean' attitude was doubly unacceptable, especially since it did not happen to be, as we have said, unique. It already foreshadowed the major heterodoxies of Prado and Spinoza. That is why, right from the dedicatory epistle to the book, Menasseh ben Israel took a particularly strong position against what he called 'the maliciousness of the Sadducees who, in these wretched times, try to convince people of the mortality of their souls in order to allow free rein to their lascivious appetites'.[42] This defensive reaction of our rabbi's was all the tougher because Uriel da Costa's rebellion was not at all restrained, as Duff and Kaan rightly point out: 'Costa's faith did not coincide with Israel's; he preferred to convert Israel: that seemed much easier to him.'[43]

It is not our intention to analyse *De la resurrección de los muertos*, but two important points must be highlighted, which are fundamental to Menasseh ben Israel's thought and which appear here for the first time: the freedom of man and the universality of salvation. From here on these two themes are at the centre of all our rabbi's thinking. As opposed to the Sadducees, who think that men, after death, go to the *sheol*, an indeterminate wilderness about which nothing is known, a silent land in which God takes no interest, Menasseh ben Israel maintains that a new life begins after death. A great admirer of the *Zohar*, he takes from it the theory of the migration of souls, which are to make a lengthy pilgrimage until, after a series of stages of purification, they reach the highest perfection.[44] For the soul cannot die because it is, according to Plato, an essence made up of pure intelligence.[45] Moreover, the description of the soul given by the author of *The Republic* is very like that of the ancient sages in *Berakhot*, the first treatise of the Talmud.[46] This coincidence is not in the least surprising as, according to Menasseh, it was the disciples of Jeremiah who, among other things, taught Plato the mystery of the

[42] *De la resurrección de los muertos: Libros III en los quales se prueva la immortalidad del alma y resurrección de los muertos*, Amsterdam, 1636, unpaginated Epistola Dedicatoria.
[43] Uriel da Costa, *Exemplar Humanae Vitae*, translated by A. B. Duff and P. Kaan, Paris, 1926, introd. p. 45.
[44] On this subject see S. Karpe, *Étude sur les origines et la nature du Zohar*, Paris, 1901, pp. 481 ff.
[45] *De la resurrección de los muertos*, p. 28.
[46] Ibid.

transmigration of souls. Our rabbi makes a point of explaining man's tendency to evil by appealing to Plato's theory of the fall of the soul. The soul is exiled on earth but this banishment is not final. This Platonism is combined with a theory of climates taken from Galen. For men's more or less wicked characters are in no way linked to ethnic or religious origins, but are due to the chance of climate, to 'characterological' type, and to the conjunction of the planets to which they are subject. However these factors are in no way inescapable. If they are unfavourable, a man can overcome them and, by a readiness to understand, acquire a saving wisdom: 'Now just as a man may be put at a disadvantage as the result of a contrary conjunction of the planets, by his disturbed temperament, or through climatic influences, he can overcome all these hostile elements, acquire both learning and virtue, so mastering nature through his own efforts'.[47] Every man 'may dwell in the tents of the Lord'. But the struggle will not finally be resolved until the end of the soul's pilgrimage. This belief was fundamental in the Kabbalah, which Menasseh ben Israel admired so much. It should be remembered that migration must be understood not as a transmigration of the soul (metempsychosis), but rather as its re-embodiment (metensomatosis), which bears witness to divine justice and mercy.[48] Since physical make up plays an important role in human behaviour, the soul might complain of having been contaminated by a body it did not choose. In order that man should have no excuses to make to God, He provided a new bodily frame, so that either a man may attain greater perfection, or a soul, which has not been able to resist evil instincts, may be punished. The *Zohar* and Plato are unanimous on this method of purification.[49] This, it goes without saying, implies the immortality of the soul and the resurrection of the dead, a general resurrection which will take place in all corners of the world. God has indeed favoured His people by giving them the six hundred and thirteen precepts of the Law and they must be generally applied. If a synthesis is required, or even a summary of conduct towards others, Lev. 19: 18 may be recalled: 'Thou shalt love thy neighbour as yourself.'[50]

Menasseh ben Israel was to take up the tradition of Jewish universalism again, insisting with force and precision on the equality of the just, to whatever nation or confession they might belong, and on the salvation of

---

[47] *De la fragilidad humana*, Amsterdam, 1642, p. 78.
[48] See G. Casaril, *Rabbi Siméon Bar Yochaï et la cabbale*, Paris, 1961, p. 113.
[49] *De la resurrección de los muertos*, p. 117.
[50] *De la fragilidad humana*, pp. 52–4.

all men of good will, answering as it were in advance the accusations of egoism and xenophobia which Spinoza was to make against the Hebrews in the *Tractatus Theologico-Politicus*.[51] Lamennais was to be more impartial than the philosopher in this matter since he later wrote:

> Whatever ideas the Jews had of their pre-eminence over other peoples, they recognized that the true God had worshippers everywhere. The Talmud recognizes that just, pious men exist in every nation on earth and that they will have a share, as good as that of the Israelites, in the world to come. Maimonides and Menasseh ben Israel taught the same doctrine.[52]

In fact our rabbi rejects any solitary enjoyment of salvation by the Jewish people alone. He devotes the ninth chapter of the second book of *De la resurrección de los muertos* to quoting and commenting on all the texts which support the universality of salvation for the just. Commenting on the words of Daniel he writes: 'It is clear that there is no special mention for the people of Israel, for Daniel does not say "many among the sons of your people", but "many of them that sleep in the dust of the earth", which includes many other nations.'[53] Menasseh ben Israel also notes that it would be iniquitous for the wicked of Israel to enjoy the same fortune as the just of other nations.

Why this insistence on the freedom of man and the universality of salvation at the heart of works which have for many years been thought to be dedicated to the exclusive use of a community with problems of cohesion? Certainly Menasseh ben Israel's first concern is, without doubt, to oppose all heterodoxy. But why, then, does he almost always publish in Latin, following up the first Latin edition with a second in Spanish? It should be noted that Latin was very little used in teaching in the Amsterdam community, since the young Baruch de Spinoza was to go to the Catholic van den Enden,[54] to learn it. In publishing in Latin, our rabbi knew that he was taking a stand in political and religious dispute, putting the whole weight of this authority, already great in 1639, behind the cause of freedom of conscience, of tolerance, and of respect for mankind. In that year, 1639, *De Termino Vitae* was published. In this work Menasseh lays less stress on the universality of salvation than on

---

[51] Chapter XVII. On this topic see H. Méchoulan, 'Juifs, Hébreux et pharisiens'.

[52] *De l'indifférence en matière de religion*, quoted by J. Salvador in *Histoire des institutions de Moïse et du peuple hébreu*, Paris, 1862, vol. 1, p. 419, Cf. *Tosefta Sanhedrin*, 13.2, 'There are just among the heathens who have a share in the future world'.

[53] *De la resurrección de los muertos*, p. 100.

[54] See the chapter devoted to this strange character in K. O. Meinsma, *Spinoza et son cercle*.

the freedom of man. For in 1634, in his *Epistolica Quaestio de Vitae Termino*, Beverovicius, a celebrated doctor, had considered whether the span of human life was definitively and necessarily fixed by God.[55] In search of wider knowledge on this question, he had obtained from numerous scholars, among whom were Barlaeus[56] and Episcopius,[57] the collection of responses which then made up the greater part of his book. The question probably went beyond the realms of the usefulness of medicine, for it formed part of the old problem of lazy reasoning already debated by the Stoics, which Leibniz summed up in these terms: 'If the future is predestined, that which must happen will happen, whatever I can do.'[58] It goes without saying that discussion of this question was on a collision course with the doctrine of predestination advocated by Calvin, a doctrine which his opponents were quick to class with Muslim fatalism. It is known that the followers of Arminius, the Remonstrants, were vigorously opposed to Gomarus, the defender of the Calvinist theses supported by the House of Orange. According to this belief, God has chosen for all time, by a free act of grace and love, certain of His creatures to be accorded the joy of perpetual glory, without His divine foresight having taken into account their faith or their deeds. Destined to sin, the rest of mankind is condemned to destruction without the possibility of salvation. Original sin defiles men definitively, and they can never wash away the stain which reduces them to a state of total moral incapacity. Only certain elect have been redeemed by the sacrifice of Christ: it is they whom God will call to Himself. Arminius, on the other hand, taught that God excludes nobody from His love, which embraces the whole human race. Everybody has the possibility, by faith and above all by deeds, of achieving bliss. Episcopius afterwards took his master's thinking further. He subordinated theological abstractions to the practice of a Christianity composed of charity, love of one's neighbour, and understanding, vigorously excluding all forms of intolerance. The secondary position he gave to dogma caused less emphasis to be put on the specific beliefs which divide mankind. This led to a great open-mindedness towards all confessions on Episcopius's part, in as much as the brotherhood which should unite people seemed more important to him than the religions which divide them. It is certain

[55] Dordrecht, 1634.
[56] According to Bayle, this writer was a fervent follower of Arminius and, as a result, shared the Remonstrants' views. See Bayle's *Dictionnaire*, s.v.
[57] We note that Bayle's article on 'Episcopius' in his *Dictionnaire* is very interesting.
[58] *Théodicée*, ed. P. Janet, Paris, 1900, p. 6.

that this generous man, whose ties of friendship with Menasseh have been documented for us by Sorbière and Paquot,[59] would have unhesitatingly subscribed to these Isaiah-inspired words of Malachi's: 'For from the rising of the sun even unto the going down of the same my name shall be great among the Gentiles; and in every place incense shall be offered unto my name.'[60] In supporting Episcopius's theories, Menasseh ben Israel was taking a definite risk. Arminius's disciple's own brother was a victim of orthodox fanaticism, which, in arming the people against him, was responsible for wrecking his house. Our rabbi himself made a point of mentioning the danger to which some writing could give rise, as we have seen in the dedicatory epistle to *De Termino Vitae*. He was giving support through this book to the Remonstrants, whose political orientation, as Kolakowski reminds us, may be summed up in these three essential criteria: religious tolerance, a federalist system of government, and pre-eminence of the civil power over the life of the Church.[61]

Schoeps demonstrates, in his *Philosemitismus im Barok*, the important part played by the Arminians in seventeenth-century philosemitism.[62] Menasseh put all his learning at the service of the Arminian theory, to which he never made any actual allusion. He expounded only the doctrine of the rabbis to his friend Beverovicius, without appearing to take sides in the conflict which was splitting his country of asylum. Our author's work is divided into three books, which cover the following topics: the span of life, the possibility of altering the date of its conclusion, and finally, the compatibility of human freedom with God's foreknowledge. We do not want to discuss the whole of this book here, but we will go over the basic points, which prove quite clearly that Menasseh ben Israel was opposed to Calvinism, as later and in other circumstances was Saul Levi Morteira.[63] The influence of the planets is not to be neglected, but it is not to be considered as the determining factor in the life of man because, if this were the case, his freedom would

---

[59] Sorbière confirms the friendship linking Menasseh ben Israel with Vossius, Barlaeus, and Episcopius in his *Sorberiana . . .* , p. 125. See also Paquot, *Mémoires . . .* , p. 398.

[60] Isaiah 1.11.

[61] See L. Kolakowski, *Chrétiens sans Église: la conscience religieuse et le lien confessionnel au XVIIe siècle*, Paris, 1965, p. 77.

[62] H. J. Schoeps, *Philosemitismus in Barok*, Tübingen, 1952, p. 21.

[63] *Tratado de la verdad de la lei de Moseh y Providencia de Dios con su pueblo*. This manuscript has never been published. It was written in Amsterdam before 1660. See H. Méchoulan, 'Morteira et Spinoza au carrefour du socinianisme', in *REJ*, cxxxv, 1976, pp. 51–65.

be reduced to nothing. Menasseh goes on to recall that the stars have no influence on the life of a Jew, except inasmuch as he neglects the Law.[64] Jews, he continues, do not consider the span of life to be definitely fixed. by divine decree for, there again, their freedom would be destroyed. Many factors, dependent on and independent of human will, come together to fix the date of death: 'All Jews without exception admit that the date of death is modifiable.' The first of the arguments advanced by Menasseh went straight to the heart of his friend, the doctor, since our rabbi, in keeping with Jewish tradition, considers that man is accountable for his health. If his life span were immutable, why should man have recourse to a doctor's skill and the remedies which God, in His great bounty, has provided? Among the Jews, whenever a man is ill, the doctor is sent for to treat him.[65] Menasseh lays equal stress on the part played by ancestry and diet, the influence of vice and virtue, the effect of climate, and, above all, the importance of piety and of repentance during the course of a life. God is not deaf to the prayers of the just. So it is not impossible for man's conduct to affect the length of his life, by natural means or with divine help. As far as the problem of human freedom is concerned, Menasseh's answer to his own question, having set out numerous theories, is that of Maimonides: it is clear that man has free will and there can be no doubt that God is omniscient; but a problem remains, that of reconciling the omniscience of God with human free will.[66] He states that he is adopting Rabbi Isaac Bar Sheshet's lucid solution, which may be expressed in these terms: the ordering of the world for all time is known to God, but that knowledge does not determine man's conduct.

A man does not act this way or that because God knows in advance that he will so act but, on the contrary, it is because a man acts according to his own will that God knows his actions for all time. Rabbi Isaac Arama, Justin Martyr, Origen, the Damascene, Chrysostom, Jerome, Augustine, and Cyril share this view. I support this solution unconditionally.[67]

Menasseh then illustrates this philosophical choice with the following example: though a person standing on the top of a tower sees men coming and going in all directions, he does not, for all that, determine their movements. All these conclusions in favour of freedom are supported by biblical authority, by the Rabbinical Commentaries, and also, not always the case in Menasseh's work, by reference to non-

---

[64] *De Termino Vitae*, pp. 18–19.   [65] Ibid., p. 43.   [66] Ibid., p. 226.
[67] Ibid., pp. 227–8. This theory is taken up again in *De la fragilidad humana*, p. 67.

Jewish thinkers. It is very likely that the young Spinoza benefited from this intellectual opening-up, which would have put him considerably in his master's debt. It is not for nothing that the authors of the *Spinoza Catalogue*, published on the 300th anniversay of the philosopher's death, wrote: ' . . . Menasseh ben Israel was also in favour of contacts with the Christian world, in a way which makes it probable that he encouraged the young Spinoza along this path, outside school as well.'[68]

It was in another work which appeared in 1642, *De la fragilidad humana*, that Menasseh, while meditating on man's weakness, went on most emphatically to refute the doctrine of predestination. Our rabbi rejects violently, from the first page of his book, the Pelagian doctrine which claimed that Adam's transgression affected nobody but himself. The whole of the first part of his discourse on the frailty of man is devoted to showing that sin is natural to him and that even the most righteous among the just is a sinner. In Menasseh's eyes there is no excuse for ignorance or even for guilty thoughts never realized in actions. It is therefore impossible to find a man, however righteous he is, who does not sin, for, as the saying goes, 'humanum est peccare'.[69] But God has given man, through the Law, the means to overcome his sad and weak condition. Totally open to evil, he is equally open to good, and may follow the divine commandments, act virtuously and rid himself of the misfortune which is the result of sin. There is a positive quality in the works of the just man which challenges his fallen state. Furthermore no good deed is empty in the eyes of God;[70] no sin, even a mortal one, can wipe out good or meritorious works. It is not striving which can overcome the tragedy of the fall. Menasseh concludes by citing Cleanthes, who was so disadvantaged socially, but who became 'a second Hercules in wisdom'. Thus 'let him who would live in the tents of the Lord and dwell on the mountain of holiness conduct himself perfectly, and be just and perfectly sincere'.[71]

The period from 1639 to 1642 was decisive not only for our rabbi, but also for the whole Jewish community. Menasseh ben Israel was officiating in one of the three synagogues in Amsterdam, *Neveh Shalom*. Now, as we know, this was to disappear after the union of the three places of worship in a single temple, whose pulpit was entrusted, in 1639, to Saul Levi Morteira. This unification had deplorable consequences for our author, who saw his very modest salary decrease from 200 to 150 florins

68 *Spinoza, troisième centenaire de la mort du philosophe*, p. 30.
69 *De la fragilidad humana y inclinacion del hombre al pecado*, p. 5.
70 Ibid., p. 48.   71 Ibid., p. 83.

a year.[72] In addition, Basnage's comment seems well-founded: 'From the age of eighteen he was chosen to expound the Talmud in Amsterdam. In this work he acquired a reputation which caused jealousy and made him enemies . . .'.[73] Indeed, over and above his loss of salary, Menasseh's self-esteem suffered greatly when he saw his less eloquent, less well-known rival, Isaac Aboab de Fonseca, become Morteira's assistant at a salary of 450 florins! In order to cope with his needs, both as head of a family and as a printer, our rabbi tried commerce and sent his brother, Ephraim, to Brazil, as he tells us in a letter, published as a postscript to *De Termino Vitae*, addressed to one of his greatest friends, Beverovicius.[74] This new enterprise explains the dedication of this work and of the second part of the *Conciliador* to the 'very noble, very wise and illustrious Gentlemen of the Council of the West Indies'. The dedication tells us that Menasseh is preparing to leave Holland for Brazil, and in his dedicatory epistle he gives an account of his activities. In 1641 he has written 350 sermons, replied to 150 letters from the best known scholars in Europe, without mentioning his books, of which he gives a list. His determination to leave Amsterdam was reinforced by a tiresome incident which took place in the spring of 1640. The commercial activities of Menasseh and his brother, who was already established in Brazil, and of his brother-in-law, Jonas Abrabanel, who was equally involved in the business, gave offence to certain influential members of the community who wanted a monopoly of dealings among the Jews. This attitude was denounced in lampoons posted at the doors of the synagogue and at the bourse, lampoons which directly called into question the power and authority of the *parnassim*. These officials took action, and after an inquiry found that the authors of the posters were none other than Jonas Abrabanel and Moses Belmonte.[75] They were temporarily expelled, by means of the minor *herem*, and made honourable amends. But their retraction was not the end of the affair, Menasseh, sick at the sight of his brother-in-law being condemned for having expressed an indignation which he himself shared, spoke publicly in the synagogue, denouncing the decision of the Gentlemen of the *Ma'amad*. Menasseh, in his turn, was expelled temporarily by the minor *herem*.[76] This episode made him still more resolute in his desire to leave the 'Jerusalem of the North', and he was

---

[72] C. Roth, *A Life of Menasseh . . .* , p. 51.   [73] Basnage, *Histoire des Juifs*, p. 998.
[74] *De Termino Vitae*, p. 237.   [75] C. Roth, *A Life of Menasseh . . .* , pp. 53 ff.
[76] Ibid. This *herem* is recorded on p. 155 of the *Livro dos acordos da Naçam* preserved in the Municipal Archives of Amsterdam. It was deliberately hidden as a result of a

about to embark for America when an unexpected event made him reconsider his decision. The Jewish community of Recife wanted to provide itself with a well-known rabbi and asked for the ministry of Isaac Aboab de Fonseca. He accepted and so the second place in the rabbinical hierarchy in Amsterdam fell vacant. 'Swallowing his pride', as Cecil Roth says, Menasseh took on the duties of his former rival. The arrival in Amsterdam, two years later, of the Pereyra brothers[77] further improved our rabbi's situation. The reason for this was that Abraham Pereyra founded a religious school whose direction he entrusted to our author. From this time on, to the end of his life, he was to enjoy relatively easy circumstances, but above all a growing reputation which he managed to acquire by dint of unremitting work, which he himself instances in describing one day's timetable:

So that you can see that I am not exaggerating, this is how I allocate my time. Each day I devote two hours to the temple, six to the school, one and a half to the Pereyras' Academy, both the public classes and individual work, of which I am president, and two to the correction of my typographical proofs, as I am alone in this work. From eleven o'clock until noon I receive all those who come to me for advice. This is all indispensable. Your Grace may be the judge of the amount of time I have to deal with my domestic cares, and to answer four to six letters a week.[78]

Menasseh ben Israel does not mention in this letter the commercial activities he was engaged in, with loathing, 'for want of a patron'.[79] It was not only in order to live free from want that he undertook trade with Brazil and Poland, but also to be able to go on printing his books. The younger of his two sons took care of the printing-works, while the elder was in charge of business matters. He was to die on a journey he was making on his father's account to Poland. In addition to the great sorrow caused by this bereavement, there was a considerable financial loss because his son was carrying goods and money, which were lost with him.

The theological discussions of this whole period, which supported

resolution passed by the Gentlemen of the *Ma'amad*, dated 8 Ellul 5409 (16 Aug. 1649). In fact the leaders of the community, who were ashamed of what had happened, had a page stuck over that on which the *herem* appeared, a page on which may be read: 'Em 8 de ÿlul 5409 foÿ resoluido polos Senhores do Mahamad que por bons Respeitos se cubrisse esta folha. Esto firmaran . . .' A 'blunder' while the work was being consulted has, nevertheless, allowed a photocopy to be made.

[77] On the Pereyra brothers see M. Kayserling, *Biblioteca española-portuguesa-judaica*, s.v. On Abraham Pereyra, see the introduction to *La Certeza del Camino*, Madrid, to be published.

[78] See Menasseh ben Israel's letter published by E. N. Adler, *About Hebrew Manuscripts*, Oxford, 1905, pp. 73–4.   [79] Ibid.

the liberals' theories and their political struggle, did not allow our rabbi to forget that his co-religionists were being hunted down, tortured, and burnt in the Peninsula and in Poland.[80] We need no further proof than the sudden appearance, in the middle of a discussion focusing on the span of life, of the problem of the forced conversion of Portuguese Jews, of their dreadful situation, and of the unenviable destiny of the countries which were making them suffer such appalling treatment. Menasseh indeed points out that the Jews make a contribution to the prosperity of the lands which give them asylum,[81] thus answering in advance Kant's accusation in the *Anthropology*.[82] Our rabbi wanted to rescue large numbers of Marranos and Jews from their tragic lot, and was looking for new countries which would give these unfortunate people a welcome. Moreover, through his friend Isaac Vossius, a Gentleman of the Chamber to Her Majesty the Queen of Sweden, he established a relationship with Christina, to whom he addressed a poem in Hebrew on the occasion of her coronation. Arckenholtz, this celebrated queen's biographer, writes that Menasseh

had it in mind to dedicate to her all four volumes of his work called *Conciliador*. In addition he offered, should the queen wish to increase her library of Hebrew books, to obtain the best for her and in the best editions. . . . It is not possible to say whether all these attentions paid by this rabbi to Christina concealed some plan to make her favourable to the introduction into Sweden of the Jewish nation . . .

and Arckenholtz concludes: 'Menasseh ben Israel was a perfectly honest man and seemed to lack no virtue save the good fortune to be a

[80] On the 1648 massacre of Jews in Poland, see Gabriel ben Josue, *La Porte de la Pénitence*, printed in Amsterdam in 1651 by Immanuel Benveniste, and translated into French by L. Wogue with an introduction by X. Korczak Branicki, Paris, 1879; also Nathan Nata Hannover, *Le Fond de l'Abîme*. On the relationship between Menasseh ben Israel and David Carcassoni, who was responsible for collecting funds for the ransoming of Jews from the diaspora communities, see David Kaufmann, 'David Carcassoni et le rachat par la communauté de Constantinople des juifs faits prisonniers durant la persécution de Chmielnicki' in *REJ*, xxv, Paris, 1892, pp. 202–16.

[81] *De Termino Vitae*, p. 147.

[82] *Kants Werke, Akademie-Ausgabe*, Bd. vii, p. 205–6 (note). 'The Palestinians who live among us have, due to their practice of usury since they were exiled, at least with most people, a reputation for deception which is not without foundation. It does indeed seem strange to conceive of a *nation* of deceivers, but it is also very strange to conceive of a nation of merchants, the majority of whom, bound by an ancient superstition accepted by the State they live in, do not seek any civil dignity, but prefer to make good this disadvantage with the benefits of trickery at the expense of the people who shelter them and at the expense of each other. In a nation of merchants, unproductive members of society . . . it cannot be otherwise.'

Christian.'[83] We will see later, in the analysis of the *Hope of Israel*, that our rabbi was more successful in his approaches to Cromwell.

Menasseh was prevented, by the many activities we have mentioned, from publishing as many works as he would have wished. A treatise on duties, entitled *Thesouro dos Dinim*, appeared in 1645. Written in Portuguese, it was addressed to a wide public of men and women, being aimed at the regulation of the life of a Jew on a day-to-day basis. We will consider later the *Hope of Israel*, which came off the presses in 1650. In 1652 Menasseh published *Nishmat Hayim*, which was sub-titled *De Immortalitate Animae*. In this work he seeks to prove that the immortality of the soul is a topic common to the Bible, the Talmud, the Kabbalah, and the Rabbinical Commentaries. Always very faithful to the Platonic doctrine of the *Phaedo*, he welcomed most warmly the key ideas of the kabbalah, which he set in opposition to those of Aristotle.

We must now make a special effort to bring out the theme of salvation for all, which appears, founded on Messianic thought, in the *Piedra gloriosa o de la estatua de Nebuchadnesar*, a work dedicated to Isaac Vossius, which Rembrandt was to illustrate.[84] This last book, designed to explain the prophecy of Daniel, reaffirms the major importance of the universality of salvation for Menasseh, who does not hesitate to reduce to certain moral imperatives the religion which is both essential and sufficient for all men to be saved. He even prunes the injunctions of the Law of Noah, to which he draws attention in Chapter IX of the second book of *De la resurrección de los muertos*. In our rabbi's work, along with the Messianic belief which he affirms in his writing from the *Hope of Israel* onwards, we find a preoccupation with morality to the detriment of dogma, to the point where the propositions we shall examine define a faith which could be common to all men and would arouse no dissension. It is probable that the influence of Grotius had some effect on the formulation of the moral rules which Menasseh proposes. The famous jurist indeed wrote: 'Let us tear egoism from our hearts, let us follow the laws of Nature like the luminous spheres which attract each other and give rise to celestial harmony.'[85] The Remonstrants' tolerance and the *pietas universalis* of men like Barlaeus should also be stressed. We can say without paradox that Menasseh's thought is less religious than Spinoza's, when he is dreaming of his 'common and universal faith', for

---

[83] *Mémoires pour servir à l'histoire de Christine reine de Suède*, Amsterdam, 1751, vol. i, p. 304.   [84] Amsterdam, 1655.

[85] H. Grotius, *Œuvres théologiques et morales* in A. Caumont, *Étude sur la vie et les travaux de Grotius*, Paris, 1862, p. 278.

the author of the *Tractatus Theologico-Politicus* insists on the need for obedience to God for those who follow the path of religion,[86] while our rabbi puts greater emphasis on the commandments of the law of Nature. When meditating on salvation for all men of goodwill, to whatever confession they belong, Menasseh bases his thoughts on the Hebrew tradition which may be summarized by the commentary on Psalm 125, in which the psalmist entreats divine bounty for the priests and the Israelites but also for virtuous men of all nations 'from which it follows that a virtuous pagan is worth as much as a High Priest descended from Aaron'.[87] True to this interpretation, Menasseh reflects on the works of the just. If God extends His mercy even to animals, why should He not show it to men endowed with reason? The Eternal takes account of each individual's merits. Some men, who meditate on Holy Scripture, interpret it in a different way; however, if a just and moral life comes out of that meditation, the distinction, in respect of merit, between Jews and non-Jews disappears, inasmuch as it is true that 'the non-Jew, who is virtuous and has the Law fresh in his mind, will not fail to gain his reward'.[88] Menasseh goes on to set out the demands of this Law in the following manner: it is necessary 'to live with equity and justice, to offend nobody, not to take another's goods for oneself, not to tarnish anyone's reputation, to be charitable to one's neighbour, and to live soberly and temperately.'[89] Our rabbi asks himself if it is possible for someone who orders his life according to these principles to find his merit unrecognized. The answer is a categorical no. From the East to the West, the name of the Lord is great for all nations, and all, in their different ways, worship a primary cause. He who lives according to the law of Nature is pious, and will enjoy the rewards of his piety, as the ancient sages proclaimed.[90]

The diaspora must be understood as a divine way of making it possible for all peoples to share in the good times to come.[91] All those who welcome the Jews, the messengers of God, with kindness will also be rewarded: the Messiah will receive them and accord them eternal happiness. Menasseh notes that the Hebrews pray to God every day for the preservation of the princes who protect and shelter Jews in their kingdoms. Jews will remember this on the Day of Judgement, and our

---

[86] Chapter 14.
[87] *Avoda Zara* 3 a.
[88] *Piedra Gloriosa* . . . , p. 243.
[89] Ibid., p. 242.
[90] Ibid., p. 243. It is entirely understood that the observance of these rules, while capable of ensuring the salvation of all, is not enough for a Jew. See the argument between Juan de Prado and Orobio de Castro in I. S. Révah, *Spinoza et le Dr Juan de Prado*, Paris–The Hague, 1959, pp. 133 ff.
[91] *Piedra Gloriosa* . . . , p. 95.

rabbi then refers by name to these temporal powers: the Emperors of the House of Austria, the King of Poland, and the Duke of Tuscany. It goes without saying that Menasseh expresses his thanks in a particularly emotional way to the Gentlemen of the States General and the Magistrates of Amsterdam, to whom he conveys the loyalty and gratitude of his co-religionists. Then, surprisingly and with great courage for a refugee in a Protestant country, he expresses his gratitude to the Popes themselves for the help and protection they give to the Jews. The final Day of Judgement is not far off, and it is the right time to count one's friends, for, writes Menasseh, if the prophecies are to be fulfilled, Israel will not fail in its duty of gratitude.[92]

In order to understand this point of view, the importance of Messianism in Menasseh's thought must now be emphasized, an importance which was already apparent in the *Hope of Israel* and which is developed in the *Piedra gloriosa*. It should be recalled that the whole Christian millenarian movement of the first half of the seventeenth century is based on the prophecy of Daniel[93] variously interpreted. For our rabbi, the statue dreamed of by Nebuchadnezzar is a symbol of the four monarchies which succeeded each other historically: the Babylonian, the Persian, the Greek, and the Roman. We do not want to give an exegesis of the prophecy of Daniel here. It is enough to know that a stone was detached from the statue without any manual assistance, that it struck its iron and clay feet, and broke them in pieces. 'In the days of these kings shall the God of heaven set up a kingdom, which shall never be destroyed: and the kingdom shall not be left to other people . . . Forasmuch as thou sawest that the stone was cut out of the mountain without hands . . .'.[94] This stone represents the fifth monarchy, that of Messianic rule. Belief in the coming of this fifth monarchy made a deep impression on the first half of the seventeenth century, although this fact has been obscured by the interest taken in the major philosophies. This millenarian hope did not only inspire simple hearts and minds, but also those of men like Milton, Newton, and Oldenburg, the Secretary of the Royal Society, and even Serrarius,[95] a friend of Menasseh ben Israel's

[92] Ibid., pp. 247 ff.

[93] On the prophecy of Daniel and the reading of it in Seventeenth-century Amsterdam and by Spinoza, see H. Méchoulan, 'Révélation, rationalité et prophétie: Quelques remarques sur le livre de Daniel', in *Revue des Sciences philosophiques et théologiques*, 64 no. 3, Paris, July 1980, pp. 363–71.

[94] Daniel 2: 44–5.

[95] On what was at stake for the millenarians, see the controversy which set Serrarius against Desmarets in *Chiliasmus enervatus ad D. P. Serrarium*, Groningen, 1664.

and of Spinoza's, who, it should be stressed, had *Esperança de Israel* in his library.[96] Peter Serrarius, whom we will meet again later, was a convinced millenarian, who acted as intermediary between Oldenburg and Spinoza in all sorts of exchanges.[97]

It is difficult today to make the imaginative leap of understanding needed to accept these beliefs. Nevertheless Denis de Rougemont reminds us that millenarianism is always a temptation:

Marxism appears at the end of the story, like a secular Apocalypse. Almost all the ingredients of salvation are found in it . . . but without a belief in the beyond of History, in this supreme Coming which transcends History, without the leap of faith in eternal life, man remains a prisoner of never-ending time. So the millennium, which is only the penultimate for the visionary, appears by contrast in Marx's utopia to be the ultimate outcome of a dialectical materialism preserved, in the end, from the shocks, errors, and tragedies which make up History.[98]

Menasseh ben Israel, like all believing Jews, never doubted that the Messiah would come and that universal peace would then be established, temporal and spiritual peace, as he himself makes clear in refuting the accusations of Christian detractors summarized by Luis de Granada in these contemptuous words: 'Those who hope for the temporal Messiah err no less than the Moors who hope for a sensual paradise. And for that reason, we are obliged to snap our fingers at the Jews' Messiah and at the Moors' paradise, since each is as vile and base as the other.'[99] It is for this reason that Menasseh declares that, in a temporal sense, the Messianic era is not, as some people think, longed for by Jews merely for the advantages a restored homeland would provide, the leisure and pleasures of a comfortable, peaceful life. Indeed, on the contrary, they hope for the coming of a temporal and spiritual monarchy wherein, by virtuous living in this life, they will find true contemplation and the soul's happiness.[100]

[96] See no. 92 of the *Catalogue van de Bibliotheek der vereniging het Spinozahuis te Rijnsburg*, Leiden, 1965.

[97] K. O. Meinsma in his *Spinoza et son cercle* recalls Serrarius's very important role as an intermediary between Spinoza, Boyle, and Oldenburg; in particular see Chap. 7. P. Vulliaud in his *Spinoza d'après les livres de sa bibliothèque*, Paris, 1934, p. 33, makes a point of mentioning Spinoza's relationship with Serrarius, a relationship which he also refers to in his book *La Fin du monde*, Paris, 1952, p. 133. On the friendship between Menasseh and Serrarius, see the opening lines of the dedication of Felgenhauer's *Bonum Nuncium Israeli . . .*, Amsterdam, 1655.

[98] *L'Avenir est notre affaire*, Paris, 1977, p. 134.

[99] *Quarta parte de la Introducción de la Fe*, Madrid, 1730, vol. vi, p. 266.

[100] *Piedra Gloriosa . . .*, pp. 58–9.

Corresponding to the Jewish hope, which is the hallmark of both Menasseh's life and his thought, is a Christian millenarian expectation, which emerges prominently very precisely in the first part of the seventeenth century.[101] This expectation, with which Menasseh was very familiar because many Christians came to him to ask for his support or his ideas, caused him not a little concern. Certainly it was a happy sign, in that it heralded the dawn of a new era,[102] but it had to be kept within the limits of the Hebrew vision of salvation. Menasseh could not accept the second coming of Christ, or the prerequisite conversion of the Jews. He also had a difficult position to defend. He had to deny no part of that which reinforced 'Judaeo-Christian friendship' and the Messianic expectation, and to accept no part of that which might alter the specifically Jewish dimension of the event.

The heralding of the end of time is as old as Christianity itself. Norman Cohn, in his celebrated work *The Pursuit of the Millennium*,[103] has retraced and analysed the major periods of this eschatological tension which is always reanimated by the misfortunes and suffering of men who look, in their chiliastic dream, for the abolition of Evil. It was incontestably the Reformation and the introduction of the Old Testament into every Protestant home which made the greatest contribution to firing imaginations and feeding hearts with great hopes of moral regeneration and earthly justice. Christians, who had always been over-fascinated by the idea of a beyond, the location of all rewards and punishments, had forgotten the role that Christ had to play on earth. Serrarius provides an answer to Luis de Granada's reasoning when he writes that if Jews had only the Messianic promises in view and paid no attention to the way, that is to say the New Testament, Christians were equally guilty of the same sort of forgetfulness, and adds: 'We, on the other hand, we are mistaken in that we only consider the way, while at the same time demonstrating a lack of enthusiasm for the promises which are the end to which the way leads us.'[104] These earthly promises are contained in the Old Testament, interest in which was continually growing in the Protestant Christian world of the seventeenth century, as

---

[101] See H. Méchoulan, 'Menasseh ben Israël au centre des rapports judéo-chrétiens en Hollande au XVIIᵉ siècle dans une lettre inédite d'Isaac Coymans à André Colvius', in *Studia Rosenthaliana*, xvi no. 1, Mar. 1982, pp. 21–4.

[102] See *Hope of Israel*, Section 36.

[103] London (revised and expanded edn, 1970).

[104] P. Serrurier, *Assertion du règne de mille ans ou de la prospérité de l'Église du Christ pour servir de réponse au traitté [sic] de Monsieur Moïse Amyraut sur ce même sujet*, Amsterdam, 1657, p. 7.

much among scholars as among simple believers. At this time of revolutionary crisis in England, in these pitiless years of the Thirty Years War so painfully experienced in central Europe, people sought in the Old Testament not only consolation, but also a social model which, if strictly followed, would put an end to injustice and the political and religious oppression which was enslaving both bodies and souls. We must remember that the countries which today make up Germany and Czechoslovakia saw their population of 16m. fall to 6m. after the Thirty Years War; to this tragic figure we must add the events of the Cossack rebellion in Poland, which resulted in the death of almost 200,000 Jews, the Civil War in England, the invasion of the Turks in 1653, the appearance of the great comets in 1618, 1648, 1652, and 1654, and the huge epidemics which particularly affected the Republic of the United Provinces.[105]

Nor is it surprising to find territory favourable to the development of Christian millenarian expectations first of all in Germany. Jacob Boehme emerges from the silence imposed by his pastor in 1618, the date of the outbreak of the Thirty Years War. The meditation of this great mystic has had a great influence on the thinkers who have come after. They have all heard the message of the shoemaker of Görlitz: 'I want to warn you, with all goodwill, that you must pay careful attention to the present epoch, for the seventh angel of the Apocalypse has raised his trumpet.'[106] The scandalous incidence of violence has reached such a pitch that the imminence of the end of time is no longer in dispute. The Book of Daniel gives the best confirmation of this statement. The coming of the fifth empire is inescapable. But the Jews must not be excluded from this Messianic regeneration, the Jews, whose seniority as a chosen people appears with all the more force because it is to the Old Testament that we turn for confirmation of more recent events. To this use of the Old Testament may be added the fascination exercised by the Kabbalah and its promises. Did not the Zohar give 1648 as the date of deliverance by the Messiah? So, and for the first time in history, relations between Jews and Christians are such that the former find themselves unburdened by the latter of all the sins of Israel. From now on universal salvation comes through the Jews, whom it is no longer

---

[105] On these epidemics and their Messianic interpretation, see K. O. Meinsma, *Spinoza et son cercle*, ch. 7.

[106] Jacob Boehme in G. Wehr and P. Deghaye, *Les Cahiers de l'hermétismae*, Paris, 1977, p. 29.

proper to hate or despise, for they are, as it were, the keepers of the keys of the Kingdom.

This second coming, so long awaited by Christians, cannot take place as long as the Jews do not have their political rights restored to them in the Holy Land, where finally they will all be reunited; hence the fundamental importance of the problem of the Ten Lost Tribes which, must at least be located geographically in anticipation of the great day of reunion. This is, moreover, the theme of the *Hope of Israel*.

There were many millenarians who were waiting for the fifth empire or the reign of the saints. It would be pointless to list them exhaustively, but proper, none the less, to mention those who had connections with Menasseh ben Israel. This survey will allow us to bring out the main themes of their eschatological beliefs, and then to see how Menasseh ben Israel responds to them.

In his reply to Felgenhauer,[107] our rabbi quotes Mochingen of Danzig, who had written to him: 'Know that I approve and respect your religious doctrines and that I, together with some of my co-religionists, would like to see Israel finally being illuminated by the true light and finding again her former glory and salvation.'[108]

Another mystic, Abraham von Frankenberg, a disciple of Jacob Boehme, wrote the *Clavis Apocalyptica*. Élisabeth Labrousse, in her fine work on the effect on Europe of the solar eclipse of 12 August 1654, *L'Entrée de Saturne au lion*,[109] tells us that *Clavis Apocalyptica* had a preface by John Dury, a correspondent of Menasseh ben Israel's, and appeared in London in 1651 in an English translation by Hartlib.[110] It is no surprise to learn that Abraham von Frankenberg corresponded with Menasseh, to whom he wrote: 'The true light will emanate from the Jews; their time is near. Every day we will hear from all quarters of miracles worked in their favour.'[111]

But, on a practical level, how could a political restoration of the Jews to Palestine be envisaged, a restoration seen as a prerequisite for the second coming of Christ on earth? Very naturally we turn to the *Rappel des Juifs* by La Peyrère, which Menasseh certainly knew, as he mentions it in his letter in reply to Felgenhauer.[112] La Peyrère does not see

---

[107] Published in *Bonum Nuncium Israeli*, pp. 87–91.
[108] Graetz, *History of the Jews*, vol. v, p. 163.
[109] The Hague, 1974.
[110] Ibid., pp. 7–8.
[111] Graetz, *History*, vol. v, p. 163. Note that a letter from Abraham von Frankenberg to Menasseh ben Israel is published in Felgenhauer's *Bonum Nuncium Israeli . . .*, pp. 92 ff.
[112] In *Bonum Nuncium Israeli . . .*, p. 90. On this matter, see Richard H. Popkin's article

himself as a prophet, but supremely as a reconciler of Jews and Christians. Does not Christ tell the Samaritan woman that 'salvation is of the Jews'?[113] The regeneration and renewal of the world depend on the return of the Jews to the Holy Land, a return whose organization he entrusts to Louis XIV. To prepare public opinion for this event, La Peyrère calls on Christians to stop despising Jews and to recognize them as brothers, inasmuch as it is true that they have been 'chosen and adopted as children of God in Jesus Christ, to be brothers of Jesus Christ'.[114] At the end of his work on the Preadamites he was to write: 'Natio sancta et electa! filii Adam qui fuit filius Dei.'[115] In order to achieve this union and the return of the Jews, La Peyrère offers the Jews a Catholicism relieved of the whole weight of dogma, so that 'Jews and Gentiles, reunited in this return, may praise God, the one with the other, making up a single Church, which will be the truly Catholic Church'.[116] The new confession proposed to the Jews is, moreover, entirely acceptable to the Israelites, La Peyrère considers, since it has to do with a faith which was that of the first Apostles. It would, moreover, unite not only Jews and Christians, but all mankind. That done, it would only remain for the generous French king to gather the Jews of the world together in his kingdom and to reconquer Palestine for them, so that the chosen people could regain its role of universal priest.

Like La Peyrère, but in a prophetic and eschatological vein, Felgenhauer, in his *Bonum Nuncium Israeli* . . . dedicated to our rabbi,[117] first insists on the unity of the Jewish and Christian peoples, all sons of Abraham.[118] Heedful of great events, of the passage of comets, and of wars, Felgenhauer describes a divine vision foretelling a new era.[119] God has given him a mandate to announce to the Jews the coming of the

'Menasseh ben Israel and Isaac La Peyrère', in *Studia Rosenthaliana*, vol. viii, no. 1, Jan. 1974, pp. 59–63.

[113] La Peyrère, *Du rappel des Juifs*, n.p., 1643. This refers to the opening lines of his book. Among other studies of La Peyrère, mention must be made of H. J. Schoeps's major work, *Philosemitismus in Barok*.

[114] *Du rappel des Juifs*, p. 11.

[115] *Praeadamitae*, in a chapter entitled '*Synagogis Judaeorum*, . . . ', placed at the end of the work and not paginated.

[116] *Du rappel des Juifs*, p. 53.

[117] On this extremely rare book, see P. Vulliaud, *La Fin du monde*, pp. 138 ff.; A. H. Silver, *A History of Messianic Speculation in Israel*, New York, 1927, pp. 164 ff., and above all H. J. Schoeps, *Philosemitismus*.

[118] *Bonum Nuncium Israeli* . . . , p. 11: 'Sive Iudaei sive gentes erimus, modo Spiritum, Fidem et Obsequium Abrahami habeamus, Unum tunc sumus in Uno, Patre nostro Deo Uno, Iudaei et Christiani . . . '

[119] Ibid., p. 13.

Messiah, who must be preceded by the prophet Elijah; Felgenhauer himself then claims to be Elijah.[120]

A more cautious friend of Menasseh's, Simon Episcopius, touches on the coming of a new era; he gives no details as to how it will come, and puts forward no date. According to him, the Gentiles will receive the first benefits and it will be in a second phase that the whole Jewish nation will be involved in Christianity's triumph.[121]

The vision of Serrarius, who, we recall, was the mutual friend of Menasseh, Felgenhauer, and Spinoza, was very different. Vulliaud writes, with reason, on this subject: 'Critics love to expand on the only visit of Leibniz to Spinoza; they are completely silent on the close relationship of the latter with Serrarius. Critics are charmed by pretty compositions, realism makes them fearful.'[122] What fear can he mean? That of seeing the rationalist, Spinoza, in touch with the mystic millenarian, Serrarius, who was giving Jews back their dominant role in the eagerly awaited Messianic adventure, and making a particular point of it. Serrarius absolves the Jews of all their former blindness because they hope for the same Messiah as the Christians: 'What Jews and Christians are now anticipating so keenly is the appearance of the true Messiah in the glory of God . . . We must show them love and respect because of the inheritance which was promised to them, and was, through grace, bestowed on us by the Lord Jesus, who is their Messiah and ours.'[123] Serrarius goes on to report that he has met a rabbi, 'a resident and doctor of the Jerusalem of today', who told him that 'all those, from among all peoples, Christians as much as Jews, who have believed in God and lived lives worthy of Him, will be raised by the Spirit of God to live with Him for ever'.[124] To support his millenarian thesis, Serrarius relies on the same prophetic authorities as Menasseh ben Israel uses in the *Hope of Israel* and in the *Piedra gloriosa*. But this new era comes through the conversion of the Jews, of which Serrarius speaks in these terms: 'As far as the conversion of the Jews is concerned, it will bring a great change. I assure you that it will give a new atmosphere and a different aspect to the earth.'[125]

Although Menasseh ben Israel was very happy with all these writings, which restored to Jews the humanity which Christendom, over the

---

[120] Ibid., p. 32.
[121] See P. Toon, *Puritans, the Millenium and the Future of Israel*, Cambridge, 1970, p. 140.
[122] *Spinoza d'après les livres de sa bibliothèque*, p. 35.
[123] P. Serrurier, *Assertion du règne de mille ans*, p. 16.
[124] Ibid., p. 37.   [125] Ibid., p. 168.

centuries, had often grudged them, he could not endorse these visions which, though varied, all had one point in common: the precondition of the conversion of the Jews to Christianity. Menasseh did not want to clash head-on with any of his friends. And in his cautious and skilful reply to Felgenhauer we can see his mistrust of all the visions and expectations which did not take account of the unique prophecies of the Old Testament, expounded *more hebraïco*. Although, in the first place, our rabbi concedes to the man he calls *mi Paule* that the coming of the Messiah will be preceded, after major upheavals, by the disappearance of all the empires of the world, he remains evasive as to an interpretation of the historical circumstances. Although he then allows that the Messiah will be preceded by the arrival of the prophet Elijah, he reminds Felgenhauer, politely but firmly, that Elijah can only stem from the Jewish nation, thus depriving this visionary of the main argument in his message. At the end of the letter, he gives an account of the large number of thinkers who share Felgenhauer's views on the reign of Israel; but here again our rabbi remains very guarded. As far as predictions of date are concerned, his reticence gives way to a categorical refusal to ally himself with those who claim to be able to calculate when the Messiah will arrive.[126] According to Menasseh, the divine revelation, which Daniel received concerning the coming of the fifth monarchy, is so enigmatic as to be beyond our understanding.

Even in the middle of a commentary on Daniel's vision, he is careful to write 'If that which the prophets declared were to be realized . . .', and not 'When the prophecies are fulfilled . . .', avoiding the use of the future by employing a conditional. This note should serve to tone down the enthusiasm which J. H. Greenstone ascribes to Menasseh in his book *The Messiah idea in Jewish History*.[127]

We have seen how Menasseh, always at the centre of the continental philosemitic and Messianic movement, responded with moderation and realism to the spiritual effervescence of his friends and correspondents. Not the least among these were English theologians and thinkers, and it would seem essential to discuss the religious and political atmosphere in the England which was to receive a visit from our rabbi in 1655.

Although England was spared the Thirty Years War, her economic, social, political, and religious situation was very unpromising in the early years of the seventeenth century. In addition to price increases, royal monopolies, a decline in maritime power, and the commercial domina-

---

[126] *Hope of Israel*, Sect. 27.   [127] Philadelphia, 1948, pp. 207 ff.

tion of the United Provinces, there were food shortages and epidemics, all things which particularly afflicted the underprivileged classes. In religious matters, the authoritarian policy of William Laud was in conflict with the Puritans. To terrible economic circumstances, this added the religious tension which was closely associated with the confrontation which set the king and his Parliament in opposition to each other.

Once the threshold of the intolerable has been reached, despair is sometimes transformed into a hope which searches for somewhere to anchor its faith, for an explanation of events and the model to follow in order to influence their course. The Bible, sold relatively cheaply, 'the Bible in pocket format', was going to provide an answer to all expectations and the key essential to an understanding of the tragic, explosive and unsettled existence. Arise Evans, the author of *Lights for the Jews*,[128] who attempted to convince Menasseh ben Israel that King Charles Stuart was the Messiah, wrote: 'Afore I looked upon the Scripture as a history of things that passed in other countries, pertaining to other persons; but now I looked upon it as a mystery to be opened at this time, belonging also to us.'[129] This state of mind is characteristic of a great spiritual upheaval. The gulf between man and God, a separation maintained by the clergy, was going to disappear, and God would speak directly to the heart of man, would work in history towards justice and freedom. A. H. Silver writes most precisely that 'All the Messianic speculation of the day was related in an essential way to Israel . . .', which was known to be in direct relationship with God.[130]

The Quakers viewed the Golden Age not as a mythical era, but as a reality, which could be located in history. It was the ancient Hebrews' State, and must at all costs be rediscovered. This was, moreover, the view of the Puritans as a whole.

Marx was not the first to condemn capital and the exploitation of one man by another; it was Isaiah in his imprecation 'Woe to them that join house to house, that lay field to field'.[131] Amos had already denounced the scandal of the iniquity of the rich and the great. It may be imagined how a believing and oppressed people would feel on reading: 'Ye that

[128] *Lights for the Jews or the means to convert them in answer to a book of theirs called The Hope of Israel written and printed by Manasseth ben Israel, Chief agent for the Jews here 1650*, London, 1656. On Arise Evans's distinctive character, see chap. 2 of Christopher Hill's book, *Change and Continuity in 17th Century England*, London, 1974.

[129] A. Evans, *An Eccho to the Voice of Heaven*, 1653, p. 17, quoted by C. Hill in *The World Turned Upside Down: Radical Ideas during the English Revolution*, London, 1972, p. 75.

[130] *A History of Messianic Speculation in Israel*, p. 173, and chap. 7 in general.

[131] Isaiah 5: 8.

put far away the evil day, and cause the seat of violence to come near; . . . and stretch themselves upon their couches, and eat the lambs out of the flock, . . .'[132]

It is hard to avoid being fascinated by the political organization of the ancient Hebrews, who were very preoccupied with social justice. Their system was dictated by God Himself, and has been well analysed by Sylvain Zac.[133] For these fervent Englishmen, it was not a matter of Utopia but of retrieving something. For this, it was enough to return to biblical purity. Servitude, misfortune, and injustice would be abolished at one stroke, by following the commandments of the Law. For Moses did not set up a monarchy, although he held a monarch's power. Only the theocratic system of government practised by the ancient Hebrews afforded equality to all, because all recognized a single God, whose Law was revealed to the whole people. Thus supreme authority will not be the prerogative of one man, but will be granted to all the chief men, who will be administrators under the control of the people. All attempts at a military bid for power are excluded by the organization of the army itself, made up of free citizens who choose themselves a general for a one-year term. Patriotism and civic duty are like extensions of the requirements of Law, since to serve the country is to serve God Himself.

On the economic front, only the use of the land and not its ownership belongs to the people, in that Moses made the soil of the State the inheritance of Israel as a whole. In order to avoid the establishment of any monopolies which might determine the power of some and the poverty of others, the year of Jubilee was instituted, as a watchful and permanent means of redistributing wealth. In short, love for others was itself a divine commandment.

English millenarian hopes were more practical and more political than those of Jacob Boehme's heirs. They demonstrated a demand for social justice and freedom much closer to the Jewish Messianic expectation. W. Schenk writes very aptly that the significance of the millennium for the Quakers was not the end of the world, but its restoration in its original purity: 'The Millennium would restore the primitive righteousness of the Jews and realize the Old Testament ideals of social justice, specially as preached by the prophets.'[134] The long-awaited

---

[132] Amos 6: 3–4.

[133] S. Zac, 'Spinoza et l'État des Hébreux', in *Speculum Spinozanum 1677–1977*, London, pp. 543–67. On this question, see also L. Mugnier-Pollet, *La Philosophie politique de Spinoza*, Paris, 1976.

[134] *The Concern for Social Justice in the Puritan Revolution*, London, 1948, p. 121.

kingdom of Christ was the fifth monarchy promised by Daniel. Newton also states that he who rejects the prophecies of Daniel also rejects Christianity itself.[135]

Biblical fervour and a political will for radical change were intertwined and complementary. England was to become a new Israel. The anonymous author of a petition declares that England and Israel are promised lands, that the laws of the two countries have the same origin, and that they constitute a changeless expression of divine will.[136] Winstanley, whose life and works have been admirably studied by Olivier Lutaud, recalls in touching terms the example of Israel and its democratic foundation in the promised land.[137]

Certainly millenarian hopes were not all cast in the same mould. The men of the fifth monarchy were not Diggers. It is not our purpose here to go into the complexities of the various sects at that time; others have done so with competence and learning. In England the work of Christopher Hill and of B. S. Capp may be noted, and in France that of Olivier Lutaud.[138] But a review of that extraordinary atmosphere of hope shared by all is fundamental to an understanding of Menasseh ben Israel's English venture. In their feverish wait for change, people were watching out for signs heralding it, some with the innocence of the simple, others with the learning of the wise.

The first of these signs was the fall of the Antichrist, which each interpreted in his own way and the date of which was precisely

---

[135] Mentioned by P. G. Rogers in *The Fifth Monarchy Men*, London, 1966, p. 139.

[136] Mentioned by J. Dykstra Eusden, *Puritans, Lawyers and Politics in Early Seventeenth Century England*, New Haven, Yale University Press, 1958, p. 122.

[137] Quoted by O. Lutaud in *Winstanley, socialisme et christianisme sous Cromwell*, Paris, Sorbonne-Paris IV publications, 1976, p. 352, Gerard Winstanley writes in *The Law of Freedom*, 1652, pp. 524–5: 'The Scriptures say, They made this Canon Land a common Treasury of livelyhood to the whole Commonwealth of *Israel*, and so disposed of it, as they made provision for every Tribe, and for every family in a Tribe, nay for every particular man in a family, every one had enough, no man was in want, there was no beggery among them. . . .

And thus the Land was divided, and the whole Land was the Common Stock, every one had a brotherly freedom therein, for the freedom of the one was the freedom of the other, there was no difference in that they were men of true faithful and publick spirits, not falsehearted. And so likewise when *Esther* prevailed with King *Ahasuerus* for freedom, she did not seek her own freedom and interest, but the freedom of all her kindred and friends; . . . if this our English Commonwealths Government carry perfect Freedom in his hand, then shall the Law go forth from *England* to all the Nations of the World.'

[138] C. Hill, *Puritanism and Revolution*, London, 1958, *Antichrist in Seventeenth Century England*, London, 1971, and *The World Turned Upside Down*; B. S. Capp, *The Fifth Monarchy Men*, London, 1972; O. Lutaud, *Les Niveleurs, Cromwell et la République*, Paris, 1967.

calculated. The propositions of Henry Denne, one of the Levellers' leaders, as reported by Christopher Hill, reveal another difficulty. For him the Antichrist is embodied simultaneously in the king, the pope, and all the bishops; they must be brought down so that freedom, equality, and justice may reign. The great Milton considered Charles I to be the Antichrist, and called for a European crusade against monarchy.[139] W. Aspinwall, a famous follower of the fifth monarchy, saw in the existence of Charles I the little horn described by Daniel in Chapter 7 of his vision. But although struggle with, and defeat of, the Antichrist were necessary, that was not sufficient to make the new era arrive. These Protestants were gripped by a thirst for universalism, expressed in William Reyner's appeal to Parliament: 'First the destruction of the Whore . . . then the destruction of Beast himselfe and all the King his partakers . . . after which followes the binding up of Sathan with its consequents . . . and the glorious restauration of the Church both of Jewes and Gentiles under the type of new Jerusalem.'[140] By whatever means the Fifth Empire was to come, all acknowledged the link between the future reign of Christ on earth and the political restoration of the Jews; R. Maton gives particular prominence to this link in his work *Israel's Redemption*.[141]

Almost all the writings which show evidence of this expectation give, as the second sign, the preliminary conversion of the Jews. The Jews, while retaining their national identities in their countries of origin, will recognize Christ as the returned Messiah, and will participate in the long-hoped-for universal religion. That is why there were feverish calculations of the date of Christ's coming and the conversion of the Jews: 1656 was the year most put forward.[142]

It is clear that in such an atmosphere the traditional view of the Jew

---

[139] *Antichrist in 17th Century England*, p. 95.

[140] *Babylons ruining earthquake and the Restauration of Zion*, London, 1644, in *Fast Sermons to Parliament*, vol. xii, July–Sept. 1644, London, 1971, p. 12.

[141] *Israel's redemption redeemed or the Jewes generall and miraculous conversion to the faith of the Gospel*, London, 1646.

[142] C. Hill notes, on this subject, that Cromwell's decision to allow Jews to settle in England in 1656 is not irrelevant to the speculations about this date. See *Antichrist . . .* , p. 115. See also David S. Katz, *Philo-semitism and the Readmission of the Jews to England 1603–55*, Oxford, 1982, pp. 99–100. In *L'Entrée de Saturne au Lion*, p. 64, Elisabeth Labrousse, quoting from R. S. Paul's *The Lord Protector. Religion and Politics in the life of Oliver Cromwell*, London, 1955, p. 333, recalls 'the influence exercised over Cromwell by his favourite chaplain, Peter Sterry, who looked for a great cataclysm in 1656 which would let loose a firestorm on the wicked, an idea which reappeared in Robert Vilvain's *Theoremata theologica: theological treatises . . .* , London, 1654, fol. 186 recto and verso . . .'.

was somewhat modified, and in a text by Edward Nicholas we see this change of attitude fully developed. For in his *Apology for the Noble Nation of the Jews* we read:

I have next to offer to your considerations the many promises made by God by the mouthes of his Prophets, for the reduction of them (the Jews) into their own countrey, still owning them for his own people, a countrey, I say, lawfully theirs, by the donation of God himself, and a propriety that no prince under heaven can plead the like. . . . Besides many more places in this (Isaias) and other Prophets, some whereof do more plainly extend to the advantage of the Gentiles.[143]

We note that Edward Nicholas does not breathe a word of a preliminary conversion. Was it tacitly understood?

A. Stern, in his short but interesting article 'Menasseh ben Israël et Cromwell',[144] reports that John Sadler, a friend of Cromwell's and a member of the Council of State, published a book called *Rights of the Kingdom*, in which he deplores the Jews' miserable lot:

How they are now, I need not say, although I might also beare them witnesse, that they are zealous in their way nor do they wholly want ingenious able men, of whom I cannot but with honour mention him that hath so much obliged the world by his learned writings, Rabbi Menasseh ben Israel: a very learned civill man and a lover of our nation. The more I think upon the great change now comming on them and all the world, the more I would be just and mercifull to them, to all. Nay, universal sweetnesse if I could a Christian overcoming all with love.[145]

Roger Williams, one of the most ardent defenders of freedom of conscience, writes in 1652: 'No opinion in the world is comparably so bloody or so blasphemous as that of punishing and not permitting in a civil way of cohabitation the consciences and worships both of Jews and Gentiles.'[146] Stern also notes that a great number of pieces written in that vein would have been forgotten if the Hanserd Knollys Society had not republished them.[147]

It was in this climate, altogether favourable to the resettlement of Jews

---

[143] London, 1648. On this apologia, see H. Méchoulan, 'Philosémitisme et politique', in *Les Nouveaux Cahiers*, Paris, Spring 1980.

[144] *REJ*, vol. vi, Paris, 1883, pp. 93–105.

[145] London, 1649, p. 48.

[146] Quoted from *The hireling ministry none of Christs or a discourse touching the propagating of the gospel of Christ Jesus humbly presented . . .* by Roger Williams of Providence in New-England, London, 1652.

[147] *REJ* vi. p. 101. Mention must also be made of N. Sokolow's no longer recent but still interesting work, *History of Zionism 1600–1918*, London, 1919, and P. Toon's remarkable study, *Puritans, the Millennium and the Future of Israel*.

in England,[148] that Menasseh formed the idea of going there, following an interview with members of an English mission in Holland. These delegates assured him in 1651 that a return of the Jews would be warmly welcomed. It is more than likely that, for his part, our rabbi, through his correspondents and friends, particularly Nathanael Homes, a millenarian pastor whom Menasseh quoted in his reply to Felgenhauer,[149] was well aware of the state of opinion which we have described. And so the religious and political impact of the Old Testament and the need to convert the chosen people to Christianity, in order to see the reign of Christ established on earth, were to be linked for Cromwell with some perhaps more realisitic requirements. As a Puritan, he had a certain interest in the People of the Book. As a statesman, he saw, above all, the commercial profit England would derive from the settlement of Jews in her lands. Did. he not have before his eyes the example of the Netherlands and Hamburg, prospering while Spain, which had not accepted their presence, was in decline? Menasseh, moreover, took the opportunity of developing this argument in a booklet addressed to Cromwell and entitled *How Profitable the Nation of the Iewes are*.[150]

Menasseh had to wait some years before being able to leave Holland, because of the war between his adopted country and England. Just before setting sail, he had a visit from an anxious emissary; did the Jewish community in Holland wish to leave that country to settle in England? The matter went as far as the United Provinces' Ambassador in London, who received as assurance that our rabbi's initiative concerned only the 'Jews' of the Iberian Peninsula.[151] Menasseh left Amsterdam on 2 September 1655, accompanied by his son, Samuel, who had already spent time in England. As Cecil Roth writes, his first concern was to get in touch with David Abrabanel Dormido, a Portuguese Jew who was serving England well by providing information on

---

[148] On this subject use may be made of C. Roth, 'The Resettlement of the Jews in England in 1656' in V. D. Lipman (ed.) *Three Centuries of Anglo-Jewish History*, London, 1961, as well as Hermann Gollancz, 'A Contribution to the History of the Readmission of the Jews', in *Transactions of the Jewish Historical Society of England*, vi, 1908–10, Edinburgh–London, 1912, pp. 189–204.

[149] In *Bonum Nuncium Israeli*, p. 90.

[150] This booklet is reproduced in Lucien Wolf's basic work, *Menasseh ben Israel's mission to Oliver Cromwell*, p. 73.

[151] *A Collection of the State Papers of John Thurloe Esq.*, London, 1747, vol. iv, p. 333: 'A letter of Nieupoort, the Dutch Ambassador, Westminster, December 31, 1655: Menasseh ben Israel hath been to see me and he did assure me that he doth not desire any thing for the Jews in Holland but only for such as sit fit [*sic* ?suffered] in the inquisition in Spain and Portugal.'

Spain's military and economic power and, in particular, on the state of her American colonies.[152]

The objects of Menasseh's approaches to Cromwell were clear, and were summed up in seven points which our rabbi set out in French:

Here are the graces and favours which, in the name of my Hebrew Nation, I, Menasseh ben Israel, request of Your Most Serene Highness, whom may God prosper and give fortunate success in all his enterprises as his humble servant wishes and desires for him.

I. The first thing which I ask of Your Highness is that our Hebrew Nation may be received and admitted into this puissant Republic under the protection and care of Your Highness as are the citizens themselves, and for the utmost security in future times, I beg Your Highness to cause (if it is agreeable to him) all his chiefs and generals of arms to swear to defend us on all occasions.

II. That it please Your Highness to permit us synagogues, not only in England, but also in all other conquered places which are in the power of Your Highness, and to allow us in all ways to observe our religion as we ought.

III. That we may have a place or cemetery outside the town to bury our dead without interference from anyone.

IV. That we may be permitted to trade in all sorts of merchandise as others are.

V. That (so that those who come may be of use to the citizens and may live without doing harm to anyone or causing scandal) Your Most Serene Highness may elect a person of quality to give information about and to receive the passports of those who enter, and after their arrival he will make it known to Your Highness and will compel them to swear and to keep fealty to you in this country.

VI. And, in order not to be a burden on the country's judges touching the quarrels and differences which may occur between members of our Nation, that Your Most Serene Highness may give licence to the leaders of the synagogue to take, with care, two arbitrators from their Nation to settle and judge all differences by proceedings in conformity with the Law of Moses, with freedom always to appeal against their sentence to the civil judges, having first deposited the sum to which the party was sentenced.

VII. That if, peradventure, there are certain laws prejudicial to our Jewish Nation, that first and before all else they may be repealed so that in this way we may live with the utmost security within the safe keeping and protection of Your Most Serene Highness.

These things being granted to us by Your Most Serene Highness, we will

---

[152] *A Life of Menasseh* . . . , pp. 212 ff. and 227. J. Thurloe, the head of Cromwell's intelligence service, mentions this individual in his papers, *A Collection of the State Papers of John Thurloe Esq.*, vol. iii, p. 750. We can find no evidence in the contemporary texts we have studied for the possible spying and journalistic activities put forward by J.-P. Alem in *L'Espionnage à travers les âges*, Paris, 1977, p. 132.

always remain very affectionate, feeling bound to pray to God for the prosperity of Your Highness and of your illustrious and very wise Council. May it please Him to give fortunate success to all Your Most Serene Highness's enterprises. Amen.[153]

In spite of the pro-Jewish atmosphere which we have described, it would be wrong to believe that Menasseh's request gave rise only to favourable reactions. There were some implacably opposed to the return of the Jews to England, of whom the best known was William Prynne.[154] John Dury, who had been sufficiently interested by Montezinos's narrative to cause the *Hope of Israel* to be written, as we shall see later, had a notably equivocal attitude towards the settlement of the Jews. This is demonstrated by the opinion he gives about the eventual return of the Jews to England in a small volume entitled *A Case of Conscience: Whether it be lawfull to allow Jews into a Christian Commonwealth? resolved by Mr John Dury. Written to Samuel Hartlib Esq.*[155]

When our rabbi presented himself at Whitehall armed with his petition, he was not admitted to the Council. Cromwell had to take the matter in hand himself and came up against an insidious opposition among the members of the Council of State, who refused to make a pronouncement too quickly, arguing that they needed to examine the request which the Lord Protector had presented to them with greater attention. The details of these negotiations have been admirably studied by L. Wolf and Cecil Roth, to whom we refer the reader who wishes to discover in greater detail the difficulties encountered by our rabbi's request.[156] He was introduced into the most cultivated circles in London. He met the Countess of Ranelagh, John Sadler, Robert Boyle, and Henry Oldenburgh, John Dury's son-in-law, who later wrote to Spinoza for information on the return of the Israelites to their homeland.[157] With a view to supporting Cromwell's tenacious efforts to break the particularly violent opposition of papists and royalists, Menasseh wrote one of his best works, entitled *Vindiciae Judaeorum*, a lively and moving piece which answered point by point all the racists' slanders.[158]

---

[153] From L. Wolf, *Menasseh ben Israel's mission . . .* , Introduction p. LXXXIII.

[154] See C. Roth, *A Life of Menasseh*, pp. 240 ff.

[155] London, 1656. On Dury's views see S. Levy, 'John Dury and the English Jewry' in *The Jewish Historical Society of England, Transactions*, IV, reprinted for W. Dawson & Sons, London, 1971.

[156] To these works may be added F. W. R., 'The Return of the Jews', in *South Place Magazine*, London, no. 3, vol. xi, Dec. 1905, pp. 33–43.

[157] Letter XXXIII in Spinoza, *Œuvres complètes*, La Pléiade ed., Paris, 1954, pp. 1240–1.   [158] London, 1656.

Cromwell's support for our rabbi was reinforced by one particular incident. A rich merchant named Robles was arrested on a charge of papism. As England was then at war with Portugal, the merchant's fortune was legally confiscated. On Cromwell's initiative, the Council of State lifted the sequestration order because the accused showed himself to be a Jew and not a Catholic. This constituted an implicit recognition of the right of Jews to live in England. As Graetz writes, 'Marranos settled in London made no mistake over the significance of this ruling; they hastened to throw off the mask of Christianity.'[159]

It would seem that Menasseh ben Israel's journey was only a qualified success, since he did not obtain the charter he had come to ask for, but, from the practical point of view, it was an incontestable victory, for the Jews very quickly were allowed to live in England, to practise their religion there, and to bury their dead there in their own cemeteries. But our rabbi was unable to rejoice fully in the outcome of his efforts. At the end of his material resources, he had to ask Cromwell for help, which was given. Then fate struck him a cruel blow with the death, at the age of thirty, of his second son, Samuel. On his deathbed Samuel asked to be buried in Holland. Menasseh had therefore to appeal a second time to Cromwell's generosity, which was not denied. Stricken and ill, Menasseh left England, and arrived at Middelburg in October 1657, where he died on 20 November of the same year. His remains were interred in the Portuguese Jewish Cemetery of Amsterdam at Ouderkerk aan de Amstel. On his tomb may be read:

> No murio por q(ue) en el Cielo
> Vive con suprema gloria
> Y su pluma a su memoria
> Inmortal dexa en el suelo.[160]

ESPERANÇA DE ISRAEL, 1650

Spes Israelis and *Esperança de Israel* appeared in Amsterdam in the year 5410 of the Creation of the World, that is in 1649/50, in the midst of the United Provinces' Golden Age. On 15 January 1650 Menasseh ben Israel signed the dedication of the Spanish version to the *parnassim* (wardens) of the community. We think it important to give the reader

---

[159] *History of the Jews*, p. 173.
[160] L. Alvares-Vega, *Het Beth Haim van Ouderkerk, Beelden van een Portugees-Joodse begraafplaats* . . . , p. 33.

this dedication in full at this point. For it provides an interesting list of the community's leaders at the time, and makes the objective of the projected work clear. It also indicates which individuals encouraged our rabbi to get his work written quickly:

'To preach good tidings unto the meek, to bind up the brokenhearted'[1]

MENASSEH BEN ISRAEL

To the very noble, very wise, and very eminent Lords, Deputies, and *Parnassim*[2] of this Holy Community of *Talmud Torah*:[3]
Joseph da Costa,
Isaac Jesurun,
Michael Espinoza,
Abraham Enriques Faro,
Gabriel de Rivas Atlas,
Isaac Belmonte,
Abraham Franco,[4] *gabbai*.[5]

Very noble, very wise, and very eminent Lords.

The famous narrative of Aaron Levi, also known by the name of Montezinos, has been widely circulated in the last few years. Since something new gives pleasure, and as there is obviously a great desire to discover the truth, my compatriots, through their letters, have pressed me most keenly to give my opinion, as also have the most brilliant, the most noble, and the most learned personalities all over Europe. I have therefore attempted to respond briefly to their request. But because a man of letters and of quality[6] in England has recently insisted firmly that I should go further into this subject, I have put this

---

[1] Isaiah 61: 1.
[2] Hebrew: administrators of a Jewish community.
[3] Hebrew: Teaching of the Law, the official name of the Jewish-Portuguese community in Amsterdam from the time of the uniting of the three communities in 1639.
[4] Many of these men played an important part in the community well before 1650. Joseph da Costa, *alias* Juan Peres da Cunha, was already Treasurer of the Beth Ya'acob, House of Jacob, community in 1619. In 1650 he left for Brazil, and two years later was *parnas* of the Jewish-Portuguese community Sur Israel, Rock of Israel, in Recife, from where he appears to have gone to New Amsterdam; see W. C. Pieterse, *Livro de Bet Haim do Kahal Kados de Bet Yahacob*, Assen, 1970, p. 184. Michael Espinosa, who came from 'Portugal, was married three times: Baruch Spinoza was born on 24 November 1632 of his second marriage to Hanna Debora, daughter of Baruch Senior and María Núñez; see J. S. da Silva Rosa, *Geschiedenis der Portugeesche Joden te Amsterdam 1593–1925*, Amsterdam, 1925, pp. 58–9. On Michael Espinosa, see the early but still important work of A. M. Vaz Dias and W. G. van der Tak, 'Spinoza merchant and autodidact: Charter and other authentic documents relating to the Philosopher's youth and his relations', in *Studia Rosenthaliana*, xvi no. 2, 1982, pp. 113–71.
[5] Hebrew: Treasurer of the community.
[6] This refers to John Dury, a theologian who had met Menasseh ben Israel in 1644 and learnt from him of Antonio de Montezinos's epic: see Goodman Lipkind's entry 'Dury, John' in *Jew. Enc.*, vol. v, p. 19. See also our Introduction, pp. 48, 59.

work into Latin[7] with particular care, for the matters it treats of are difficult and out of the ordinary, and no-one has tackled them with the required vigour. I here express my opinion with simplicity and modesty as I always do in my books, without ever upsetting people's minds, or openly setting myself against anyone. And so I hope that all will welcome it warmly, and most particularly you, Gentlemen, to whom I dedicate and consecrate it in your capacity as Governors and *Parnassim* of this very noble Community.

I set great store by the opportunity which I have been given to write a work of such weight and importance, at a time when people as wise as they are zealous are to be found. I have entitled it *Mikveh Israel*—Hope of Israel — taking this title from Jeremiah 14:8, 'The hope of Israel, the saviour thereof'. For its sole objective is to show that this hope which sustains us, that of the advent of the Messiah, is an expectation of happiness to come. Although the coming will be difficult, it is none the less inevitable, for it is founded on the absolute promise of the Lord, may He be Blessed.

And now, very wise and very eminent Lords, I beg you to welcome this humble offering kindly and, if it lacks scholarship, to value it at least for the theme which it develops. Accord it all your attention, bearing in mind all the skill and care I needed to deal with so many questions in such a short treatise. In this way you would give me enormous encouragement to undertake much greater pieces of work. I entreat the Lord to give you a long and happy life, so that you may ever be inclined to love virtue and Literature.

Amsterdam, 13 *Sebat* of the year 5410.[8]

So the *Hope of Israel* came out in 1650, simultaneously in Spanish and Latin. It was from this latter version that Moses Wall made his translation of the work for English readers. Without making a comparative study of the three texts, which would be a work of specialized scholarship, some comments are, none the less, necessary. Even though we have no textual proof, we may be almost completely certain that the *Hope of Israel* was written first in Spanish.[9] For there are a number of errors in the Latin version which cannot in any way be attributed to Menasseh ben Israel. We do not propose to make an exhaustive list of these mistakes, but will now give a few examples of them. They provide evidence of the existence of a non-Jewish translator who had Menasseh

[7] The Latin edition, *Mikveh Israel, Hoc est Spes Israelis*, also dates from 1650.

[8] According to the Jewish dating of Creation (AM) this would be 15 Jan. 1650.

[9] Without accepting Sorbière's opinion on the preparation of the Latin version as a 'proof', we have to consider it. For he writes: 'Latini linguae non ita peritus erat ut aut scribere aut ex tempore loqui posset expedite, sed editos lusitanice Consiliatorem, de Resurrectione et de Creatione verterant Dionysius Vossius, Vorstius et alii amici', in *Soberiana ou bons mots, rencontres agréables, pensées judicieuses et observations curieuses de M. Sorbière*, Paris, 1684, p. 125.

ben Israel's full confidence in a way which was sometimes prejudicial to the text.

Menasseh ben Israel could not have thought he was the Messiah who would lead the Jewish people back to their homeland, and yet, speaking of the rediscovered Ten Tribes, the Latin text has ' . . . postquam illas in patriam reduxero'. The purpose of the *Hope of Israel*, as we will show in our introduction, is to prove that the American Indians are definitely not the descendants of the Ten Lost Tribes, and yet we find in the Latin text 'Mihi ex parte probanda videtur Hispanorum in India habitantium sententia, qui communi consensu astruunt Indos a X tribubus procedere. Nec sane in totum falluntur' (p. 21). How could our rabbi, who was also a printer and complained in his letters of spending too much time correcting proofs, have let pass these inaccuracies which undermine the sense of his doctrines? There are other errors, less serious but still significant. For how could a Spanish speaker like Menasseh distort in the Latin version so many names of places, towns, and people connected with South America and the Iberian Pensinsula?

Unfortunately for our rabbi, his English translator was not a first-class Latin scholar. He added to the mistakes and introduced other ambiguities. In addition he tended to transcribe passages which made hardly any sense, for want of a clear understanding of the text. How are we to understand the presence of Hebrew caciques, the transformation of the door of a mosque into the port of Mysketa, and the assertion of the Chinese Jew who had allegedly learnt his own language from a child? Moses Wall was no more familiar with Jewish culture, as is demonstrated, for example, by the problem he had with the passage in which a Hebrew neologism appears in the mouth of Eldad ha-Dani. We might also mention the misunderstanding which makes it seem that Montezinos was ostracized by the Jewish community of Amsterdam, whereas Menasseh ben Israel reports that the traveller was unwilling to derive any material profit from relating his remarkable adventures. The proper names are even more corrupt in the English version than in the Latin.

There is another curious point, worthy of note: Menasseh ben Israel did not supply his Latin translator with the same edition as the Spanish vesion he gave his community. In fact it is impossible to follow the Latin and English versions in the Spanish because the texts differ in the way the chapters and paragraphs are presented and divided. Some of them have a construction foreign to their Spanish counterparts. Paradoxically some expositions are fuller, indeed more detailed, in the Latin than in the Spanish. We are thinking in particular of the passage in which

Menasseh ben Israel gives an account of his wife's renowned ancestry. More often however, certain passages are either less developed or absent. An example of this is the pasage concerning the future coming of the Messiah in the context of a debate with the Jesuit, Matteo Ricci.

All the errors have been corrected, sometimes in the text itself where they impair comprehension, but more often in a note. We have also taken care to correct the mistakes in biblical quotations which are frequent and reproduced in their entirety by Moses Wall.

It is not possible to draw doctrinal conclusions from all the differences between the Spanish and the Latin–English texts. Nevertheless the reader who wants to make a detailed study of our rabbi's text cannot avoid a comparison of Moses Wall's text with the Spanish version.

This book has its origins in an amazing tale told, on his return from the Americas, by a Jewish traveller, Antonio de Montezinos, of whom we shall have more to say later. It is sufficient here to know that he claimed to have found the descendants of the Lost Ten Tribes.[10]

Menasseh ben Israel was asked to give his opinion of this story by many Christian friends, among whom without doubt the most important was John Dury, to whom he replied as follows: '. . . I, to give you satisfaction, have written instead of a Letter a Treatise, which I shortly will publish and whereof you shall receive so many copies as you desire.'[11] Montezinos's account disturbed many people, in fact, as a letter from John Dury to Thomas Thorowgood shows.[12] The former stated that he had heard many rumours about the Ten Tribes while he was in the Netherlands. We will quote that part of the letter which is relevant to our subject:

[10] 'In 721 BC the Assyrian king, Sargon, took possession of Samaria. The Kingdom of Israel was brought down. It was a catastrophe without precedent in the history of Israel. The conquerors had a policy of deportation and exchange of populations. Deported to Assyria, ten of the twelve tribes of Israel vanished from the historical scene. Later on the idea of the 'Lost Tribes' was to haunt Jewish minds for a long time.' See J. Eisenberg, *Une histoire des Juifs*, Paris, 1970, p. 37.

[11] Letter from Menasseh ben Israel to John Dury dated 25 November 1649 at Amsterdam, in T. Thorowgood, *Iewes in America or probabilities that the Americans are of that race*, p. xvii. Curiously enough, in the sixteenth century one Antonio Montesino of Lima stated, according to the writings of Luis Lopez, Bishop of Quito, that 'The Indians of the islands and mainland of the Indies . . . are Hebrews descended from the Ten Lost Tribes of Israel'. See André Néher, *Jewish Thought and the Scientific Revolution of the Sixteenth Century: David Gans*, Oxford, 1985, II, 3, 4.

[12] *An epistolicall discourse of Mr John Dury to Mr Thorowgood concerning his conjecture that the Americans are descended from the Israelites. With the history of a Portugall Iew Antonio Monterinos [sic] attested by Menasseh ben Israel to the same effect*, Saint James, 27 Jan. 1649, unpaginated, in T. Thorowgood, *Iewes in America . . .*, London, 1650.

. . . a little before I came from the Low Countries, I was told of a Jew who came from America to Amsterdam, and brought to the Jews residing there, newes concerning the ten Tribes; that hee had been with them upon the border of their Land, and had conversed with some of them for a short space and seen and heard remarkable things whiles he stayed with them. . . . I heard that a Narrative was made in writing of that which he had related . . . I have procured it from the Low Countries, and received a Copie thereof in French, attested under Manasseh ben Israel his hand, that it doth exactly agree with the originall, as it was sent me . . . And because I was not satisfied in some things, and desired to know how farre the whole matter was believed among the Jewes at Amsterdam, I wrote to Manasseh ben Israel, their chiefe Rabbi about it, and his answer I have gotten in two Letters, telling me that by the occasion of the questions which I proposed unto him concerning this adjoined Narrative of Mr Antonie Monterinos (*sic*), hee to give me satisfaction, had written insteed of a Letter, a Treatise, which hee shortly would publish, and whereof I should receive so many copies as I should desire: In his first Letter dated Novem. last 25, he saies that in his treatise he handles of the first inhabitants of America, which he believes were of the ten Tribes; moreover, that they are scattered also in other Countries, which he names, and that they keepe their true Religion, as hoping to returne again into the Holy land in due time.

In his second Letter, dated the twenty three of December, he saies more distinctly thus: 'I declare how that our Israelites were the first finders out of America. . . . I thinke that the ten Tribes live not onely there, but also in other lands scattered every where; these never did come backe to the second Temple, and they keep till this day the Jewish Religion. . . . So then at their appointed time, all the tribes shall meet from all the parts of the world into two provinces, namely Assyria and Egypt, nor shall their kingdome be any more divided, but they shall have one Prince the Messiah Sonne of David. I do also set forth the Inquisition of Spaine, and rehearse divers of our Nation, and also Christians, Martyrs, who in our times have suffered severall sorts of torments, and then having shewed with what great honours our Jewes have been graced also by severall Princes who professe Christianity. I prove at large, that the day of the promised Messiah unto us doth draw neer, upon which occasion I explaine many Prophecies &c.'

By all which you see his full agreement with your conjecture concerning the Americans, that they are descended of the Hebrewes.[13]

Most commentators and critics of the book have seen our rabbi only as a dreamer seized with Messianic enthusiasm, ready to believe in a fairy-tale type of story. However this extract from Dury's long letter allows us to put forward what seems to us the only possible explanation of the genesis of the work. For we are struck by the period of time which

---

[13] Ibid.

elapsed between hearing the tale from Montezinos, who arrived in Amsterdam in 1644, and the hurried, precipitate and somewhat undisciplined composition of the *Hope of Israel*. Indeed the many mistakes in relation to quotations indicate that Menasseh ben Israel did not have time to check them all.[14]

It must be recognized that our author carried out his work at a considerable pace. In Section 24 of the book he mentions the third part of his *Conciliador*, which appeared in 5410, that is to say after 7 September 1649.[15] Elsewhere, in Section 30, he reports the martyrdom of Tomás Treviño de Sobremonte taking place in Mexico *this year*, in fact on 11 April 1649.[16] Allowance must be made for the time which will have elapsed between the *auto-da-fé* in Mexico and the report of it reaching Amsterdam. So it was, in all probability, during the autumn of 1649 that Menasseh wrote *Spes Israelis* and *Esperança de Israel*, adding this work to his many daily occupations.

We are even more surprised to learn, by means of Antonio José Saraiva's fine article, that Menasseh ben Israel and Antonio Vieira had discussed at length problems relating to the arrival of the Messiah, in the course of a visit the celebrated Jesuit paid to the United Provinces in 1647.[17] Why then five years silence on the part of our rabbi? As a religious official, he was reluctant to give his backing to a story which was so extraordinary in content. But once the tale was known, made use of, and distorted by the Christians, he had to claim it as a Jewish piece of good news, and then put it in the context of existing explanations concerning the problem of the Ten Tribes. For Montezinos's account, transmitted by Dury to Thorowgood, was used to back up John Eliot's evangelistic mission to the Americas.[18] Menasseh ben Israel wants to put a very quick end to the explanation of the Jewish origin of the Indians suggested by Dury and supported by Thorowgood.[19] The Indians are

---

[14] Menasseh ben Israel made extensive use, especially as far as quotations were concerned, of Gregorio García's work of synthesis, *Origen de los Indios del Nuevo Mundo e Indias Occidentales*, Valencia, 1607, a compilation of all the hypotheses put forward at the time about the origins of the Indians of the New World.

[15] The beginning of the Jewish year 5410 corresponds to this date.

[16] See below, no. 193.

[17] A. J. Saraiva, 'Antonio Vieira, Menasseh ben Israël et le Cinquième Empire' in *Studia Rosenthaliana*, vol. vi, no. 1, Jan. 1972, pp. 44–50.

[18] See L. Glaser, *Indians or Jews?*, Los Angeles, 1973, p. 37. See also the interesting bibliography in L. Wolf, *Menasseh ben Israel's mission. . .*, p. 152.

[19] The book's title, *Iewes in America, or probabilities that the Americans are of that race*, is eloquent in itself. See, for example ch. 4, pp. 48–53, 'Answer about their becoming so barbarous'.

not descended from the Lost Ten Tribes, and they have nothing in common, morally or physically, with the ancient Hebrews. The *Hope of Israel* reminds us firmly of this.[20]

Menasseh is fully aware of the importance of his book which he recognizes without false modesty, as he declares in his dedication to the *parnassim*: 'I set great store by the opportunity which I have been given to write a work of such weight and importance.' This is clearly not an anodyne piece of rabbinical advice. Indeed he very sensibly takes his title from a verse of Jeremiah: 'O the hope of Israel, the saviour thereof in time of trouble, why shouldest thou be as a stranger in the land, and as a wayfaring man that turneth aside to tarry for a night?'[21] But, as rabbi of a community whose members had, for the most part, lived as Marranos in the Iberian Peninsula, as himself the son of a Marrano, and as a great admirer and relative by marriage of Isaac Abrabanel the writer of several books and commentaries on the coming of the Messiah, Menasseh ben Israel knew very well the explosive charge the word *esperanza* had in Spain, as much for Judaizing New Christians as for the Old Christians who used to deride the Marranos' Messianic hopes. The term *esperanza* had a particular resonance for the entire population. The Spanish theatre used this word to indicate, in a satiric manner, a specifically Jewish mentality. Not all the uses the dramatists and great authors of the Golden Age made of it may be mentioned here, writers such as Lope de Vega, Tirso de Molina, Calderón, and Quevedo.[22]

And so, for the first time in a Christian Europe where Jews were not usually allowed Messianic expectations, when, that is, they were not actually being mocked for their unfounded hope, our rabbi, in a widely understood language, let off a bombshell, a book whose 'sole objective is to show that this hope which sustains us, that of the advent of the Messiah, is an expectation of happiness to come. Although the coming

---

[20] See, for example, Sect. 7. Many, even among the few authors who have studied Menasseh, have misread *Esperança de Israel*. John Dury, in the text we have mentioned, set off on the wrong track. He was followed by Kayserling, who wrote concerning this work: 'In this essay he [Menasseh] sought to investigate the traces of the settlement of the missing Ten Tribes, and he arrived at the conclusion that the American Aborigines were descendants of those tribes; that is to say, the wild Indians were of Jewish descent', in 'The life and labours of Menasseh ben Israel', *Miscellany of Hebrew Literature*, p. 16.

[21] Jeremiah 14: 8.

[22] See M. Herrero Garcia, *Ideas de los Españoles del siglo XVII*, Madrid, 1966, pp. 629–35; Y. H. Yerushalmi, *From Spanish Court to Italian Ghetto* . . . , p. 305; Y. Kaplan, 'The Attitude of the Leadership of the Portuguese Community in Amsterdam to the Sabbataian Movement, 1665–71', in *Zion*, xxxix, 3–4, 1974, p. 200 (in Hebrew).

will be difficult, it is none the less inevitable'.[23] For Menasseh ben Israel chose to address Jews in Spanish, aiming the Latin version of his work more particularly at the scholarly world.[24]

Menasseh ben Israel's book opens with Montezinos's narrative which some, today, would consider rather unreliable; it continues with travellers' tales in the style of the period, and a long list of ancient and contemporary quotations. Throughout he asserts and supports *coram publico* the fundamental truth that Judaism feeds on: the imminence of the Messiah's coming.

The publication of the *Esperança de Israel* was quite an event, at a time when Jewish authors kept works dealing with the Messiah within their own community. For they well knew the dangers they would encounter in giving foolish publicity to the certainties to which they adhered. In 1650 Menasseh ben Israel, with quotations from a good many Jewish and Christian writers, calmly introduced Jewish Messianism into the Republic of Letters. In acceding to his friend John Dury's request, he was also responding to Spanish derision of the Marranos' *esperanza*.[25] It was only in Holland, which was two centuries ahead of the rest of Europe in respect of freedom and tolerance, that this new page of Jewish history could be written, and that, in 1650, what the great historian Salo Wittmayer Baron calls the 'Late Middle Ages and Era of European Expansion'[26] could emerge.

In truth, our rabbi's book rests on two foundations. The first is none other than the *Relación de Aharón Levi, alias Antonio de Montezinos*, which the author gives before his own comments. The second consists of Jewish Messianism such as is expressed through Messianic movements which have arisen in various countries at various times, in Hebrew treatises from the Middle Ages to the sixteenth century, and finally in the popular mind in forms still poorly explained. If we do not accord this Messianism its rightful place in the book's scheme, we are condemned to seeing it as merely a non-essential aspect of the work.

The character whose 'extraordinary journey' opens the *Hope of Israel* lived for only a short time within a Jewish community. Antonio de

[23] Dedication to the *parnassim*.

[24] On the choice of Spanish by the writers of this period, see J. Caro Baroja, *Los Judíos en la España moderna y contemporánea*, vol. i, p. 207.

[25] Was it to prevent this derision becoming a permanent feature that, two and a half centuries later, when Santiago Pérez Junquera reprinted the book *a plana y renglón*—respecting the pagination and lineation of the original—he altered its title to 'Origen de los Americanos. Miqweh Israel. Esto es Esperanza de Israel ... sobre el origen de los Americanos', seeking to stress only the American pretext for its being written?

[26] *A Social and Religious History of the Jews*. Volumes ix to xvi are devoted to this period.

Montezinos, *alias* Aaron Levi, was a New Christian. He was born in Portugal in the town of Villaflor, a well-known centre of Marranism.[27] He was descended from Jews converted in 1497. Like many others, and for reasons we do not know, he set off for the Western Indies where he lived until 1644.[28] He then set sail for Amsterdam, reaching it on 19 September. He stayed only six months in this city and went to sea again. Taking into account the date of his arrival and the length of the crossing, he will have reached his destination, namely the Jewish community of Recife, or Pernambuco, in Brazil, which was the first community in the New World, towards the end of 1645. He died two years later, probably during the Brazilian summer of 1647/8. According to Menasseh ben Israel, he was forty years old in 1644. Born about 1604, he was relatively young when he died, having spent the best years of his life in a Marrano's state of dissimulation and anxiety. But his brief visits to Jewish communities, both in Amsterdam and Recife, must have intrigued, if not troubled, the 'various people of the Portuguese Nation' to whom he related his adventures. The few details we have about this man are almost all from sources in Amsterdam. Although it is true that he spent all he had in accomplishing what he saw as his mission to Amsterdam, he refused all assistance from the community, and recoiled from the idea of deriving the slightest profit from his efforts. For travellers used sometimes to stop in Jewish communities to get help, especially if they were the bearers of sensational news. We have examined the registers of the community which contain all the recipients of alms from the 'Nation' of Amsterdam in 1644 and 1645: his name does not appear.[29]

Menasseh ben Israel interviewed Antonio de Montezinos during the course of the six months he spent in Holland. And our rabbi reports: 'Before me and in the presence of several people of quality, he took a solemn oath that all that he had said was true.' We do not know what impression he made on the Jewish community of Recife, since that community's register was only started some months after his death.[30] However when he wrote the *Hope of Israel*, our learned rabbi already knew that 'on his death bed, he [Montezinos] took the same oath, at a time when it is better not to commit perjury'.[31]

[27] Cf. Arch. Nat. Paris, E 3706/12, no. 198, a royal declaration of 22 July 1697, relating to Portuguese Jews in Bayonne, which states that out of thirty-six individuals who had come from Portugal, nine were from Villaflor.
[28] See below Section 13.
[29] Municipal Archives of Amsterdam, PA. 334, 19.   [30] See below n. 166.
[31] Cf. the aphorism 'No man is found to lie at the hour of death', *Ketubot* 18b.

Would an innocent reading of Menasseh ben Israel's work convince a modern reader of the truth of Antonio de Montezinos's account? We cannot be sure. On the other hand it is beyond doubt that even before our rabbi took up his pen to record it at the beginning of his *Hope of Israel*, this story had made a considerable impact on Jewish hearers, and had also spread to Christian circles. For the Jews of Amsterdam and Pernambuco, the tale had more than Messianic echoes, it was a direct signal, tidings of the end of exile. For Christians, as we have seen, and especially for Protestants, it posed a problem of 'ethnography': were the American Indians descended from the Lost Ten Tribes of Israel? It also made a number of people face the question of the nearness of the second coming.

We should also note that there were texts available in Amsterdam written by Antonio de Montezinos to Abraham Israel Pereyra, the man who was for many years the most important of the community's leaders and one of the most faithful followers of Shabbetai Zevi, the false Messiah.[32] Whatever Antonio de Montezinos's tale consists of, it was calculated to set the most sober spirits among the Jews of Amsterdam bubbling over with excitement.

The adventure began in Spanish New Granada—now the Republic of Colombia—between the river port of Honda on the Magdalena[33] and the *Audiencia* of Quito. Our Antonio de Montezinos crossed the Cordilleras with some Indians whom he engaged to carry his goods. On the way, some of them were complaining about their ill fortune, and their leader, a certain Francisco, made a curious remark which Montezinos heard but to which he paid no attention. And yet Francisco was alluding to 'a hidden people' who would avenge the Indians for all the ills heaped on them by the Spanish.

[32] Noted by C. Roth in 1934, this correspondence cannot now be found. See C. Roth, *A Life of Menasseh ben Israel*, p. 331. Elizabeth Levi de Montezinos has looked in vain for these manuscripts. See her article 'The Narrative of Aharon Levi alias Antonio de Montezinos' in *The American Sephardi*, vii–viii, 1975, pp. 63–83, and particularly p. 79. In a recent letter, Elizabeth Levi de Montezinos has been kind enough to give, for our benefit, additional data from her family tradition, which stresses the sense of honour attached to the oath. In spite of a long letter from Richard D. Barnett, the eminent archaeologist and specialist in Sephardic Jewish history, and of mail addressed to a company, which still exists in London, we have had no further luck. The reference would be to a copy of Menasseh ben Israel's book containing a part of this correspondence.

[33] We are delighted, at this point, to thank Flor Romero de Nohra, Counsellor of the Colombian Embassy in Paris, who has helped us reconstruct Montezinos's itinerary. The location of Honda is 5° south, 74° west, 150 km. north-west of Bogotá. Ships used this port until 1965, and in colonial times it was the most important in New Granada.

A fair time elapsed during which Montezinos reached Cartagena of the Indies.[34] There our traveller was arrested by the Inquisition. In prison he had plenty of time to reflect on his past. The remark made by the Indian, Francisco, came back to him and led him to say to himself, 'These Indians are Hebrews.' He promised himself that if he escaped from the jail of the Inquisition, he would get to the bottom of the matter. The Inquisition did release its victim. Faithful to his resolve, Antonio de Montezinos returned to Honda and, amazingly, found Francisco again. He repeated his mysterious words to Montezinos, and appeared willing to travel with him.

As soon as they left the town, Montezinos began to question his companion. The revelations really began there, for it was unthinkable to talk of Judaism within a town. The dialogue between the Indian and Montezinos, in the depths of the countryside, away from all inquisitive eavesdroppers, is typical of the behaviour of Marranos who used to confess their true faith to each other in that way. Our traveller declared that he was a son of Israel, and the Indian, whose confidence he won with difficulty, proposed an arduous journey across the mountains. The trek lasted for more than a week and, one morning, the two men reached the bank of a great river which the narrator compares to the Douro; it was the Río Cauca. Beyond this river lived some strange 'Indians' who came to meet Montezinos and recited to him the Jewish profession of faith in Hebrew: 'Hear O Israel, the Lord our God is one God.' Our traveller was not, however, allowed to cross the river. But the 'Indians' came over several times to give him a curious message consisting of nine propositions. These men claimed to be descended from Abraham, Isaac, Jacob, and Reuben. One day they would come out of hiding; to do this they were waiting for messengers who knew how to write.

In spite of all his efforts, Antonio de Montezinos was not able to cross the river to visit the Indian settlement, nor to learn more about it. Some 300 'Indians' came by canoe to meet him, and to speak to him in the same manner. In addition to what they said, Montezinos noted their physical appearance: 'Those men are somewhat scorched by the sun, some of them wear hair long down to their knee, others of them much as we commonly cut it. They were comely of body, well accoutred . . .' The Spanish version also specifies: 'They were tall, handsome, they cut a fine figure.' Their appearance thus bore little resemblance to that of the indigenous people who, in those days, were described as being rather ugly.

[34] This city is more than 1,000 km., as the crow flies, from Quito.

At the end of three days, laden with provisions and presents, Antonio de Montezinos and Francisco took their leave of these strange 'Indians', and retraced their steps. On the way Francisco explained to his companion the mystery of these Israelite 'Indians'. Having arrived in the country many moons ago, they were repeatedly attacked by new arrivals, the true Indians, Francisco's own ancestors. The Israelites were driven back but nevertheless caused many casualties among the Indians. Weary of war, the last *Mohanes*[35] prophesied that truth was on the side of the sons of Israel, that at the end of time they would leave their hiding-place and become the masters of the world. The Indians should therefore join them so as to share their fortunate destiny. From that time there existed a secret alliance between many Indians and the sons of Israel. Furthermore at Honda Montezinos was introduced by his companion to three young natives. The account ends with their words:

Upon a time you shall see us and shall not know us. We are all our brethren by God's singular favour ... As for the country, be secure, for we rule all the Indians. After we have finished a business we have with the wicked Spaniard, we will bring you out of your bondage by God's help, not doubting but he who cannot lie will help us, according to his word.

So Antonio de Montezinos delivered to the communities of Amsterdam and then of Pernambuco a message whose implications were manifold: there exist *ab antiquo* some descendants of one of the Lost Ten Tribes, that of Reuben, in a very distant and secret land, New Granada in America. As immediate allies they have a number of Indians and as potential allies all the Indians. They are all working in practical ways for the redemption of Israel. Even though Montezinos did not lay particular stress on this point, his account contained an invitation to the Jewish community, in the ninth proposition, to 'send twelve men ... who are skilful in writing'. Why were the Israelites of the Western Indies asking the Jewish community to send them some scholars? To obtain information from them, the nature of which remains unclear, to institute a dialogue? The question is not tackled, not at least in the account as it has come down to us.

This was a remarkable revelation. Jews and Christians knew about it well before it was published in the prologue of *Esperança de Israel* and of *Spes Israelis*. Everyone was aware of its extaordinary nature. Menasseh ben Israel's dedication to the leaders of the Amsterdam community leaves no doubt about its impact. Does it appear a fabrication as most

---

[35] The text explains these as *sorcerers*.

historians have considered it to be?[36] Was Montezinos just an adventurer like the many who used to visit Jewish communities long ago? Did he have a vision of the political redemption of the people of Israel? Does his odyssey contain verifiable elements?

To our knowledge, only Elisabeth Levi de Montezinos has recently attempted to do him justice. She begins by referring to a family tradition handed down by her father, Jacob Levi de Montezinos, according to which messengers came to Amsterdam to invite Antonio de Montezinos to go to London. But, because he wanted to keep the route leading to the Israelites of the Andes secret, he had to refuse their offer.[37] Above all she lays stress on the recent discovery of documents of the Inquisition which in part confirm what Montezinos said. Here we give a translation of an extract from the note of the Holy Office which she publishes in the original Spanish:

Antonio Montessinos, born at Villaflor in the Kingdom of Portugal (of whom mention has been made in previous dispatches) who concealed himself and fled, was caught in this city [Cartagena of the Indies] with sequestration of goods and locked up in the secret prisons on 3 September 1639, after a testimony of complicity made against a certain Montessinos, accused of Judaism: he is suspected of being the same as the man who has been apprehended. This has all been done with the agreement of Fr. Manuel Rodríguez de Araujo, a religious of St Francis, Commissioner of the Holy Office in an area of this bishopric, and in the presence of the *licenciado* Don Francisco Rege Corvalán, *consultor*. As the Inquisition had not yet been established, there was no tribunal, and so there was a certain delay in sending out the notices of the hearing, until 14 December of last year 1640. It was on that date that he was given the first monition [38] to which he remained *negativo* . . .[39]

The second hearing was held on 4 February 1641 accompanied by the second monition, in the course of which he made the same denial; he did the same at the third [hearing] and following the third monition which took place on the seventh of the same month. On the nineteenth, not having been able to be certain of the person's identity, by ordinary act and without *consulte*, the case was suspended in view of the long period during which he [the prisoner] has been locked up

---

[36] It is enough to quote Cecil Roth, who writes: 'The fantastic character of this account needs no elaboration.' *A Life of Menasseh ben Israel*, p. 330, n. 1.

[37] 'The Narrative of Aharon Levi . . .', pp. 78–9.

[38] The prisoner is then asked to clear his conscience and to make a confession if he wants to benefit from the indulgence of the Holy Office.

[39] Archivo Histórico Nacional de Madrid, sección Inquisición Cartagena de las Indias, libro 1012, fo. 158. Here we thank most warmly Pilar León Tello, curator at the Archivo Histórico Nacional of Madrid, who kindly transcribed and sent us the text of this report. To be *negativo* is to refuse to confess to religious offences.

without complete justification. For this reason, forthwith, he came out of the prison of the Inquisition and got back the poor goods which had been sequestered.[40]

It should be mentioned that another document of the same type—namely a communication from the tribunal of Cartagena of the Indies to the Supreme Council of the Inquisition in Madrid—was noted in 1966 by Lucía García de Proodian, who was not aware of its significance.[41] We have been able to obtain this second document which, while containing some differences of detail, confirms the first. These texts make it clear that our hero was well and truly incarcerated in the Inquisitorial jails of Cartagena of the Indies from 3 September 1639 to 19 February 1641, that is for almost eighteen months. By not giving way before the Inquisitors, by remaining *negativo*, he risked going to the stake, had his identity been proved. The tribunal, however, let him go for want of evidence showing that he was indeed the individual against whom there were testimonies which would have allowed them to charge him with Judaism. So it is understandable that Menasseh ben Israel wrote: 'He [was] set at liberty through God's mercy . . .'

The chronological authenticity of the events which Montezinos describes is more difficult to establish. Although he reached Amsterdam on 19 September 1644, he relates that it all began two and a half years previously, that is in March 1642. At that time he met the Indian, Francisco, for the first time, and made the long journey to Cartagena of the Indies, where he was imprisoned and then released. He had time to return to Honda, to find the Indian, Francisco, again and journey with him as far as the Israelites' hiding place, to return from it—a trek which took some three weeks—and finally to make the sea crossing to Amsterdam. Unless he accepts this hurried chronology on the one hand, and on the other *a second imprisonment at the end of 1642*, the historian is forced to consider either that the sequence of events as reported to us is incorrect, or that Antonio de Montezinos's memory was not entirely accurate. What is certain is that he spent time in the dungeons of the

---

[40] 'The Narrative of Aharon Levi . . .', pp. 82–3. There is a facsimile in this article of the Inquisition document (Archivo Histórico Nacional, Madrid, section Cartagena de las Indias, fo. 49).

[41] Archivo Histórico Nacional, Madrid, libro 1012, fos. 158–9. Lucía García de Proodian in *Los Judíos en América, sus actividades en los Virreinatos de Nueva Castilla y Nueva Granada, s. XVII*, Madrid, 1966, document 196 *bis*, p. 532, only mentions one Antonio Montesinos as being among the prisoners whose cases had not been tried at Cartagena of the Indies.

Holy Office *one year before* his first meeting with the Indian, Francisco, and not *after* as he relates.

The most acceptable solution seems to us to be the following: at the beginning of 1639 at the latest, Antonio de Montezinos met the Indian, Francisco, for the first time. He then went to Cartagena where he was arrested. For eighteen months he languished in the secret prisons of the Inquisition. While there, reflecting on his past life, he came to the conviction that the 'Indians' whom he had met were Jews. Freed from the clutches of the Holy Office on 19 February 1641, he had time to get back to Honda and the hidden Israelites, and, no doubt, to return to Cartagena, before making for Amsterdam.

The identity of the man raises fewer problems. As he says himself in his account, as the Inquisitorial dispatches indicate, as doubtless other Jews in Amsterdam who came from the same place attested, he was certainly born at Villaflor. He was, he says, the son of Luis de Montesinos.[42] A *licenciado*, by the name of Luis Montesinos, is to be found in 1624 in the Kingdom of Quito, among seven individuals who testified before the Holy Office against a certain Tello de Valasco.[43] Was this our traveller's father or a man of the same name? If it were he, Antonio de Montezinos would have belonged to a distinguished family, as Menasseh ben Israel maintains, a typically Marrano family whose members had no hesitation in denouncing people to the Inquisition.[44]

The historian might be tempted to conclude critically that Montezinos, broken by his long imprisonment, which was only punctuated by the three hearings, purely and simply imagined that the descendants of one of the Lost Tribes of Israel, that of Reuben, were living in a lost refuge in the Andes, and that it fell to him to reveal these facts to his Jewish brothers living in a free land. This leaves the oath sworn by our

[42] We do not know on what Seymour B. Liebman based his assertion that this Luis de Montesinos was a member of the Portuguese Jewish community in Amsterdam. See *The Inquisitors and the Jews in the New World: Summaries of procesos, 1500–1810 and Bibliographical Guide*, Coral Gables, Fla, 1976, p. 161. In his note on this individual, Liebman refers to the document mentioned above, n. 40, but erroneously has the arrest occur in 1641.

[43] John Leddy Phelan, *The Kingdom of Quito in the 17th Century. Bureaucratic Politics in the Spanish Empire*, London, 1967, p. 260.

[44] In the main the denunciations arose when prisoners awaiting trial, in the hope of getting clemency from the court, finally denounced their 'accomplices' (I. S. Révah, 'Les Marranes . . .', p. 42). They were also the work of Marranos, not as yet under suspicion, who wanted to create a good impression on the Holy Office, or to take vengeance on rivals or enemies. Needless to say, denunciation was an evil which afflicted the entire population of the Peninsula, to the point where many Old Christian moralists condemned the practice.

traveller on the truth of his tale, the first time in Amsterdam and a second time in Pernambuco, 'taking the same oath at his death'.[45] In the Spanish version, Menasseh goes on to say 'at a time when it is better not to commit perjury'.[46] Such an oath would not have been taken lightly, as it involves the eternal life.

As far as attitudes of mind are concerned, it matters little whether the tale is authentic or imaginary. It had an extremely strong impact on the 'Nation' of Amsterdam, on well-read Jews and Christians,[47] and indeed on Menasseh ben Israel, who was to write, from the starting-point of this amazing adventure, its Messianic sequel *Esperança de Israel*. In the short term, it was responsible for the birth of a vast literature. In the medium term, it supported our rabbi's political initiative for the admission of Jews into England. In the long term, it predisposed the minds of the Jews of Amsterdam to accept, in 1666, with certainty and jubilation, the news that the Messiah had appeared in Smyrna in the person of Shabbetai Zevi. Thus Montezinos's story had less value for itself than for the whole scheme of Jewish Messianism, in which it appeared just at the right moment.

Messianic expectation is the most essential characteristic of the Jewish people. Set out in treatises written in the Middle Ages or in modern times, expressed belatedly as an article of faith by Maimonides, very often fundamental in texts and daily life, it is always implicit in Jewish attitudes of mind, both popular and learned. The discourse of the Jewish people is constantly permeated by the fact of Messianism, which even if not always expressed, is always quietly lived by. This discourse is firstly that of the traditional sources, the Bible, Talmud, and Midrash. It is secondly and supremely that of the daily liturgy and of those festivals when the imminent coming of the Messiah, the son of David, is recited three times a day and in the grace after meals. We do not propose to review the history of Jewish Messianic thought at this

---

[45] See Sect. 13. [46] See para. 17 and above n. 31.

[47] We may wonder whether the Marrano poet, Antonio Enríquez Gómes, who wrote the *Romance al divín mártir Juda Creyente*, the only one of his works which may be understood without a key, while in France, had any knowledge of Montezinos's account before it was published by Menasseh ben Israel. The writer left France for Spain at the end of 1649 or the beginning of 1650, but he must have written his poem between 1647 and 1649. For, in this work heralding the Messianic age, he speaks of the Fifth Empire, the Empire of the Messiah and of its Indian frontiers, previously hidden: 'Saldrá a luz un nuevo imperio/Con los términos indianos,/No visto ni descubierto.' The connection was not made by the last editor of the text, Timothy Oelman, in his 'Antonio Enríquez Gómez's "Romance al divín mártir, Juda Creyente"' in *Journal of Jewish Studies*, xxvi, 1–2, 1975, lines 494–6.

point; it has been excellently dealt with elsewhere.[48] We intend only to bring out the special contribution which Jewish sources have brought to the coming of the Messiah. This contribution has varied over the course of history: the Jewish people were not established as such before the Exodus from Egypt, for many centuries they formed a political entity which they lost and found again for a time, they then endured an interminable exile . . .

Has the vision of the coming of the Messiah been modified by historical circumstances? Has it been refined from a purely material model towards a spiritual viewpoint?[49] Without getting involved in a discussion of this type, we are well aware that several coexisting elements combine to make up the Jewish Messianic image. The first is the reign of the King-Messiah, the son of David, a just, peaceful, and happy reign. The second—which was particularly valuable when Israel was in captivity—is the real emancipation of the Jewish people from all foreign domination, and the end of the diaspora. The third is the setting up of a better human order with all nations recognizing the Unity of God. The coming of the Messiah is then a public and tangible event, both national and universal.

There are many pieces of Biblical evidence for the Messianic promise. Some are explicit, others have been clarified by commentators who have interpreted the hidden meaning of certain verses of Scripture. It might almost be said that the whole Bible speaks of nothing but the Messiah: 'Rabbi Hiyya bar Abba said, in the name of Rabbi Johanan: all the prophets without exception have only prophesied for the days when the Messiah will come.'[50] It would not be useful here to set out a catalogue of all the Messianic promises in the Bible. However in the sixteenth century, after the expulsion from Spain in 1492 which was a tragedy for Israel, Isaac Abrabanel undertook a compilation, in treatise form, of all Biblical texts heralding the Messiah. To this end he wrote the last part of his Messianic trilogy, under the title of *Mashmi‘a Yeshu‘ah*, Announcing Salvation.[51]

---

[48] There is a great deal of literature on this subject. We might mention Julius H. Greenstone, *The Messiah Idea in Jewish History*; Joseph Sarachek, *The Doctrine of the Messiah in Medieval Jewish Literature*, New York, 1968; Abba Hillel Silver, *A History of Messianic Speculation . . .*, and of course Gershom G. Scholem's great book, *The Messianic Idea in Judaism*, London, 1971, which gives all the useful references.

[49] A. H. Silver sees 'the Messianic Idea' in revolutionary terms in *A History of Messianic Speculation . . .*, p. ix.

[50] Sanhedrin 99 a.

[51] From Isaiah 52:7. This work examines and comments on the biblical texts which concern the Messiah at close hand or from afar. It was published for the first time in 1526

The Messianic hope is present in the Hebrew people's infancy: the divine promise given to Abraham foretells a state of bliss, which, through him, will be spread among all peoples: 'And I will make of thee a great nation, and I will bless thee, and make thy name great; and thou shalt be a blessing: And I will bless them that bless thee, and curse him that curseth thee: and in thee shall all families of the earth be blessed.'[52] Taken up by all the patriarchs, and made for one moment a reality by King David whose reign, idealized, became the prototype for that of the Messiah, the Messianic hope is recalled by the prophets, either to rebuke the Hebrew people in times of injustice, or to comfort them in moments of political weakness or exile. In the Messiah's time, broadly speaking, Israel will live freely on the earth, each under his olive tree and under his vine, governed by a just king of the House of David. God will have taken vengeance on those who oppressed his people, but He will give a share of His blessing to those who recognize His Name.

The figure of the Messiah, as G. Scholem has noted,[53] remains imprecise: it is the transformation of men and of the world that the prophets are clear about. Isaiah paints a picture of the Messianic era promised to Israel and to the nations of the world:

And it shall come to pass in the last days, that the mountain of the Lord's house shall be established in the top of the mountains, and shall be exalted above the hills; and all nations shall flow unto it. And many people shall go and say, Come ye, and let us go up to the mountain of the Lord, to the house of the God of Jacob; and he will teach us of his ways, and we will walk in his paths: for out of Zion shall go forth the law, and the word of the Lord from Jerusalem. And he shall judge among the nations, and shall rebuke many people: and they shall beat their swords into ploughshares, and their spears into pruninghooks: nation shall not lift up sword against nation, neither shall they learn war any more.[54]

Zechariah explains in a single verse that all this will be achieved by the total conversion of all nations: 'And the Lord shall be king over all the earth: in that day shall the Lord be One, and his name be One.'[55]

The historical situation has instilled in the exiled, persecuted, and degraded Jewish people an attitude combining patience and impatience,

---

and reprinted many times, notably in Amsterdam in 1647. Menasseh ben Israel, whose family links with Isaac Abrabanel are known, certainly made use of it when writing the *Esperança de Israel*. On another Messianic work by Isaac Abrabanel, see n. 71.

[52] Genesis 12: 2–3.
[53] *Messianic Idea in Judaism*, p. 44.
[54] Isaiah 2: 2–4.
[55] Zechariah 14: 9. This verse forms part of the Jewish Liturgy. It is the culmination of the *'Alenu* prayer ('It is our duty') which concludes the three daily services of Judaism.

conflicting and complementary, the one inciting the other. Messianism, as a spiritual force, has given rise to various currents of thought within rabbinical Judaism, to feverish or tranquil speculation about the time of its advent, and to the popular demonstrations which are what the Messianic movements actually were. Scholem has shown that this force, when faced with the discipline of exile, expressed itself on different levels. Its alignment was strictly conservative in the precepts of the Law, both written and oral taught by rabbinical tradition, which aimed at preserving the Jewish way of life right up to the moment of the Messiah's arrival. It also looked back at an idealized past which it sought to see reborn. God was entreated to give back to Israel the period of blessings which had been lost: 'Renew our days as of old' say Lamentations (5: 21) read on 9 Av, the anniversary of the destruction of the Temple of Jerusalem. This expectation was also Utopian inasmuch as it envisaged a state of affairs which never had existed, in comparison with which anything real was marked by an irreparable inferiority and meanness. Even the concept of Utopia is inadequate, for the Messianic world does not merely entail a dream with which the people of Israel may lull themselves, but a reality so close that they must at all times remain cool-headed, adhere to the strict criteria laid down in Scripture, and, when a false Messiah arises, refrain from giving way to the unbalancing effect of a coming which is immediate but imperfect. Conservative, restitutory, 'Utopian', Jewish Messianism drew from a common source of hope in which Israel found strength, peace, and a reason to live.

Faced with the strength of popular Messianic feeling, medieval rabbinical thought developed two major forms. In one, which Scholem calls Apocalyptic, the Messiah will put a very sudden and miraculous end to Israel's exile, gathering those who have been dispersed into their ancestral land, and restoring the kingdom of the Son of David. All this would happen in a period of terrible wars, at the end of which God would avenge His people and strike down His enemies. The world will be renewed and the prophets' visions fulfilled to the letter. According to some writers, the rabbis would, on the whole, have nothing to do with the Apocalyptic view which would threaten the solid edifice of rabbinical standards, the *halakhah*. Another tendency, which may be described as Rationalist, was also expounded. This reduced Messianic perspectives to acceptable proportions. Thus, for Maimonides, the words of the prophets 'should be seen figuratively'. He writes: 'Do not believe that the Messiah must perform signs and miracles, or institute a new state of affairs in the world . . . '. Indeed, but Maimonides does not cast doubt on either the restoration of the people of Israel and of the House of David, or the transformation of the earthly world: 'In those days', he proclaims, 'there will be neither famine, nor war, nor jealousy, nor discord, for the earth will be possessed in abundance. The whole world will have no other care than the knowledge of God.'[56]

The real question was to know not what the Messiah would do, but when he would do it. Many Jewish authors were eager to elucidate the characteristics of the world of the Messiah, so different from the historical world of exile. But they were all, influenced in this by the genius of their people, tempted to determine the exact date of the beginning of the new era. Since the Scriptures contain the divine word, they should provide the means of making Messianic computations, if certain verses can be adequately interpreted. Periods of political turmoil and Jewish persecution were very helpful in this type of calculation. In this way Maimonides keeps to a family tradition that the secret of the coming of the Messiah is to be found in the prophecy of Balaam in Numbers 23:23: 'At the due season shall it be told to Jacob and Israel what God hath wrought.'[57] This prophecy was made in the Year of Creation 2488. After the same period of time again, that is to say in AM 4976 or AD 1216, the prophecy will be fulfilled and the Messiah will come. The calculation with which Menasseh ben Israel must have been familiar, that of Don Isaac Abrabanel, was based on a classic verse, in this case Daniel 7:25: ' ... and they shall be given into his hand until a time and times and half a time.'[58] These periods, equal in length to that of the First Temple (410 years), added to the date, according to Jewish tradition, of the destruction of the Temple (AD 68) give the year 1503.[59] The upheavals of the end of the fifteenth century and the expulsion from Spain may well have convinced Isaac Abrabanel that the time was near.[60]

Jewish history has relegated the recording of these calculation to its obscure margins. It has also attempted, less successfully, to write off the amazing movement of popular enthusiasm which was what the Messianic movements constituted. Nineteenth-century historians were contemptuous not only of the Messianic calculations but also of the

[56] Maimonides, quoted by G. G. Scholem in *Jewish Messianism*, pp. 25–6, 27–32.

[57] Quotation in this case taken from the Revised Version, London, 1884, incorporating footnotes 4 and 5 to Numbers 23:23.

[58] Quotation taken from the Revised Version.

[59] See A. H. Silver, *A History of Messianic Speculation* ... , pp. 74–5.

[60] See B. Netanyahu, *Don Isaac Abrabanel, Statesman and Philosopher*, Philadelphia, 1968, pp. 218–19.

individuals around whom the 'intense Messianic expectation'[61] took shape. Current opinion accords these critical events their importance as a concrete expression of Israel's historic attitude of mind. There were many such movements at the time of the Second Temple, and one of them was fundamental to the birth of Christianity.[62] During the whole of the Middle Ages, particularly among Sephardic Jews, Messianic manifestations arose in various places from the Yemen to Iraq and Persia. The period of the Crusades was especially productive of Messianic agitations.[63]

It is probable that the arrival of Antonio Montezinos initiated a new phase of interest on the part of the Jews of Amsterdam in everything to do with Messianism, a phase which was to culminate in the affair of Shabbetai Zevi, the false Messiah. But, in 1650, the work under review reinforced the fundamental hope which was at the root of the Jewish soul. All the same the attitude, in this matter, of the Portuguese community of the banks of the Amstel, from its beginnings up to 1644, remains relatively unknown. The historian may judge that this community, whose material and intellectual prosperity was obvious, would have kept the expectation of a new era under wraps or, at the least, not made it their first preoccupation. Could these well-to-do merchants have cheerfully anticipated imminent removal to the Holy Land? Would they have been content with a theoretical Messianism, such as that which Emmanuel Lévinas now censures when he writes: 'Nothing is more hypocritical than the Messianic prophetism of the established bourgeois.'[64] We have already stressed the exceptional nature of the birth and expansion of this community: its members felt that their return to the Jewish Faith in its integrity, after three generations of a precarious and sinful existence in a land of idolatry, was miraculous. Was not their reunion with living Judaism a shining example of divine care, and a necessary part of the foundations for the Messianic age? 'The minor miracle of seeing themselves completely reintegrated into the practice of their faith led them to accept the idea of immediate redemption and the

[61] G. G. Scholem, *Jewish Messianism*, p. 26.
[62] On the fundamental role of Messianism in the early days of Christianity, see G. Puente's remarkable book, *Idéologie et histoire. La formation du christianisme comme phénomène idéologique*, Paris, 1982.
[63] A. Z. Aescoly, *Jewish Messianic Movements: Sources and Documents on Messianism in Jewish History from the Bar-Kokhba Revolt until Recent Times*, Jerusalem, 1956 (in Hebrew). This work shows how, in a given region, an individual claiming to be the Messiah could drive Jews into taking action to shake off the yoke of external authority and to reconquer the Holy Land.
[64] *Difficile liberté: Essais sur le Judaïsme*, Paris, 1963, p. 130.

final triumph which the prophecies promised to the Lord's chosen people.'[65]

At the present time, such texts as might enlighten us on Messianism in Amsterdam before 1644 are, in essence, certain manuscripts which set out to convince immigrants from the Iberian Peninsula of the truth of Judaism and the falsity of Christianity. These texts were devoted to demonstrating that the Messiah had not yet come, and consequently to stressing the validity of the divine promise. But, as we have seen, even in the atmosphere of intellectual freedom prevailing in the Republic of the United Provinces, publication of these manuscripts would have been unthinkable. It is only in the last few years that these texts have begun to be published and studied. The remarkable inventories of these documents made by L. Fuks and R. Fuks-Mansfeld have, without doubt, made possible a new understanding of the Jewish attitude of mind in Amsterdam in the first half of the seventeenth century.[66] In these circumstances debates on Messianism were necessarily oral and circulated in manuscript form.

There are, however, some indications to confirm João Lúcio de Azevedo's statement, previously cited. Admittedly, little is known of the impact on the Portuguese community of the arrival in Amsterdam in 1623 of the false Messiah, Philip Ziegler.[67] Admittedly, the objects of Jacob Judah Leon's 'architectural' work are not explicit in his writings, which must, nevertheless, be added to our assessment of the manifestations of Messianic enthusiasm in Amsterdam.[68] In 1642 this rabbi published his *Retrato del Templo de Selomoh*.[69] The book described the Temple of Solomon in depth and detail: it was illustrated with his own

[65] The facts may be compared with this assessment by the great historian, João Lúcio de Azevedo, taking into account J. S. da Silva Rosa's classic history, *Geschiedenis der Portugeesche Joden te Amsterdam, 1593–1925*, Amsterdam, 1925, in *Lusitania*, vol. iii, fasc. ix, Apr. 1926, p. 435.

[66] *Hebrew and Judaic Manuscripts in Amsterdam Public Collections*, (1) *Catalogue of the Manuscripts of the Bibliotheca Rosenthaliana, University Library of Amsterdam*, (2) *Catalogue of the Manuscripts of Ets Haim, Livraria Montezinos, Sephardic Community of Amsterdam*, Leiden, 1973–5.

[67] H. I. Bloom, *The Economic Activities of the Jews of Amsterdam in the Seventeenth and Eighteenth Centuries*, p. 24.

[68] We owe this information to the very learned curator of the Bibliotheca Rosenthaliana in Amsterdam, A. K. Offenberg, who has made a detailed study of the works of Jacob Judah Leon (Templo). Readers are referred to his remarkable study, 'Bibliography of the works of Jacob Jehudah Leon (Templo)', in *Studia Rosenthaliana*, vol. xii, no. 1–2, July 1978, pp. 111–32.

[69] Middelburg, 1642. We note that Spinoza had this book in Latin in his library. See no. 82 of the *Catalogus van de Bibliotheek der Vereniging Het Spinozahuis te Rijnsburg*.

etchings, and supplemented with models of the building. This very exceptional piece of work had been undertaken at the insistence of the Dutch mystic, Adam Boreel, who was interested by the reconstruction of the Temple.[70] It is very likely that Jacob Judah Leon, who received his nickname of *Templo* from this project, was 'stimulated by the thought of the imminence of the restoration' of Israel to its historic homeland, and of the Temple. The work's success and the disappearance of the many copies of the famous model constitute an expression of Messianism in Jewish Amsterdam. It should also be mentioned that it was not merely due to the quirks of publication that Isaac Abrabanel's great works on the Messiah's coming, taken from traditional Jewish sources and his own conjectures, were printed in Amsterdam without the name of the publisher.[71]

Although Messianic expectation was nourished by verses of Scripture as well as by daily liturgy, it looked, above all, for 'signs' which might be found in current events. A somewhat unkind report, which M. de Bonrepaus, the French Ambassador at the Hague, wrote towards the end of the seventeenth century, makes the Jews appear constantly on the look-out for news: 'They pay as much attention to the news as they do to business, and comment on it at length on Saturdays and Sundays, while Christians of all denominations are concerned with their religious duties.'[72] That is how Montezinos's tale was spread so widely by word of mouth among the community: its publication was not, at a pinch, essential, and it was really in response to requests from outside that Mennasseh ben Israel had it printed in 1649.

Three events which could be interpreted as 'signs' happened in 1648 and 1649. The Treaties of Westphalia proclaimed, to a certain extent at least, freedom of conscience;[73] above all they marked the end of Spanish supremacy, and therefore of that of Catholicism. In this sense,

---

[70] On Adam Boreel, see Walther Schneider, *Adam Boreel*, Giessen, 1911; A. H. Silver, *A History of Messianic Speculation*, p. 192. On Jacob Templo, see C. Roth's article, 'Templo, Jacob Judah (Aryeh) Leon (1603–75)' in *Enc. Jud.* 15: 998–9.

[71] On Isaac Abrabanel's Messianic works, see above n. 51. This author also wrote *Ma'yenei ha-Yeshu'ah*, the Fountains of Salvation, from Isaiah 12.3, a work in which he gives an interpretation of the eschatological chapters of the Book of Daniel. This treatise was printed in Amsterdam in 1647. See B. Netanyahu, *Don Isaac Abravanel*, pp. 209 ff. The third part of Isaac Abrabanel's Messianic triptych is *Yeshu'ot Meshiho*, Karlsruhe, 1828.

[72] Quoted by Leon Vignols, 'Le Commerce hollandais et les congrégations juives à la fin du XVIIe siècle' in *Revue historique*, 15th year, vol. xxxiv, 1890, p. 330.

[73] On this point, see S. W. Baron, *A Social and Religious History of the Jews*, vol. ix, pp. v–vi.

for a good many Jews in Amsterdam, who were former victims of the Spanish Inquisition, 1648 might have been the dawn of redemption. Furthermore Jewish refugees now arriving in Amsterdam were still in a state of terror as a result of the massacres perpetrated by Chmielnicki's Cossacks in Poland.[74] Might not these horrors be the birth pangs of the Messiah spoken of by the traditional texts? Finally, did not the news of the beheading of Charles I herald the overthrow of the things of this world and the beginning of the longed-for new era?

In spite of its undoubted effect on the Jewish community of Amsterdam, we have seen that Montezinos's account, to which Menasseh ben Israel gives considerable importance throughout the work under review, had no practical consequences. For no expedition designed to verify the traveller's statements was organized. And yet if the Lost Tribes had been found again, if it had been thought that they would confront the hated domination of Spain militarily, might it not have been concluded that the Messianic age had begun? The punishment in Deuteronomy 28: 64, 'And the Lord shall scatter thee among all people, from the one end of the earth even unto the other; and there thou shalt serve other gods, which neither thou nor thy fathers have known, even wood and stone', found its confirmation in the presence of Israelites 'at the other end of the earth' in the New World. Daniel 12: 7 provided consolation which seemed to fit the facts: 'And I heard the man clothed in linen, which was upon the waters of the river, when he held up his right hand and his left hand unto heaven, and sware by him that liveth for ever that it shall be for a time, times, and an half; and when he shall have accomplished to scatter the power of the holy people, all these things shall be finished.'

We cannot accept the explanation of the origin of *Esperança de Israel* put forward by the historian Peter Toon. He suggests that our rabbi progressively changed his mind, explaining in this way Menasseh's resolve to publish the text of Montezinos's account and his own commentary under a resolutely Messianic title.[75] We have already set out what seems to us to be Menasseh ben Israel's actual motivation.

To be honest, our rabbi's views on the existence of a Jewish ethnic group in New Granada are of little significance in the history of

---

[74] Chmielnicki and a horde of Cossacks and Tartars laid Poland waste to avenge Polish tyranny over the Ukraine. See C. Roth, *A Life of Menasseh*, pp. 204–5, and N. N. Hannover, *The Depth of the Abyss (Yeven Metsulah)*.

[75] *Puritans, the Millenium and the Future of Israel*, p. 118.

Portuguese Jewish opinion in Amsterdam. In bearing witness to the
depth, the importance, and the topicality of the current Messianic hope,
he echoed these attitudes all the more readily since, as Cecil Roth says,
he had acquired a genuine Messianic inheritance by marriage.[76] If the
Amsterdam Jews' hope of redemption has to be fitted into the framework set out by Gershom Scholem, it should be described as
'restitutory', in that it is moving towards the restoration of their ruined
kingdom and of their Temple to the Jewish people. Of the two possible
forms of the longed-for coming, it seems that it was the apocalyptic
vision which prevailed: the time was near, the prophecies would be
fulfilled 'soon and in our time'. Menasseh ben Israel's work is more than
a piece of literature derived from classical learning, accounts of ancient
and more recent travels, and current Messianism. In it may be detected
a tactical and pragmatic intention to harness European millenarian
enthusiasm for the benefit of the Jewish people.

The nineteenth-century historian was very severe in respect of these
'chimeras'; the present-day historian is inclined to smile and repeat
Joseph Sarachek's brusque judgement: 'The Messianic doctrine does
not fascinate and enthrall the modern Jew as it certainly did the Jew of
the past.'[77] But, as we have demonstrated, the Jewish world was very far
from being the only one to be conscious of the excitement aroused by the
Messianic promises. Writing his *Esperança de Israel, sub specie aeternitatis*,
Menasseh ben Israel—and this was not the least of his virtues—did not
neglect the historical circumstances. He certainly considered that the
time was ripe to prepare England to accept Jews. For as their dispersal
throughout the world was essential to the coming of the Messiah, our
rabbi saw in this an opportunity to line English chiliastic enthusiasm up
behind the establishment of his co-religionists in England. It is also possible that, in seeking to secure this right of abode, he had it in mind that
tolerance, even in Holland, is always a function of the number of those
to be tolerated. Menasseh ben Israel remains not only a true witness of
his age and his people, the 'Spanish and Portuguese Jewish Nation of
Amsterdam', but also a man who made his mark on the religious and

[76] We have already seen that he was married to Rachel Abrabanel, a descendant of the
famous sixteenth-century statesman, philosopher, and harbinger of the Messiah, Isaac
Abrabanel. He had certainly read and reflected on, perhaps printed, Abrabanel's
Messianic trilogy. Cecil Roth goes so far as to write: 'By alliance with it [the family], the
young Amsterdam rabbi might have the satisfaction of knowing that the blood of the
ancient royal house of Israel, from which the promised Messiah was to descend, would
course in the veins of his children', *A Life of Menasseh ben Israel*, p. 36.

[77] *The Doctrine of the Messiah in Medieval Jewish Literature*, p. 310.

political history of Judaism, something which not all who comment on
his work have seen, as they dip their pens in the ink of facile irony.

The English version of the book is divided into thirty-nine unequal
sections. Across time and space, these thirty-nine sections tackle the
detailed problem of the hidden Jews of the New World, and the more
general one of the Lost Tribes of Israel with, as a fixed point of reference,
the absolute certainty of the advent of the Messiah. The subject matter
is arranged in three groups: the Indians, the Ten Tribes, the Messiah.

As might be expected, the first section sets out the themes of the book,
making it clear from the start that there are only *hypotheses* about the
Lost Tribes, but a *certainty* as to the prophets' promises. There are three
different theories about the origin of the American Indians: that of
Venegas, for whom their ancestors were Carthaginians, that of Arias
Montanus, for whom the Indians are descended from Joktan, the father
of Ophir and himself a grandson of Noah,[78] and finally that of certain
Spaniards who believe that the Indians are the offspring of the Lost Ten
Tribes of Israel. This opinion is examined at the end of Section Two.
Taking a text from 2 Esdras [4 Esdras in the Vulgate which Menasseh
used], Menasseh ben Israel deduces from it the possibility that the Lost
Tribes went to the Americas, and he supports this sentiment with
Father Malvenda's explanation. Some epigraphical evidence, namely a
Hebrew inscription found in the Azores, is discussed very seriously by
our rabbi, who goes on to enumerate the many rites and customs
common to the Hebrews and the Indians. According to some accounts,
buildings which might be synagogues were to be found in the New
World, erected by 'a white and bearded people'. Our author deduces
from this that they could have been constructed at a remote period by
some Israelites. This would not be impossible, for the distant islands of
which the Bible speaks could be none other than America. Menasseh
concludes that some Jews reached America at a very early date, and goes
on to give accounts of the existence in the New World of white men who
are bearded—while the Indians have no beards—warlike, and *hidden*.
Did not Alonso de Erzilla, in his prophetic verses, foretell the discovery
of lands previously hidden by divine will? Sections Eight to Thirteen
confine their attention to the various Indian populations which could be
decended from the Israelites who had gone to America. In the wake of
the great sixteenth- and seventeenth-century adventurers, Menasseh
ben Israel plunges into the mysterious forests of South America. He

[78] Genesis 10: 21–9.

recounts the epic journey and discoveries of Aguirre, as told by Juan de Castellanos; tells of the comely, bearded men described in 1622 by Gaspar de Bergara; and mentions other similar encounters which some people of Pernambuco in Brazil may have had. He dwells upon a similar discovery by Pedro Hernández de Queiros, according to whom these peoples who kept evading the explorers were monotheists. Finally he reports that a Flemish mariner came seeking the Jews of Amsterdam to tell them about a white and bearded tribe he had met in the New World; an expedition was envisaged but never undertaken. The navigator died shortly after making this discovery. Menasseh ben Israel then, very naturally, recalls Montezinos's account. Rather strangely for the uninformed reader, the section ends with a prediction by Jacobus Verus of Prague about the comet of 1618 which foretold the decline of Spain.[79] This section is very important because it concerns events to come, thus taking its place in the Messianic dimension without which all the travellers' tales are mere anecdotes.

Sections Fifteen to Nineteen deal with the problem of the Lost Ten Tribes of Israel. They were not all exiled to the same place. Some even went to China. We have the Jesuit Matteo Ricci's account of the Jews of China. To this Menasseh ben Israel added Alvaro Semedo's evidence and a piece of Scriptural confirmation (Section 16). Next come the statements of Abraham Ortelius on the presence of Jews in Tartary, the history of the Naphtalites and their wars, and the travels of David Reuveni and Eldad ha-Dani. Our rabbi also demonstrates the existence of descendants of the Ten Tribes in Asia (Section 17). There were also some in Africa, in the kingdom of Prester John; a good many prophetic verses foretold this settlement in Africa (Section 18). Their presence in Media was vouched for in ancient times by Kings, Tobit, and Flavius Josephus (Section 19).

After setting out the tribal geography of the Israelites through the ages, Menasseh ben Israel devotes a long, powerful section to the river which, in Jewish mythology, holds back the Ten Tribes until the time appointed by God for their return. This is the Sambatyon, a turbulent river which cannot be crossed, as it carries rocks along with it, but which stops flowing on the Sabbath day. However the Israelites cannot cross it on that day, for that would be to violate the holy day. The Talmud, the

---

[79] In his book, *Los Judíos en la España moderna y contemporánea*, vol. ii, p. 450, J. Caro Baroja speaks very soundly of Menasseh ben Israel's theses on the decadence of Spain which 'independently of the theological causes he was looking for, should satisfy not only the Jews but also the Dutch, and Protestants in general'.

Targum Jonathan, the Midrash, Josephus, and Pliny have all described this river. Moses of Gerona and Benjamin of Tudela identify it with the Gozan; Abraham Farissol with the Ganges. Was it to be found in the Indies? It is true that many lands remain unexplored, many rivers unknown, many peoples hidden; for example, there was the discovery, in Spain, of the Batuecas, a people who were living away from the mainstream of history, and who were discovered by chance. This Section Twenty is central to *Esperança de Israel*, because the return of the Lost Tribes is the corner-stone of the Messianic advent within the whole scheme of the Redemption. Menasseh ben Israel builds up and develops his theories as a faithful lover of and believer in the ancient and medieval Jewish traditions, and as a well-informed geographer, aware of issues raised by sixteenth- and seventeenth-century world expansion.

At the end of Section 21 our author gives an account of the faithfulness of the Ten Tribes' religious observance, and puts forward, in Section 22, some hypotheses to explain the permanence of their exile. For no one returned to the Holy Land at the end of the captivity in Babylon.

Section 23 deals with Messianic redemption and its various forms. The Spanish version, which was aimed at the Jewish public and not distributed in the same way as the Latin and English version, develops this theme in Chapter XIII. The number 13 is the sum of the numerical values of the letters which make up the Hebrew word *ehad* (1+8+4), One being the supreme divine attribute; 13 is also the number of articles of faith drawn up by Maimonides.

By the dawn of the Messianic age, the diaspora will have reached its greatest spread.[80] The exiles of Judah and the exiles of Israel will converge on the Nile before assembling in the Holy Land. Only then will the return from captivity, predicted by the prophets, be accomplished. Although the figure of the Messiah remains in the shadows, Jewish tradition puts the wars of Gog and Magog before the redemption. It also accepts that there will be two Messiahs in succession, one the son of Ephraim or of Joseph who will die, and the other the son of David, the Messiah of Glory (Section 26). This redemption will materialize when the Tribes of Israel flood into Egypt and Assyria, the antechambers of the Holy Land. That is why these two countries are the object of divine benediction. For these reasons the Messiah's coming is, at once, both a national and a universal blessing (Section 27). The

---

[80] Isaiah 11:11.

thorny matter of the date remains. Menasseh ben Israel apparently breaks with the systems of his predecessors who, by scrutinizing the Scriptures in various ways, calculated the Messianic year or cycle of years [81] (Section 28). Sorrows and long periods of waiting will precede the coming of the Messiah (Section 29).

The calamities which were dreaded and predicted have already happened. The 'fourth beast' of which Daniel 7: 7 speaks is none other than the Spanish Inquisition. And our rabbi tells the stories of the martyrdom of its victims: two Christians burnt for Judaizing, the Franciscan, Diogo da Asunção (Asumpção), and the young Lope de Vera y Alarcón, and many Judaizing New Christians who went to the stake in the New World. Although Menasseh ben Israel does not suggest any date for the fulfilment of the Promise, he makes it quite clear, as a historian of contemporary events, that it will be fulfilled soon (end of Section 29). If these disasters and martyrdoms are not enough, our rabbi has two more pieces of evidence, also taken from contemporary history. The first is the recognition by world leaders of the worth of certain Jews. The second is the cruel fate of the royal families of Spain and Portugal, clear evidence of divine punishment of the persecutors of the Jewish people (Section 34). Thus redemption is at hand (Section 35).

Section 37 summarizes, in seven propositions, Menasseh ben Israel's statements in respect of the Ten Tribes and the regrouping of the whole Jewish people, who were to recover their lost homeland and have their sovereignty restored.

In his conclusion our rabbi returns to Montezinos's account, which he regards as the most admissible of those referring to peoples who were hidden and different from the Indians. He reaffirms that the Indians have nothing in common with the descendants of the Lost Tribes living in the New World. To account for the Israelites' coming to America, he suggests there was a natural upheaval which would have allowed them to cross the Bering Strait witout getting their feet wet. Is there not much of the same sort of thing in the writings of many classical authors? From here on there is nothing unreasonable in Montezinos's statements, and our rabbi concludes his work by endeavouring to support the veracity of the traveller's account while, in a few areas only, clarifying obscure or difficult points presented by this famous tale.

---

[81] In the Jewish lunar calendar, the number of months is calculated within nineteen-year cycles in such a way as to avoid getting behind the solar year and the sequence of seasons.

This analysis of *Esperança de Israel* does not convey the amazing richness of this little work, in which are interwoven Scriptural texts, Talmudic and Rabbinical Commentaries, descriptions of faraway places and strange peoples, exhausting journeys in virgin forests, mysterious discoveries, and dramatic episodes in the history of Judaism and, above all, of Marranism. In this slim volume Menasseh succeeds in the formidable task of leading the Jewish reader, normally confined inside a restricted world, limited by the community and by rabbinical culture, across the vast expanses of the continents and oceans, while still keeping him within and under the solid, consoling protection of the strictest orthodoxy. And the late Morris Epstein quite rightly observes that 'evidence of the remarkable power of the legend is nowhere better seen than in the career of Rabbi Manasseh ben Israel of Amsterdam'.[82] Using a flood of themes, episodes, and quotations which anyone might find chaotic, precipitate at the very least, our rabbi puts together all that is known about the Lost Tribes, constructing from it a unity within a Messianic framework. He suffuses it with the certainty that the Tribes' reappearance is imminent and the Israel's exile will end.

Menasseh has more than satisfied the demands of his Christian friends who, as we have seen, only expected a letter giving his opinion on Montezinos's story. While remaining silent on the very foundation of Christianity, namely that the Messiah had already come, he has feverishly composed a *manifesto* according to which crypto-Judaism, or Marranism, as well as the Portuguese Jewish community of Amsterdam, and thereafter the entire Jewish world will burst open Israel's medieval imprisonment to take on an expanding world on equal terms.

A book's success may be gauged by seeing how many editions it runs to, and analysing the reactions it provokes. The success of the *Esperança de Israel* is in keeping with its unusual nature. It is not a learned rabbinical treatise, and is not much cited by the great holders of important chairs. The author is still considered to be a talented worker not blessed with any originality, despite the praises heaped on him in his day. His other works have hardly been republished at all, notwithstanding their learned content. On the other hand the *Esperança de Israel* has had a remarkable existence.

In spite of the fact that Menasseh ben Israel took advantage of his book's success in England, and that a considerable Christian literature

[82] Allen H. Godbey, *The Lost Tribes: A Myth. Suggestions towards Rewriting Hebrew History*, New York, 1974. See Epstein's prologue p. xviii.

was produced to refute his theories, the clearest proof of the success of this work is to be found in its editions and, above all, in its translations. How far did reading the *Esperança de Israel* prepare the minds of the Portuguese community in Amsterdam for an enthusiastic reception of Shabbetai Zevi's Messianic proclamation in 1666? It is not easy to be sure, but it is striking to note that in this same year, 1666, a Dutch version of the work, *De Hoop van Israël*, appeared in Amsterdam. This was clearly designed to enlighten the Dutch public about Jewish Messianism. In particular it must have been the source of a very large number of Hebrew translations; but there were no scholarly editions. These translations are chiefly interesting for their number, a sure sign of wide distribution, and for their low price. The Hebrew versions are in small fascicules and were distributed, from the eighteenth to twentieth centuries, throughout the Jewish communities of Eastern Europe. The reason for their existence, as indicated by the publisher, was that previous editions were out of print and a copy of the book had been found by chance.

The success of the *Esperança de Israel* explains why the first historian of Zionism, Nahum Sokolow, devoted so much space and attention to Menasseh ben Israel, as the bard of the Jewish national idea.[83] But contrary to what Sokolow thought, it was not this idea which contributed most to the dawning of Zionism. It was the booklets in Hebrew, peddled in Russia and Poland and read in Jewish families in the evenings, which without doubt worked underground, conveying the miraculous and the real, Holy Scripture and secular knowledge, the scent of distant lands and the imminence of the Return. The Sephardic Messianic manifesto beat a royal way through the steppes, forests, and villages of the Ashkenazi Jews.[84]

Historians of Jewish thought assert nowadays that, after the failure of Shabbetai Zevi's Messianic movement, Jewish Messianism completely changed its form. It took refuge in small groups, which were viewed with suspicion, and was replaced by Hassidism, which reduced its importance: 'apocalyptic' Messianism had had its day.[85] It only remains to

[83] *History of Zionism 1600–1918*, New York, 1969, vol. i, pp. 21–46.

[84] Generally speaking, Messianic literature is essentially the work of Sephardic authors. The Marrano phenomenon had a great influence not only on its development but also on its popular impact. See Gerson D. Cohen, *Messianic Postures of Ashkenazim and Sephardim (Prior to Sabbethai Zevi)*, The Leo Baeck Memorial Lecture 9, New York, 1967.

[85] See G. G. Scholem's essay, 'La Neutralisation du messianisme dans le hassidisme primitif' in the collection *Le messianisme juif. Essais sur la spiritualité du judaïsme*, Paris, 1974, pp. 267–301.

discover its impact, to measure its actual influence on popular Jewish literature. It is with this in mind that we have briefly set out the following inventory and description of the Hebrew editions of the *Esperança de Israel*, without any claim to be exhaustive.

The success of the book's Hebrew title itself is astonishing. Some major New World communities took the name of *Mikveh Israel*: first that of Curaçao, whose Hebrew name appeared in a letter written on 13 October 1654,[86] then that of Philadelphia, whose Hebrew name is inscribed on a document of 1773.[87] In 1870 the Alliance Israélite Universelle founded near Jaffa the first Jewish School of Agriculture, which was to play a fundamental role in the colonization of the Holy Land. It was given the name of *Mikveh Israel*, the Hope of Israel. As Charles Netter explained in a letter in January 1872: ' ... *Mikveh* is founded by a "gathering" of Israelites from the whole world, many of whom "hope" that it will be the first step towards a reunion on the land of our ancestors.'[88]

The numerous commentaries to which this book gave rise, especially among Christians, were frankly unfavourable. It is not part of our plan to report all the judgements passed on the *Esperança de Israel*, but to give a general overview of its effect.

Among the earliest critics, mention must be made of Spencer, who, from 1650 on, strongly disputed the credibility of Montezinos's story. His tale is described as 'a double heresy containing not the least ounce of truth'.[89] Hamon L'Estrange, a year later, while agreeing with Menasseh ben Israel that the Americans are not Jews, did not handle our rabbi gently and showered him with sarcastic remarks.[90]

In the Dutch Puritan chiliastic accord,[91] the *Hope of Israel* struck a false note, because the work reaffirmed a specifically Jewish expectation. People were aware of this as soon as the Latin edition addressed

---

[86] Isaac S. and Suzanne A. Emmanuel, *History of the Jews of the Netherlands Antilles*, Cincinnati, 1970, p. 51.

[87] Henry J. Morais, *The Jews of Philadelphia, their history from the earliest settlements to the present times; a record of events and institutions and of leading members of the Jewish community in every sphere of activity*, Philadelphia, 1894; see also Bertram W. Korn's recent clarification, the article 'Philadelphia' in *Enc. Jud.*, 13: 369.

[88] Text quoted in George Weill's excellent article 'Charles Netter ou les oranges de Jaffa' in *Les Nouveaux Cahiers*, no. 21, Summer 1970, p. 19, n. 61.

[89] *An Epistle to the learned Manasse ben Israel* . . . , London, 1650, pp. 4–5.

[90] *Americans are no Iewes or the improbabilities that the Americans are of that race*, London, 1651, pp. 75–6.

[91] See P. Toon's book, *Puritans, the Millennium and the Future of Israel*, appendix 3, pp. 137 ff.

to the English Parliament was sent out. Universal peace was to come through the Jewish people's return to their homeland, and there would be no place for a preliminary conversion to Christianity in that much longed for event. Hulsius, the celebrated theologian, did not subscribe to Menasseh's assertions, which he recorded calmly, however.[92] By contrast, Witsius accused our rabbi of ineptitude in his discourse.[93] And the problem of the Lost Ten Tribes continued to preoccupy many writers up to the beginning of the nineteenth century, as Lynn Glaser shows in his book, *Indians or Jews?*

Spizel has explained the objectives of the *Hope of Israel* in terms of our rabbi's wish to reinforce his co-religionists' weakening Messianic hope.[94] This view is not devoid of sense if we reflect, on the one hand, upon the peaceful existence offered them by Holland and, on the other, upon the very strong Christian Messianic pressures put on the Jews in Holland throughout the seventeenth century. We need no further proof of this than these lines taken from a letter from Coymans to the celebrated Colvius, friend and correspondent of Menasseh ben Israel: 'The conversion of these people [the Jews] to Christianity (of which we have some prophecies) will be truly miraculous, almost as much so as the resurrection of the dead, for they base themselves firmly on contrary prophecies, which they say predict the conversion not only of Christians but of all the peoples of the earth to Judaism . . . '.[95] We may also note the views of Daniel de Breen, whose Messianic dreams were accompanied by polemical writings directed against the Jews.[96]

The first object of *Esperança de Israel* was to challenge the Christian use of the Old Testament. Verging on the paradox, it could be said that Menasseh ben Israel was obliged to make use of Montezinos's account and to place it in the collection of prophecies and reports which make up the texture of *Esperança de Israel*. Then our rabbi takes advantage of an unlooked-for opportunity to present a work which witnesses to and passes on Israel's eternal trust in its God, a trust which also implies

---

[92] *Theologiae Iudicae*, Breda, 1653, pp. 41 ff.

[93] *Ægyptiaca . . .* , Amsterdam, 1683, p. 371. I. Bartolocci de Celleno commented more dispassionately on Menasseh ben Israel's statements in his *Bibliotheca Magna Rabbinica*, Rome, 1675, pp. 119 ff.

[94] *Elevatio Relationis Montezinianae de repertis in America Tribubus Israeliticis, et discussio argumentorum pro origine gentium Americanarum Israelitica a Man. ben Israel in Spe Israelis conquistorum*, Basle, 1661, p. 127.

[95] See H. Méchoulan, 'Menasseh au centre des rapports judéo-chrétiens en Hollande au XVIIe siècle . . . '.

[96] See L. Kolakowski's great book, *Chrétiens sans Église*, p. 200.

duties. The first of these is, without any doubt, that they should not forget the distressing condition of the diaspora, even though the Amsterdam community was not experiencing the full weight of this distress. It is not for nothing that our rabbi headed the dedication of his work to the *parnassim* of the 'Nation' with a quotation, of which he gives only a fragment, from a verse of Isaiah (61: 1): 'The Spirit of the Lord God is upon me; because the Lord hath anointed me to preach good tidings unto the meek; he hath sent me to bind up the brokenhearted, to proclaim liberty to the captives, and the opening of the prison to them that are bound.' Taken literally, this verse may be applied to a people experiencing the harsh pangs of exile. Menasseh ben Israel gives them the consolation they have the right to expect from a learned and distinguished rabbi.

But did the Portuguese of Amsterdam really need their Messianic hopes strengthened? They clearly knew that a stopping-place, however pleasant it was on the banks of the Amstel, could only be a temporary refuge. It was a stage on the long road of exile which would lead Israel into her kingdom, the fruits of which were to be shared with all just members of the human race, thus ushering in an era of universal peace.

Esperança de Israel is an apparently anodyne work, because its author took up a position of non-conflict with others. All the same, when he castigates the hated Inquisition, our rabbi is capable of using the very harshest words. But, when his discourse is put in its historical context, and the millenarian enthusiasm of the period is accorded its full importance, Menasseh ben Israel's wisdom becomes fully apparent. He reaffirms, calmly and confidently, the superior status of the divine promises made to his people. The Christian world was quick to notice this challenge, and its reaction may be measured by the force with which it disparaged it. Moreover, thanks to Menasseh ben Israel, Jews learnt anew that genuine communication could be established with Christians. And Christians, by being prepared to have dicussions with our rabbi, such a good representative of the 'Nation', were relieved of the feeling of contempt[97] which always impoverishes and degrades those who express it much more than those who are its victims.

---

[97] Father Mersenne provides an example of this attitude when writing to Rivet about Menasseh ben Israel as follows: 'As for the Jew's books you wrote to me about, I do not think we should expect too much, as this type of person is often very ignorant and usually without method in what they do.', in *Correspondance du P. Marin Mersenne*, Centre National de la Recherche Scientifique édition, Paris, 1969, vol. iii, p. 329.

We are indebted to Eric Méchoulan for the following comment: the repellent image of the Jew, so often used in literature, has been employed in like manner by Victor Hugo in

Menasseh ben Israel has interpreted a melody whose theme was known by all his own people. It was in that context that his composition, with its newness, its strangeness, and its exoticism, took up the song of hope which the former Marranos of the 'Jerusalem' of the North had never quite lost and were now finding again.

In 1650 the author of *Esperança de Israel* led the Jewish people out of their isolation, heralded the imminent coming of a new era, and set out the divine plan for the destiny of the House of Israel which would be one day, according to Isaiah, the light of the world.

his play *Cromwell*. The writer shows us the rabbi with the hideous characteristics of a trafficker and astrologer, which proves that it is possible to be the greatest writer of the age and yet maliciously misrepresent the role of Jews in history.

Wall's English Translation of the Latin Text

NOTE ON THE ENGLISH TRANSLATION

MOSES Wall's English translation of the Latin text of Menasseh ben Israel's *Spes Israelis* was published in facsimile by Lucien Wolf in 1901 from the second, corrected, version of 1652. The reader who wishes to refer to Wall's exact text can therefore refer to Wolf's facsimile edition. This was the text available to English readers at the time of the public controversy before the resettlement of the Jews in England in 1656 and is therefore a document of historic importance. It is, however, difficult for the modern reader to follow it easily because of the spelling, capitalization, and syntax, and also to identify the places, persons, authors, and works mentioned by Menasseh. Accordingly, while trying to keep the style, wording, and general atmosphere of Wall's translation, the spelling, use of capitals and, where unavoidable, the syntax have been modernized. Biblical quotations have been kept as in Wall's version, but chapter and verse references are to the Hebrew Bible. Where the text cites a name or gives a biblical quotation wrongly, this has been corrected either in the text or in a note.

THE
HOPE OF ISRAEL

Written
By *MENASSEH BEN ISRAEL*,
An Hebrew Divine, and
Philosopher.

Newly extant, and Printed at *Amsterdam*, and Dedicated by the Author, to
the High Court, the Parliament of *England*,
and to the Councell of State,

The second Edition corrected and amended.

Whereunto are added,
*In this second Edition, some Discourses
upon the point of the Conversion of the*
JEWES.

By MOSES WALL.

LONDON
Printed by *R. I.* for *Livewell Chapman* at the
Crowne in *Popes-Head Alley,* 1652.

THE EPISTLE DEDICATORY

To the Parliament, the Supreme Court of England, and to the Right Honourable the Council of State, Manasseh ben Israel prays God to give Health and all Happiness:

It is not one cause alone (most renowned Fathers) which uses to move those, who desire by their meditations to benefit mankind, and to make them come forth in public, to dedicate their books to great men; for some, and those the most, are incited by covetousness, that they may get money by so doing, or some piece of plate of gold or silver; sometimes also that they may obtain their votes, and suffrages to get some place for themselves or their friends. But some are moved thereto by mere and pure friendship, that so they may publicly testify that love and affection, which they bear them, whose names they prefix to their books; let the one, and the other, please themselves, according as they delight in the reason of the dedication, whether it be good or bad; for my part, I best like them, who do it upon this ground, that they may not commend themselves, or theirs, but what is for public good.

As for me (most renowned Fathers) in my dedicating this discourse to you, I can truly affirm that I am induced to it upon no other ground than this, that I may gain your favour and good will to our Nation, now scattered almost all over the earth; neither think that I do this, as if I were ignorant how much you have hitherto favoured our Nation; for it is made known to me, and to others of our Nation, by them who are so happy as near at hand, to observe your apprehensions, that you do vouchafe to help us, not only by your prayers; yea, this has compelled me to speak to you publicly, and to give you thanks for that your charitable affection towards us, and not such thanks which come only from the tongue, but as are conceived by a grateful mind.

Give me leave therefore (most renowned Fathers) to supplicate you, that you would still favour our good, and further love us. Truly, we men do draw so much the nearer to Divine nature, when by how much we increase, by so much we cherish, and defend the small and weak ones; and with how much diligence do you perform this, most renowned Fathers! Who, though you seem to be arrived to the highest top of felicity, yet you do not only not despise inferior men, but you so wish well to them, that you seem sensible of their calamity; you knowing how acceptable to God you are by so doing, who loves to do good to them who do good. And truly it is from hence, that of late you have done so great things valiantly, and by an unusual attempt, and things much to be observed among the Nations. The whole world stands amazed at these things, and the eyes of all are turned upon you, that they may see whither all these things do tend, which the great Governor of all things seems to bring upon the world by so great changes, so famously remarkable, of so many Nations; and so all those things, which God is pleased to have foretold by the Prophets, do and shall obtain their accomplishment. All which things of necessity must be fulfilled, that so Israel at last being brought back to his own place; peace which is promised under the Messiah, may be restored to the world; and concord, which is the only Mother of all good things. These things I handle more largely in this Treatise, which I dedicate to you (most renowned Fathers). You cannot be ignorant that it is not only not unprofitable, but very useful for states and statesmen to foresee the issue (which yet is ever in God's hand) of human counsels, that so they may observe, and understand from Divine truth, the events of things to come, which God has determined by his Spirit in his holy Prophets. I know that this my labour will not be unacceptable to you, how mean soever it be, which I trust you will cheerfully receive, because that you love our Nation, and as part of it, the author of this discourse. But I entreat you be certain that I pour out continual prayers to God for your happiness. Farewell, most renowned Fathers, and flourish most prosperously.   MENASSEH BEN ISRAEL

MENASSEH BEN ISRAEL TO THE COURTEOUS READER

There are as many minds as men about the origin of the people of America and of the first inhabitants of the New World and of the West Indies;[1] for how many men soever they were or are, they came of those two, Adam and Eve;[2] and consequently of Noah, after the Flood. But that New World does seem wholly separated from the old. Therefore it must be that some did pass thither out of one (at least) of the three parts of the world, i.e. Europe, Asia, and Africa; but the doubt is, what people were those, and out of what place they went. Truly, the truth of that must be gathered, partly out of the ancient histories, and partly from conjectures; as their habit, their language, their manners, which yet do vary according to men's dispositions; so that it is hard to find out the certainty. Almost all who have viewed those countries, with great diligence, have been of different judgements. Some would have the praise of finding out America to be due to the Carthaginians, others to the Phoenicians, or the Canaanites; others to the Indians or people of China; others to them of Norway, others to the inhabitants of the Atlantic islands, others to the Tartars, others to the Ten Tribes. Indeed everyone grounds his opinion not upon probable arguments, but light conjectures,[3] as will appear farther by this book. But I having curiously examined whatever has hitherto been written upon this subject do find no opinion more probable, nor agreeable to reason, than that of our Montezinos, who says, that the first inhabitants of America were the Ten Tribes of the Israelites, whom the Tartars conquered, and drove away; who after that (as God would have it) hid themselves behind the Cordillera Mountains.

[1] Recent studies of this question are by Lee Eldridge Huddleston, *Origins of the American Indians, European concepts (1492-1729)*, and by Lynn Glaser, *Indians or Jews?*. We note that the problem of the origin of the Americans gave rise to a copious literature from the beginning of the sixteenth century.

[2] Menasseh ben Israel's emphasis on this is explained by his opposition to Isaac de La Peyrère's thesis set out in *Praeadamitae sive Exercitatio super versibus . . . epistolae D. Pauli ad Romanos quibus inducuntur homines ante Adamum conditi*. On Isaac de La Peyrère, see Jean-Paul Odos' unpublished thesis, *Recherches sur la vie et l'œuvre d'Isaac de La Peyrère (1595?–1676)*, Grenoble, 1974. Menasseh had it in mind to write a *Refutatio libri qui titulus Praeadamitae . . .* , see the list of works given at the end of his *Vindiciae Judaeorum*.

[3] We have corrected a translation error in the text which gives 'high conjectures' for 'levibus conjecturis'.

I also show that, as they were not driven out at once from their country, so also they were scattered into divers provinces, i.e. into America, into Tartary, into China, into Media, to the Sabbatical River,[4] and into Ethiopia. I prove that the Ten Tribes never returned to the Second Temple, that they yet keep the Law of Moses, and our sacred rites; and at last shall return to their Land, with the two Tribes, Judah and Benjamin; and shall be governed by one Prince, who is Messiah the Son of David; and without doubt that time is near, which I make appear by divers things; where, Reader, you shall find divers histories worthy of memory, and many prophesies of the old Prophets opened with much study and care. I willingly leave it to the judgement of the godly, and learned, what happy worth there is in this my book, and what my own Nation owes me for my pains: It is called *The Hope of Israel*; which name is taken from Jeremiah 14: 8: Oh the hope of Israel, the Saviour thereof. For the scope of this discourse is, to show, that the hope in which we live, of the coming of the Messiah, is of a future, difficult, but infallible good, because it is grounded upon the absolute promise of the blessed God.

And because I intend a continuation of our famous historian, Josephus' History of the Jews;[5] I entreat and beseech all learned men, in what part of the world soever they live (to whom I hope that shortly this discourse will come) that if they have any thing worthy of posterity, that they would give me notice of it in time; for though I have collected many acts of the Jews, and many histories out of the Hebrews, the Arabians, the Grecians, the Latins, and other authors of other Nations; yet I want many things for this my enterprise, all which I am willing to perform, that I may please my Nation; but rather to the glory of the blessed God, whose Kingdom is everlasting, and his Word infallible.

[4] This refers to the *Sambatyon*, a mythical river beyond which the Lost Ten Tribes of Israel are hidden; it comes up frequently in the body of the work.

[5] Menasseh ben Israel mentions this work as complete and ready for printing in the list of his works at the end of *Piedra gloriosa o de la estatua de Nebuchadnesar*, Amsterdam, 1655, with the title *La historia Iudaica, o continuación de Flavio Josepho hasta nuestros tiempos*. The manuscript was never printed, and has not been found.

THE AUTHORS OF OTHER NATIONS, WHICH ARE QUOTED IN THIS TREATISE

Abraham[us] Ortelius
Agathias
Augustinus [Augustine]
Alexis Venegas
Alonsus Cemedro [Alvaro Semedo]
Alonsus Augustinianus [Alonso
  Augustiniano]
Alonsus [Alonso] de Erzilla
Alonsus Venerus [Alonso Venero]
Arias Montanus

Baronius
Berosus
Boterus
Bozius

Constantinus [Constantin
  Lempereur]

Diodorus Siculus
Dion [Cassius]
Duretus

Eselius Geradus
Eusebius Cesariensis

Famianus [Famiano] Strada
Franciscus [Francisco] de Ribera
Franciscus [Francisco] Lopez de
  Gomara

Garcilassus [Garcilaso] de la Vega
  [Inca]
Genebrardus
Goropius
Guil[laume] Postel[lus]
Guilielmus Blawius [Blaeu]

Guil. Schilkardus

Henricus Alangre [Henri van
  Langren]
Hugo Grotius

Jacobus Verus [Vere]
Joan. de castillanos [Juan de
  Castellanos]
Joan. de Bairos [João de Barros]
Joan. Juan Román [y Zamora]
Joan. [Jean] de Laet
Joan. [Juan] Huarte
Josephus [José] d'Acosta
Joan. van Linschoten

Lescarbotus [Lescarbot]
Lucanus [Lucan]

Manuel Sá
Marcilius Ficinus [Marsilio
  Ficino]
Marinus

Nicola[u]s Trigautius [Trigault]

Origines [Origen]
Orosius
Osorius Lusitanus [Osorio
  Lusitano de Fonseca]

Petrus De Cieza [Pedro de Cieza
  de Leon]
[Petrus] Plancius
Petrus [Pedro] Simon
Petrus [Pedro] Hernandes de
  Quiros

Petrus Teixera [Pedro Texeira]
Pineda
Plato
Plinius [Pliny]
Pomarius
Proclus
Porphyrius [Porphyry]
Possevinus [Possevin]
Plutarchus [Plutarch]
Picus Mirandulanus [Pico de la Mirandola]
Ptolemaeus [Ptolemy]

Semuel Bochardus [Samuel Bochart]
Solinus
Strabo
Suetonius Tranquillus

Tacitus
Thomas Malvenda

Xenophon

Zarate

THE HEBREW BOOKS, AND AUTHORS

Talmud Hierosolymitanum [Jerusalem Talmud]
Talmud Babylonicum [Babylonian Talmud]
Paraphrasis Chaldaica [Targum]
R. Simhon ben Johay [Simeon bar Yohai = Zohar]
Seder Holam [Olam]
Rabot [Midrash Rabbah]
Jalkot [Yalkut Shimoni]
[Midrash] Tanhuma
Joseph ben Gurion [Jossipon]
R. Sehadia [Saadiah] Gaon
R. Moseh de Egypto [Maimonides]
R. Abraham Aben [Ibn] Ezra
R. Selomoh Jarhi [R. Solomon ben Isaac or Rashi]
Eldad Danita [The Danite]
R. David Kimhi
R. Benjamin Tudelensis [of Tudela]
R. Moses Gerundensis [Nahmanides]
R. Abraham bar R. Hiy[y]a
Don Shac [Isaac] Abarbanel
R. Joseph Coen [Ha-Cohen]
R. Abraham Friscoll [Farissol]
R. Mordechay Japhe [i.e. Samuel ben Isaac Japhe Ashkenazi]
R. Mordechay reato [Mordecai Dato]
R. Hazarya a-Adomi [Azariah dei' Rossi]

THE RELATION OF ANTONIO MONTEZINOS

In the 18th of the Month of Ellul: the 5404 year from the world's creation,[6] and according to common compute, in 1644, Aaron Levi, otherwise called Antonio Montezinos, came into this city Amsterdam, and related to Menasseh ben Israel and other chieftains of the Portuguese Nation, inhabitants of the same city, these things which follow.

It was two years and a half since that, going from the port of Honda in the West Indies to the Papian jurisdiction, he conducted some mules of a certain Indian, whose name was Francisco de Castillo, into the province of Quito, and that there was one in company with him and other Indians, whose name was Francisco,[7] who was called by all Cazicus [Cacique]. As they went over the Cordillera Mountains, a great tempest arose, which threw the laden mules to the ground. The Indians being afflicted by the sore tempest, every one began to count his losses; yet confessing that all that and more grievous punishments were but just, in regard of their many sins. But Francisco bade them take it patiently, for that they should shortly enjoy rest: the others answered that they were unworthy of it; yea that the notorious cruelty used by the Spaniards towards them was sent of God, because they had so ill treated his holy people, who were of all others the most innocent. Now then, they determined to stay all night upon the top of the mountain. And Montezinos took out of a box some bread, and cheese and junkets, and gave them to Francisco, upbraiding him, that he had spoken disgracefully of the Spaniards; who answered that he had not told one half of the miseries and calamities inflicted by a cruel and inhumane people; but they should not go unrevenged, looking for help from an unknown people.

After this conference, Montezinos went to Cartagena, a city of the Indies, where he being examined [by the Inquisition],[8] was put in prison; and while he prayed to God, such words fell from him: Blessed

---

[6] That is 19 September 1644. We do not understand why the Hebrew versions give the date as 11 August 1644. Antonio de Montezinos must have stayed six months in Amsterdam (see below, Section 13), that is until mid-March 1645.

[7] We have restored 'Francisco' in the text. It is surprising that the translator thought to Anglicize this name as 'Francis'. On the whole, proper names appearing in the text retain their Latin form and the numerous errors of the Latin version.

[8] We have restored a translation omission to the text. The Latin version states: '. . . ubi inquisitione habita . . .'

be the name of the Lord,[9] that has not made me an idolater, a barbarian, a blackamoor, or an Indian; but as he named Indian, he was angry with himself and said, the Hebrews are Indians; then coming to himself again, he confessed that he doted, and added; can the Hebrews be Indians? Which he also repeated a second, and a third time; and he thought that it was not by chance that he had so much mistaken himself.

Thinking farther of what he had heard from the Indian, and hoping[10] that he should find out the whole truth, therefore as soon as he was let out of prison, he sought out Francisco believing that he would repeat to him again what he had spoken. He therefore being set at liberty through God's mercy went to the Port of Honda, and according to his desire, found him, who said: he remembered all that he had spoken when he was upon the mountain. Montezinos asked that he would take a journey with him, offering him all courtesies, giving him three pieces of eight that he might buy himself necessaries.

Now when they were got out of the city, Montezinos confessed himself to be a Hebrew, of the tribe of Levi, and that the Lord was his God; and he told the Indian that all other gods were but mockeries. The Indian being amazed, asked him the name of his parents. He answered Abraham, Isaac, and Jacob. But, said he, have you no other father? He answered, yes, his father's name was Ludovico Montezinos. But he was not yet satisfied. I am glad (said he) to hear you tell this, for I was in doubt to believe you while you seemed ignorant of your parents. Montezinos swearing that he spoke the truth, the Indian asked him if he were not the Son of Israel, and thereupon began a long discourse; who when he knew that he was so, he desired him to prosecute what he had begun, and added, that he should more fully explain himself, for that formerly he had left things so doubtful, that he did not seem to be assured of anything. After that both had sat down together and refreshed themselves, the Indian thus began: If you have a mind to follow me your leader, you shall know whatever you desire to know; only let me tell you this, whatsoever the journey is, you must foot it, and you

---

[9] The Latin text has 'Benedictus sit nomen Adonay . . .'. We note that the Hebrew form of the name of God, while given in the Latin version, never appears in the English text. The Latin gives Adonay in full, something which pious Jews did not do. The phrases spoken by our character are part of the 'Dawn Blessing' which forms the first part of the Morning Prayer as follows: 'Blessed art thou, O Lord our God, King of the World, who has not made me a Gentile.' Perhaps the various versions of our text were used by the Marranos of the New World.

[10] The English translation does not state that Montezinos took an oath to find out the truth. This oath appears in the Latin and Spanish versions.

must eat nothing but parched maize, and you must omit nothing that I tell you. Montezinos answered that he would do all.

The next day being Monday, the Cacique[11] came again, and bid him throw away what he had in his knapsack, to put on shoes made of linen packthread, and to follow him, with his staff. Whereupon Montezinos leaving his cloak, and his sword, and other things which he had about him, they began the journey, the Indian carrying upon his back three measures of maize, two ropes, one of which was full of knots, to climb up the mountain, with a hooked fork; the other was so loose,[12] for to pass over marshes and rivers, with a little axe, and shoes made of linen packthread. They being thus accoutred, travelled the whole week, unto the Sabbath day, on which day they resting, the day after they went on till Tuesday, on which day about eight o'clock in the morning, they came to a river as big as the Douro. Then the Indian said: here you shall see your brethren, and making an ensign with the fine linen of Xylus,[13] which they had about them instead of a girdle. Thereupon on the other side of the river they saw a great smoke, and immediately after, such another ensign made as they had made before. A little after that, three men, with a woman, in a little boat came to them, which being come near, the woman went ashore, the rest staying in the boat; who talking a good while with the Indian in a language which Montezinos understood not. She returned to the boat and told to the three men what she had learnt of the Indian. Always eyeing him, they came presently out of the boat and embraced Montezinos, the woman after their example doing the like. After which, one of them went back to the boat, and when the Indian bowed down to the feet of the other two and of the woman, they embraced him courteously, and talked a good while with him. After that, the Indian bade Montezinos to be of good courage, and not to look that they should come a second time to him, till he had fully learned the things which were told him at the first time.

[11] The original text has 'Cazicus came again'. The translator took Cazicus for a proper name, whereas it is a Latinized form of *cacique*, a Spanish word for an Indian chief. In the Spanish text may be read: '. . . vino a su aposento el Indio'.
[12] Poor translation for 'solutum'. In the translation given in T. Thorowgood, *Iewes in America or probabilities that the American Indians are of that race*, London, 1650, it is correctly translated '. . . untied, to be made use of in the marshes and passages of rivers'.
[13] This is a misunderstanding of the original Latin, which says 'factoque ex duabus Xyli syndonibus'. The word 'Xyli' here is intended for the genitive of Xylon (cotton). The passage should read 'and making out of two pieces of cotton cloth'. The original Spanish says 'y haziendo vandera de dos panos de algodon'. What Montezinos and his companion did was to construct a flag out of their two cotton waistbands. (L. Wolf, *Menasseh ben Israel's Mission to Oliver Cromwell*, n. p. 154.)

Then those two men coming on each side of Montezinos, they spoke in Hebrew the 4th verse of Deuteronomy 6, *Shema Israel, Adonai Elohenu Adonai Ehad*;[14] that is, Hear, O Israel, the Lord our God is one God.

Then the Indian interpreter being asked how it was in Spanish, they spoke what follows to Montezinos, making a short pause between every particular.

1. Our fathers are Abraham, Isaac, Jacob and Israel,[15] and they signified these four by the three fingers lifted up; then they joined Reuben, adding another finger to the former three.

2. We will bestow several places on them who have a mind to live with us.

3. Joseph dwells in the midst of the sea, they making a sign by two fingers put together, and then parted them.

4. They said (speaking fast) shortly some of us will go forth to see, and to tread under foot; at which word they winked, and stamped with their feet.

5. One day we shall all of us talk together, they saying Ba, ba, ba; and we shall come forth as issuing out of our mother the earth.

6. A certain messenger shall go forth.

7. Francisco shall tell you somewhat more of these things, they making a sign with their finger that much must not be spoken.

8. Suffer us that we may prepare ourselves; and they turning their hands and faces every way, thus prayed to God: Do not stay long.

9. Send twelve men, they making a sign, that they would have men that had beards, and who are skilful in writing.[16]

The conference being ended, which lasted a whole day, the same men returned on Wednesday and Thursday and spoke the same things again, without adding a word. At last Montezinos being weary that they did not answer what he asked them, nor would suffer him to go over the river, he cast himself into their boat. But being forced out again, he fell into the river, and was in danger to be drowned, for he could not swim. But being got out of the water, the rest being angry, said to him: attempt not to pass the river nor to enquire more than we tell you; which the Indian

---

[14] This is the supreme profession of faith for all Jews.

[15] The Indian's apparent error is explained by the number of fingers correctly representing the patriarchs, since Jacob is the same as Israel. See Genesis 32: 28.

[16] These remarks seem particularly obscure, and were apparently no clearer to Menasseh, who avoids commenting on them.

interpreted to him, the rest declaring the same things both by signs and words.

You must observe that all those three days the boat stayed not in the same place, but when those four who came went away, another four came, who all, as with one mouth, repeated all the fore-mentioned nine particulars. There came and went about three hundred.

These men are somewhat scorched by the sun, some of them wear their hair long, down to their knees, others of them shorter, and others of them much as we commonly cut it. They were comely of body, well accoutred, having ornaments on their feet and legs, and their heads were compassed about with a linen cloth.

Montezinos says, that when he was about to be gone on Thursday evening, they showed him very much courtesy, and brought him whatever they thought fit for him in his journey; and they said that they themselves were well provided with all such things (i.e. meats, garments, flocks, and other things) which the Spaniards in the Indies call their own.

The same day, when they came to the place where they had rested, the night before they came to the river, Montezinos said to the Indian: you remember, Francisco, that my brethren told me that you should tell me something. Therefore I entreat you that you would not think much to relate it. The Indian answered: I will tell you what I know, only do not trouble me, and you shall know the truth, as I have received it from my forefathers; but if you press me too much, as you seem to do, you will make me tell you lies. Attend therefore I pray to what I shall tell you.

Your brethren are the sons of Israel, and brought thither by the providence of God, who for their sake wrought many miracles, which you will not believe, if I should tell you what I have learned from my fathers. We Indians made war upon them in that place, and used them more hardly that we now are by the Spaniards. Then by the instigation of our magicians (whom we call *Mohanes*) we went armed to that place where you saw your brethren, with an intent to destroy them; but not one of all those who went thither came back again. Whereupon we raised a great army, and set upon them, but with the same success, for again none escaped; which happened also the third time, so that the Indies were almost bereft of all inhabitants but old men and women; the old men therefore, and the rest who survived, believing that the magicians used false dealing, consulted to destroy them all, and many of them being killed, those who remained promised to discover somewhat that was not known. Upon that they desisted from cruelty, and they declared such things as follow:

That the God of those Children of Israel is the true God; that all that which is engraven upon their stones is true; that about the end of the world they shall be lords of the world; that some shall come who shall bring you much good, and after that they have enriched the earth with all good things, those Children of Israel going forth out of their country, shall subdue the whole world to them, as it was subject to them formerly. You shall be happy if you make a league with them.

Then five of the chief Indians (whom they call Cazici) who were my ancestors, having understood the prophecy of the magicians, which they had learned of the wise men of the Hebrews, went thither, and after much entreaty, obtained their desire, having first made known their mind to that woman, whom you saw to be for an interpreter (for your brethren will have no commerce with our Indians) and whoever of ours enters the country of your brethren, they presently kill him; and none of your brethren do pass into our country. Now by the help of that woman we made this agreement with them.

1. That our five Cazici should come to them, and that alone at every seventy months' end.

2. That he to whom secrets should be imparted should be above the age of three-hundred moons or months.[17]

3. And that such things should be discovered to none in any place where people are, but only in a desert, and in the presence of the Cazici. And so (said the Indian) we keep that secret among ourselves because we promise ourselves great favour from them, for the good offices which we have done to your brethren. It is not lawful for us to visit them, unless at the seventy months' end. Or if there happens anything new, and this fell out but thrice in my time: first, when the Spaniards came into this land; also, when ships came to the Southern Sea;[18] and thirdly, when you came, whom they long wished for, and expected. They did much rejoice for those three new things, because that they said, the prophecies were fulfilled.

And Montezinos also said that three other Cazici were sent to him by Francisco, to Honda, yet not telling their names, till he had said, you may speak to them freely, they are my fellows in my function of whom I have told you; the fifth could not come for age, but those three did

---

[17] Three hundred moons are equivalent to twenty-five years, the period described by Menasseh in his conclusion as 'of trial'.
[18] The Pacific Ocean.

heartily embrace him. And Montezinos being asked of what nation he was, he answered, an Hebrew, of the tribe of Levi, and that God was his God etc.,[19] which when they had heard, they embraced him again, and said: upon a time you shall see us, and shall not know us; we are all your brethren, by God's singular favour; and again, they both of them bidding farewell, departed, everyone saying, I go about my business; therefore none but Francisco being left who, saluting Montezinos as a brother, then bade him farewell, saying, farewell my brother, I have other things to do, and I go to visit your brethren, with other Hebrew Cazici.[20] As for the country, be secure, for we rule all the Indians. After we have finished a business which we have with the wicked Spaniards, we will bring you out of your bondage, by God's help; not doubting, but he who cannot lie, will help us, according to his word. Endeavour you in the meanwhile that those men may come.[21]

[19] It should read 'and that Adonay was his God'.

[20] It appears that this should read 'with other cazici'. The Latin phrase which actually mentions the 'Cazici hebraei' has no equivalent in the Spanish version.

[21] This last obscure phrase does not appear in the Spanish version, nor in the version of Montezinos's story printed in T. Thorowgood, *Iewes in America* . . . , and vouched for by Menasseh.

THE HOPE OF ISRAEL

1. It is hard to say what is certain among the so many, and so uncertain, opinions concerning the origin of the Indians of the New World. If you ask, what is my opinion upon the relation of Montezinos, I must say, it is scarce possible to know it by any art, since there is no demonstration, which can manifest the truth of it; much less can you gather it from divine or human writings. For the Scriptures do not tell what people first inhabited those countries. Neither was there mention of them by any till Christopher Columbus, Amerigo Vespucci, Hernando Cortes marquess del Valle, and Francisco Pizarro went thither. And though hitherto I have been of this mind, that I would speak only of solid and infallible things (as those things are which concern our Law), and the obscurity of the matter making me doubt whether it would be worth while for me to attempt it;[22] yet at last I was content to be persuaded to it, not that I look to get credit by it, but that my friends, and all who seek for truth, that have put me upon this work, may see how very desirous I am to please them.

I shall speak somewhat in this discourse of the divers opinions which have been, and shall declare in what countries it is thought the Ten Tribes are; and I shall close, after that I have brought[23] them into their own country, which I shall prove by good reasons, following the revelations of the holy prophets, who I believe cannot be expounded otherwise, whatever some think. Yet I intend not to dispute these things, but, according to my custom, shall lay down fairly, and faithfully, the opinions of the Jews only.

2. You must know therefore that Alexo Venegas[24] says that the first colonies of the West Indies were of the Carthaginians who first of all

---

[22] In fact five years passed between Montezinos's story being told in Amsterdam and the writing of the book. See our introduction.

[23] The Spanish text gives '. . . y concluire con la infalible reducion dellos a la patria . . .'. The use of the first person singular here is inadmissible; however the error is not the fault of Moses Wall, but of the Latin translator who writes '. . . postquam illas in patriam reduxero . . .'. It is unthinkable that Menasseh ben Israel took himself for the Messiah. So it should read 'and I will conclude by showing that their return to their homeland is inescapable'. This provides additional proof that Menasseh did not write the Latin version himself, and had not read the manuscript before printing.

[24] *Primera parte de las diferencias de libros que hay en el universo*, Salamanca, 1572. See bk. II, ch. 22.

inhabited Hispaniola[25] and, as they increased, spread to the island of Cuba; from thence to the continent of America; and after that towards Panama, New Spain,[26] and Peru. And he grounds his assertion on that reason, that as the Carthaginians (who of old did most use the seas) so those of Peru and the inhabitants of New Spain did make use of pictures instead of letters.

But this opinion does not satisfy because they anciently were white men, bearded and civil in converse; but contrarily those of Panama, Santa Marta,[27] Cuba, and the Leeward Islands went naked. Furthermore, who can think that the language which he says they first spoke, should be so soon changed that it should be wholly another? And there is no agreement between the one and the other.

Arias Montanus[28] thinks that the Indians of New Spain and Peru are the offspring of Ophir, the son of Joktan, the grandson of Eber. And he backs his opinion, by the name Ophir, which by transposition of letters, is the same with Peru. And he adds that the name *Parvaim* in the dual number,[29] signifies the isthmus between New Spain and Peru, which first was called Ophir, then Peru; and that these countries are that Ophir,[30] from whence King Solomon brought gold, precious stones, etc., as in I Kings 9:28 and 10:11 and II Chronicles 9:18 and 9.10. This opinion seems more probable than the other, and may be backed by another name of the river Piru, which according to Gomara,[31] lies in the second degree from the equinoctial line, 222 miles from Panama; as also by the name of the province Yucatan, which may be derived from Joktan the father of Ophir.[32] But besides that this notation is somewhat far-fetched, it crosses what José Acosta affirms in his *Hist. Ind.* Book I,[33] that the

---

[25] The original English text, like the Latin, is wrong here. The Spanish version allows 'New Spain' to be corrected to Hispaniola, present day Haiti. We have made this correction in the text.   [26] Contemporary name for Mexico.

[27] Menasseh ben Israel, like many Jewish authors, was somewhat reluctant to use the term 'Saint'. That is why 'X Marta' appears in the Spanish version.

[28] *Communes et Familiares Hebraïcae Linguae Idiotissimi Biblia Regia*, vol. vii, *Liber Phaleg*, Antwerp, 1572, p. 11.

[29] In Hebrew the ending -*aïm* indicated the dual in some words.

[30] The original text gives 'Peru' here. It is not known why Moses Wall anachronistically links the name of King Solomon with Peru, while the Latin and Spanish texts correctly have 'Ophir'. We have corrected the text.

[31] Francisco Lopez de Gomara, *Primera y segunda parte de la historia general de las Indias*, in *Bibl. aut. esp.*, Madrid, 1852, vol. xxii, p. 164.

[32] On this ancestry, see Genesis 10:29 and 1 Chronicles 1:23.

[33] *Historia natural y moral de las Indias*. See the *Bibl. aut. esp.* edn., Madrid, 1954, vol. lxxiii, bk. 1, ch. 13, p. 22.

name Peru was unknown to the Indians themselves before those
Spaniards gave that name. Add to this what Garcilaso de la Vega in
the first part of his Commentary of Peru, c.4,[34] says, that when a
certain Spaniard, Blasco Núñez de Balboa,[35] lived in that country,
and asked a fisherman what was the name of that province, he
answered Beru (which was the fisherman's own name, he thinking
that was the question) and he further said that the name of the river
where he fished was called Pelu. Hence you may see that Peru is
made of both those words, which also many Spaniards beside him
testify. Besides, who can think that Solomon, neglecting the Eastern
Indies, a place so rich and abounding with all things, should send a
fleet so far off as to the Western Indies. Also we read in I Kings 9: 26
that Solomon made ships in Ezion-Geber on the shore of the Red
Sea, which also Jehoshaphat did, with Ahaziah, as Ezra says in II
Chron. 20: 36;[36] and it is certain that those of those countries went
that ordinary way to India. And it will not follow that, because Holy
Scripture sometimes says that they went to Tarshish and sometimes
that they went to Ophir, therefore both those places are the same,
since Tarshish is not, as some think, Carthage, or Tunis, in Africa;
for the navy of Solomon did not sail from Jaffa, a port of the
Mediterranean, but from Ezion-Geber, a port of the Red Sea, from
which they could not sail to Carthage, but to the Eastern Indies. The
answer of Isaac Abarbanel[37] to the argument cannot be admitted,
when he says that an arm of the Nile ran into the Red Sea and
another arm ran into the Mediterranean by Alexandria in Egypt;
since it was never heard that ships of great burden did swim in those
rivers; and would not he then have built his navy in the port of
Alexandria? It is more true that Tarshish is the Ocean, or Indian
Sea; and because they came into the Ocean, after they have sailed
over the Red Sea, which is but narrow, therefore Scripture says,
'they sailed to Tarshish'. Rabbi Jonathan ben Uziel follows this

---

[34] *Primera parte de los comentarios reales que tratan del origen de los Yncas*, Lisbon, 1609.
[35] A Spanish officer who was the first to reach the Pacific Ocean on 25 September
1513. Tragically he was executed on the orders of Governor Pedro Arias de Ávila in 1517.
On this episode, see A. Rubio, *La ruta de Balboa y el descubrimiento del Océano Pacífico*,
Mexico, 1965, and P. Chaunu, *Conquête et exploitation du Nouveau Monde*, Paris, 1977, p.
133.
[36] For the authorship of the Chronicles, attributed by Jewish tradition to Ezra, see *Baba
Bathra* 14b.
[37] *Commentaire sur les premiers prophetes* (in Hebrew), Leipzig, 1686. On th subject of
I Kings 9: 26, Abarbanel does not clarify this geographical point.

opinion, and in his Paraphrase, for Tarshish, puts 'the Sea'[38]. The same is said by Francisco de Ribera in his commentary on Jonah,[39] and also Rabbi Joseph Ha-Cohen in his Chronicle.[40] These ascribe the word Tarshish to the Indian Sea, because Ophir is the same country, called of old, 'the Golden Chersonese'; and by Josephus, 'the Golden Land',[41] and today Malacca. From which they brought ivory, because of the great number of elephants which are there, of which there are none in the Western Indies. Solomon's navy stayed in those ports of India three years because they traded with the inhabitants! I know that the learned Grotius and the famous de Laet[42] think differently but I shall not insist on confuting their opinions because I study brevity. I like, in part, the opinion of the Spaniards who dwell in the Indies, who by common consent affirm that the Indians come of the Ten Tribes. And truly they are not altogether mistaken[43] because, in my opinion, they were the first planters of the Indies, as also other people of the Eastern Indies came by that strait[44] which is between India and the Kingdom of Anian. But that people, according to our Montezinos, made war upon those inhabitants the Israelites, whom they forced up to the mountains and the inland countries, as formerly the Britons were driven by the Saxons into Wales.

---

[38] *Targum ha-qadosh Yonathan ben Uziel, Targum Hierosolymitanum in quinque libros Legis*, Basle, 1607. In fact Jonathan renders Tarshish as *Afriqa* in 1 Kings 10: 22, and as *yama*, the sea, in Isaiah 2: 16, 23: 1, 10, 14, 40: 9, 66: 19, Ezekiel 27: 12, 25, 38.13, and Jonah 1: 3.

[39] See *In Ionam* in *In duodecim prophetas*, Cologne, 1600, p. 130.

[40] *Dibre ha-yamim le-malkhe Ṣarfat u-malkhut Otoman ha-Togar*, s.i. [Sabionetta], 1554. We have not found the place to which the author refers. See Jacky Kessous, 'La "Chronique" de Joseph ha-Cohen' in *Archives Juives*, xiii, 1977, pp. 44–53 and 56–75.

[41] *The Works of Flavius Josephus*, trans. by William Whiston, Edinburgh, n.d., *Antiquities*, viii, 6: 4, '. . . the land that was of old called Ophir, but now the Aurea Chersonesus, which belongs to India . . .'.

[42] See H. Grotius, *De origine gentium Americanarum*, s.i., 1642, and *De origine gentium Americanarum dissertatio altera*, Paris, 1643; also J. de Laet, *Notae ad dissertationem Hugonis Grotii De origine gentium Americanarum*, Paris, 1643, and *Responsio ad dissertationem secundam Hugonis Grotii De origine gentium Americanarum*, Amsterdam, 1644.

[43] This basic error comes from the Latin text. In fact it was to disprove the Jewish origin of the American Indians that Menasseh wrote the work. The Spanish text makes it quite clear: '. . . los españoles que habitan en dichas Indias sienten generalmente que los indios proceden de los 10 tribos pero erran manifiestamente.' So it should read: 'Having refuted the preceding opinions, it must be pointed out that the Spaniards living in the Indies on the whole consider that the Indians have their origin in the Ten Tribes, but they are clearly wrong.'

[44] This strait was subsequently given the name of the Danish explorer, Bering.

3. The first ground of that opinion is taken from IV Esdras 13: 39–45 etc. (which we quote as ancient though it be Apocryphal)[45] where it is said that the Ten Tribes which Shalmaneser carried captive, in the reign of Hoshea, beyond Euphrates, determined to go into countries far remote, in which none dwelt, whereby they might better observe their Law. And as they passed over some branches of Euphrates, God wrought miracles, stopping the course of the flood till they had passed over; and the country is called Arsareth. From which we may gather that the Ten Tribes went to New Spain and Peru, and possessed those two Kingdoms, till then without inhabitants. Genebrard, quoting Esdras concerning the wanderings of the Ten Tribes,[46] says that Arsareth is Grand Tartary, and from there they went to Greenland, for America has lately been found to be on that side farther from the sea than it is upon other sides, being almost an island, and they might pass from Greenland by Davis Strait into the country of Labrador, which is now called India, being fifty miles distant thence as Gomara says in his *History*.[47] The same journeying of the Ten Tribes into India is confirmed by that which Father Malvenda reports,[48] that Arsareth is that promontory which is near to Scythia or Tartary, near the sea called by Pliny Tabis, where America is parted from the country of Anian by a narrow sea, which also on that side parts China, or Tartary, from America.[49] So that there might be an easy passage for the Ten Tribes through Arsareth or Tartary into the kingdoms of Anian and Quivira, which in time might plant the new world, and firm land which in bigness equals Europe, Asia, and Africa put together. Alonso Augustiniano counts from the shore of the North Sea from the country of Labrador 3,928 miles and from Sur 3,000 miles. But Gomara counts from India by the North and the South 9,300 miles:[50] which space is big enough for the Ten Tribes, that they may there spread in places hitherto unknown.

4. He strengthens this opinion that in the island of San Miguel, which

---

[45] The Jews of Amsterdam of crypto-Jewish origin read the Vulgate and were reasonably familiar with the Apocrypha.

[46] *Chronologia Hebraeorum Major*, Paris, 1578.

[47] *Primera y segunda parte de la historia general de las Indias*, p. 162.

[48] *De Antichristo*, Rome, 1604, see bk. vi, ch. 32.

[49] Pliny, *Naturalis Historiae libri XXXVII*, bk. vi, ch. 17 (20).

[50] The original text 'But Gomara counts from India by the south and Sur 9300 miles' does not make sense and derives from the faulty Latin text. The Spanish text is perfectly clear '. . . y Gomara 9300 de tierra de Indias por la costa del Norte y Sur'. We have corrected the text.

belongs to the Azores, the Spaniards found sepulchres under the ground, with very ancient Hebrew letters, which Genebrard has printed in *Chronicles I*, p. 159.[51] From which we gather that in that inscription there is a mistake in the letter T, so that the sense of it is 'How perfect is God. Sehalbin is dead. Know God.' Unless you would have them to be proper names and to signify him that is dead and his father, in which sense for M you must read B, and then the sense will be 'Meetabel Seal, the son of Matadel;'[52] such names ending in -el are common in Scripture, as Raphael, Immanuel, and the like. Let it suffice him who is pleased with neither of those conjectures, that Hebrew letters were formed there. And though that island is remote from the West Indies, yet it might be by accident that they might put in thither.

5. That seems to me to be the purpose which Garcilaso de la Vega says in his commentary on Peru III c.1[53] that in Tiahuanacu, in the province of Callao, among other antiquities, this is worthy of memory (being situated at the lake which the Spaniards call Chuquiuitu) that among the great buildings which are there, one was to be seen of a very great pile, which has a court 15 fathoms broad; a wall that compasses it, 2 furlongs high; on one side of the court is a chamber 45 foot long and 22 broad; and the court, the wall, the pavement, the chamber, the roof of it, the entrance, the posts of the two gates of the chamber, and of the entrance are made of only one stone; the three sides are an ell thick; the Indians say that that House is dedicated to the Maker of the World. I conjecture that building to be a synagogue, built by the Israelites; for the authors who wrote about the Indies tell us that the Indians never use iron or iron weapons. Also the Indians were idolaters and therefore it could not be that they should build a house to God. Father Acosta, *Ind. Hist. VI*, c.14[54] mentions such buildings as are in that place; and he reports that he measured a stone which was 38 foot long, 18 foot broad and six foot thick. Cieza de Leon in his first part of the *Chronicles of Peru* c.87[55] related that in the city Guarnanga, which is

[51] *Chronologia Hebraeorum Major.*
[52] The Hebrew in the first case is אל תם מה the מ [Tet] in the second word being regarded as a mistake for ת [Taw]. In the second case, the Hebrew is שעל בן מתרעאל
מהטבאל
[53] *Primera parte de los comentarios reales que tratan del origen de los Yncas.*
[54] *Historia natural y moral de las Indias.*
[55] P. Cieza de León, *La crónica del Perú*, Seville, 1553. The Latin version mistakenly refers to ch. 83. We have corrected this in the text.

situated by the river Vinaque, there is a vast building which, because then it seemed almost ruined by time, therefore had lasted many years. He asked the neighbouring Indians who built that great pile. He learned that it was made by a people (who were bearded and white as the Spaniards) who came thither a long time before (and stayed some time after) the Indians reigned there; and the Indians said they had received it from their fathers by tradition. The same Cieza, c.105[56] of the *Antiquity of Tiguanac*, says that what the Indians boast to be very ancient can by no means be compared with that building, and other things. From all which you may well gather that the first inhabitants of that place were the Israelites of the Ten Tribes, because they were white and bearded.

6. To this opinion add an argument taken from what logicians call *a simili*; for he that will compare the laws and customs of the Indians and Hebrews together, shall find them agree in many things. Whence you may easily gather that the Indians borrowed those of the Hebrews (who lived among them) before or after they went to the unknown mountains. The Indians of Yucatan and of Acuzamil circumcise themselves. The Totons of New Spain and Mexicans (as Román y Zamora in the *Republica de Indias* testifies)[57] rend their garments if there happen any sudden misfortune or death. Gregorio Garcia in *Monarchia Ingasonum*[58] says that Guainacapac, hearing that his son Atagualpa fled for fear of the army of his enemy, rent his garments.[59] The Mexicans and Totons, or the Totonacazenses, kept fire continually upon their altars, as God commanded in Leviticus.[60] Those of Peru do the same, in their temples dedicated to the Sun. The Nicaraguans forbid their women lately brought to

---

[56] The chapter number has been corrected. It refers to the *Chronicles of Peru*, ch. 105, entitled 'Del pueblo de Tiguanaco y de los edificios tan grandes y antiguos que en el se ven'.

[57] In making this reference the translator, like Menasseh ben Israel, makes a double mistake. For he writes '(as Roman and Gomara in the generall History of the Indians testifie)'. One error concerns the author's name: Román y Zamora, not Gomara who was the writer of the celebrated *Historia general de las Indias*. The other is in the title given, as Menasseh wished to quote Román y Zamora's book, *Repúblicas de Indias idólatras y gobierno en Mexico y Peru antes de la conquista*, Madrid, 1575. We have verified the reference which may be found in the Madrid edition, 1897 (*Colección de libros raros y curiosos que tratan de América*), vol. i, p. 177.

[58] Menasseh ben Israel makes an error in the title of Gregorio García's work which is in fact called *Origen de los indios de el Nuevo Mundo e Indias occidentales*, Valencia, 1607, See bk. 3, ch. 3, para. 3, p. 227. On the use of this work by our author, see the Introduction.

[59] For the rending of garments as a sign of mourning, cf. Genesis 37: 29.

[60] 'The fire shall ever be burning upon the altar; it shall never go out.' (Leviticus 6: 13).

bed to enter their temples till they are purified.[61] The inhabitants of Hispaniola think that those sin who lie with a woman a little after her childbirth.[62] And the Indians of New Spain do severely punish sodomy.[63] Many of the Indians bury their dead on the mountains, which is also the Jewish custom;[64] and Garcia says the name Chanan is found in those countries.[65] You may wonder at this, that the Indians every fifty years celebrate a jubilee with great pomp in Mexico, the metropolis of the whole province.[66] Also that on the Sabbath day all are bound to be present in the temple, to perform their sacrifices and ceremonies. They also were divorced from their wives if they were not honest. The Indians of Peru, New Spain, and Guatemala did marry the widows of their dead brethren.[67] May you not judge from these things that the Jews lived in those places and that the Gentiles learned such things of them? Add also to what has been said, that the knowledge which the Indians had of the creation of the world and of the universal flood, they borrowed from the Israelites.

7. The fourth ground of this opinion is that the Indians are of brown colour and without beards; but in the New World white and bearded men were found who had never commerce with the Spaniards; and whom you cannot affirm to be any other than Israelites, because also as they could never be overcome so shall they never be fully known, as appears by what follows. Father Pedro Simon, a Franciscan, in his history of the discovery of the mainland[68] says that in the reign of Charles V, he commanded one Philip d'Utré thither, to discover and plant those countries; that he found them unknown towards the

---

[61] For the analogous Hebrew custom, cf. Leviticus 12: 4: '. . . (she shall not) come into the sanctuary, until the days of her purifying be fulfilled.'

[62] Cf. Leviticus 12: 2 and 12: 5.

[63] Cf. Leviticus 18: 22: 'Thou shalt not lie with mankind, as with womankind: it is abomination.' On the similarity between certain Hebrew and Indian rites, see G. García, *Origen de los Indios* . . . , bk. 3.

[64] This information is taken directly from G. García, *Origen de los Indios* . . . , bk. 3, p. 227. There are many examples of Jewish cemeteries on high ground. The best known is that of Montjuich in Barcelona. On this matter see G. Nahon, 'Les cimetières' in *Art et archéologie des juifs en France médiévale*, ed. Bernhard Blumenkranz, Toulouse, 1980, pp. 73–94.

[65] In spite of a chapter entitled 'De algunos vocablos hebreos que se hallan en las Indias' (bk. 3, ch. 7, 2) there is no mention of Chanan in the book.

[66] For the Jubilee among the Hebrews, see Leviticus 25: 10 ff.

[67] On levirate marriage, see Deuteronomy 25: 5–6.

[68] *Primera parte de las noticias historiales de las conquistas de Tierra firme en las Indias occidentales*, Cuenca, 1626. See bk. 5.

north of America in the province of Omeguas which is near the
province of Venezuela, and now is called Caracas. And having
learned of their neighbours the greatness of that people both in
wealth and in war, he determined to war upon them. When they had
marched a good way, they at last found a rich city full of people and
fair buildings; and not far off two husbandmen tilling the ground,
whom they would have made prisoners, that they might be inter-
preters. But when they saw themselves set on, they fled apace
towards the city; but Philip d'Utré and his soldiers followed them
hard upon horseback and had almost taken them whereupon the
husbandmen stood still, and with their spears wounded Philip in the
breast, piercing through his breastplate made of wool to keep off
arrows. He, wondering at the dexterity of that people, judged it a
wiser course not to make war upon that province and people so
expert in war and who dared to resist armed men. Therefore he
retreated with his company. And to this day none go to that people,
neither is it known which way to go to them. It is probable that they
are Israelites whom God preserves in that place against the day of
redemption. Alonso de Erzilla testifies the same thing in part 2 of his
Araucana, canto 27, where, describing those places, he speaks thus
in Spanish:

> Some countries there, so populous are seen
> As one continued city; which have been
> Never as yet discovered; but unknown
> To other nations, have lain hid alone;
> Not found by foreign sword, nor foreign trade
> Do either seek, nor suffer to be made,
> But unacquainted lie, till God shall please
> To manifest his secrets; show us these.[69]

8. Juan de Castellanos, Vicar of Pamplona in New Granada in Peru,
says[70] that, when Gonzalo Pizarro had revolted from his people, he

---

[69] These lines appear in Spanish in the Latin version. As the translation is very free, we
give the original here:
> Ves las manchas de tierra tan cubiertas
> Que pueden ser a penas divisadas,
> Son las que nunca han sido descubiertas,
> Ni de estrangeros pies jamás pisadas,
> Las quales estarán siempre encubiertas,
> Y de aquellas celages occupadas
> Hasta que Dios permita que parezcan,
> Porque más sus secretos se engrandezcan.

[70] In *Elegías de varones ilustres de Indias*, Madrid, 1589.

sent some to search out new countries of the Indians who lived eastwards, whose number could never be known, because (as some say) their country is above two thousand miles in length, if you compute from the head of the river Marañon, which runs nearer the Andes of Cuzco, to the place where it runs into the sea; where therefore the river began to be navigable, Pedro de Orsua, a captain, went by water and his soldiers with him in vessels called canoes. When they were too small for the force of the stream, he built brigantines on the banks of the river Guariaga, which washing the province Chachapoyas runs into the Marañon. He was scarce gone aboard his brigantines when one of his soldiers named Aguirre,[71] a stout man, killed him and by common consent succeeded the slain Orsua. When they had gone a little way, they found a plain without a mountain, where many houses stood on each side of the bank of the Marañon, built by the Indians. They still went on for forty-eight hours together and saw nothing but tall, and white, houses, which they feared to go into, because the inhabitants were numerous and because they heard the noise of hammers, for which cause they thought the inhabitants to be goldsmiths. They went on still and now sailed in the North Sea but always near to the shore of the province of Margareta, where Aguirre was caught by the inhabitants and hanged; for they heard that he had killed his captain, Pedro de Orsua.

9. Gaspar de Bergara[72] (whom I have often spoken with) went from the city of Loxa, which is in the province of Quito in the kingdom of Peru, and accompanied the colonel Don Diego Vaca de la Vega going to seek a new country.

In the year 1622 they came to the province of Yargoasongo, which had been discovered by Captain Salinas; and they passed the Cordilleras mountains, where the river Marañon is not above a stone's cast over. In the province of the Maynas Indians they built a city, whose name was Francisco de Borja.[73] In his company were

---

[71] On Lope de Aguirre, a Spanish adventurer born 1518 died 1561, Luis Silva Lezacta, *El conquistador Francisco de Aguirre*, Santiago (Chile), Editorial universitaria, 1953, may be consulted. See also *Aguirre ou la fièvre de l'indépendance: Relation véridique de l'expédition de l'Omagua et de l'El Dorado (1560–1) de Francisco Vazquez*, trans., introd., and annot. by Manoël Faucher, Paris, 1979.

[72] We have found nothing on this one of our rabbi's informants.

[73] The original text, departing form the Latin version, gives 'S. Francisco de Borja at Esquilache'. This refers to the town of San Francisco de Borja, founded by Francisco de Borja y Acevedo, Prince of Esquilache, who was Governor and Captain General of Peru from 1615 to 1621. During his term of office he subdued the Mayas Indians, and founded the town which bears his name.

one hundred Indians in canoes. Having conquered those Indians and compelling them to swear fealty to the king of Spain, the colonel, being instructed by the Maynas, went to other places, after he had put a garrison into his new city. Having sailed fifty leagues[74] in the river (he found some cottages of the Indians which there hid themselves) by favour of many rivers which there run into the Marañon. When they had sailed into the river Guariaga, where Pedro de Orsua had built his brigantines, and was killed by Aguirre, they asked the Indians whom they had taken (who were called Guariaga, from the river's name) what people live on the river's side. They told the colonel that, five days journey off, there live men of tall stature, comely in presence, and have as great beards as the Spaniards have, valiant and warlike, who are not skilled in canoes, though the rest of the Indians use no other. He presently returned the way he came.

10. At Pernambuco, about forty years since, eight Tabajares Indians had a mind to look out new countries and to see whether the land that was beyond, and unknown, was inhabited. They having spent four months in travelling westward, they came to mountains, to whose top they got with difficulty, and found a plain which a pleasant river encompasses, by whose bank side dwelt a people who loved commerce; they were white and bearded, and this five of the Tabajares (for three perished by the way and only five returned) told to the Brazilians after nine months.

11. In our time, under king Philip III, Captain Pedro Fernández de Queiros being returned out of India (where he had spent most of his life) to Rome, showed a table of lands yet undiscovered.[75] From there he went to Madrid, and five ships were given him by the governor of Panama (to whom he was sent) to perfect his design. He began to journey and had scarcely entered the South Sea when he found land which he called the Isle of Solomon and Jerusalem,[76] for reasons which he told me. He in his course of sailing always kept

[74] The Spanish version gives 500 leagues.

[75] In the Spanish version, Menasseh makes it clear that he got this information from the very learned Jacob Rosales. He was Immanuel Bocarro Francês, the Portuguese doctor, astronomer, astrologer, and poet who returned to Judaism at Livorno under the name of Jacob Hebraeus Rosales. On the discovery of the Pacific islands bordering America, Fernández de Queiros, *Historia del descubrimiento de las regiones austriales*, Madrid, 1876–80, may be consulted.

[76] These are the Solomon Islands in the Melanesian archipelago. Although the Solomon Islands are often mentioned in travellers' tales and notably in the history of their discovery by Álvaro de Mendaña (see P. Fernández de Queiros, *Historia del descubrimiento*,

close to the shore of those islands; he saw those islanders of a brown colour, and took many; others dwelt in greater islands and more fruitful; these were white and wore long garments of silk; and the pilot being bid to bring his ship near the shore, he split his ship upon a rock (and the islanders running greedily to the sight), which being sunk, the captain went thence, looking for firm land which he found to be forty degrees beyond. And he went three hundred miles to the shore; and when he perceived the country to be inhabited by the smoke which he saw, and would put into a port on the side of the river, there ran to him many white men, of yellow hair, tall like giants, richly clothed, and of long beards. But one of the vessels being wrecked in the haven's mouth, he was forced to put out to sea. Whereupon the islanders sent two Chalossi of a brown colour (as the inhabitants were of the first island) with sheep and other provisions and fruits, but desiring and threatening them, if they did not depart. The captain brought these Chalossi to Spain, from whom the Spaniards could learn nothing but by signs; and instead of answers (when they were asked), would show their beards, as if such those were, who were their lords, and had sent them; and, if they were asked about religion, they would hold up their fingers to heaven, implying that they worshipped but one God. A little while after, they died in Spain. The captain returned to Panama, having left his two ships which were wrecked and when the Governor sued him, by means of the Senators who are over the affairs of the Indians,[77] he was dismissed and returned with his ships to Spain. But the king created him marquess of the countries found out by him and commanded to give him a good army wherewith to compass his designs. But he scarce got to Panama when he died, not without suspicion of being poisoned by the Governor.[78]

12. That which I am about to tell shall serve for proof of that which I said of the Western Indians. A Dutch mariner told me that not long since he was with his ship in America, seven degrees towards the north between Marañon and the great Para, and he put into a harbour in a pleasant river, where he found some Indians who understood Spanish, of whom he bought meats and dye-wood. After he had

we have not been able to find a text in which they are called Solomon and Jerusalem Islands.

[77] This refers to the members of the Council of the Indies, one of the most important councils in the apparatus of the Spanish Monarchy.

[78] This detail does not appear in the Spanish version.

stayed there six months, he understood that that river extended eighteen leagues towards the Caraib Indians, as far as the ship could go; and that the river is divided there into three branches, and they sailing two months on the left hand, there met white men, and bearded, well bred, well clothed and abounding with gold and silver; they dwelt in cities enclosed with walls and full of people; and that some Indians of Orinoco went thither and brought home much gold, silver and many precious stones. Which he, having understood, sent thither some seamen; but the Indian, who was their guide, died by the way, and so they did not proceed but stayed there two months and trucked with the Indians who were sixty leagues from the sea. That province is called Isbia and is subject to Zeeland; they have no commerce with the Spaniards and the inhabitants travel securely every way. I heard that story by accident from the Dutch master of the ship; whence some of us, guessing them to be Israelites, had purposed to send him again to enquire more fully. But he died suddenly last year, whence it seems that God does not permit that those purposes should take any effect until the end of days.

13. Yet I give more credit to our Montezinos being a Portuguese and a Jew of our order, born in a city of Portugal, called Villaflor,[79] of honest and known parents, a man about forty years old, honest and not ambitious. He went to the Indies, where he was put into the Inquisition, as the successor of many who were born in Portugal and descended from them, whom the King of Portugal, Don Manuel, forced to turn Christian: 'O, wicked and unjust action', says Osorio; and, a little after, 'this was done neither according to law, nor religion'. And yet to this day they privately keep their religion, which they had changed, being forced thereto. He, being freed from the Inquisition, very diligently sought out these things and oft spoke with those men, and then was not quiet till he came hither, and had told us the good news. He endured much in that journey, and was driven to great want, so that no house would give him food, or give him money for his work.[80] I myself was well acquainted with him for

[79] The Latin and English versions give the French form 'Villefleur'. It is hard to understand why this one French form was used, and it cannot be attributed to Menasseh ben Israel. We have corrected it in the text.

[80] The English translator has misinterpreted this passage, in which Menasseh emphasizes the honesty of Montezinos, who did not want to profit from the hospitality he might have enjoyed, and which other travellers had exploited unscrupulously. The Latin and Spanish texts are perfectly clear on this. It should read 'for he did not want to be anyone's guest, or to derive any benefit from his efforts'.

six months together that he lived here; and sometimes I made him take an oath in the presence of honest men, that what he had told me was true. Then he went to Pernambuco,[81] where, two years after, he died, taking the same oath at his death. Which if it be so, why should I not believe a man that was virtuous and having all that which men call gain. And who knows but that shortly the truth of that prognostic may appear, which our Montezinos learned from the Mohanes, answerable to that which Jacobus Verus,[82] an astrologer of Prague wrote after the apparition of the Comet in the year 1618 and dedicated to her Highness the Princess Palatine,[83] where he thus discourses: the Comet going towards the south intimates that the cities and provinces which God threatens are those of the Western Indies, which shall revolt from the king of Spain, who will find that loss greater than he imagined, not that the Indians rebel against him of themselves but that they are provoked to it, being stirred up by others. Neither did the Comet only foretell that, but the eclipse of the sun, which was in the country the year before. Thus far the astrologer. Our ancient rabbis say, though we do not believe the astrologers in all things, yet we do not wholly reject them, who sometimes tell the truth.[84]

14. Thus far of the Western Indies, of which Isaiah may be understood (because it lies in the midst of the sea, and also has many islands) in Isaiah 60: 9: 'The isles shall wait for me, and the ships of Tarshish first, to bring their sons from far, their silver and their gold with them.' Jeremiah 31: 10: 'Hear the word of the Lord, O ye nations, and declare it in the isles afar off, and say, He that scattereth Israel will gather him.' Psalm 97: 1: 'The Lord reigneth, let the earth rejoice, and the multitudes of isles be glad.' Where part of the Ten Tribes dwell unknown to this day.

---

[81] Site of the first Jewish community in the New World, called Sur Israel. He lived there from Spring 1645 to Spring 1647. He died one year before the community began its register, now preserved in the Municipal Archives of Amsterdam, PA 334, no. 1304, published by Arnold Wiznitzer, 'O livro de Atas das Congregações Judaicas "Zur Israel" e Maurícia, Brasil, 1648–53', in *Anais da Biblioteca Nacional*, Rio, vol. 74, 1953, pp. 213–40. One Isaque Monttosinos Mesquitta signed a resolution on 15 September 1651, but it is unlikely that he was related to our traveller.

[82] We have found no mention of this astrologer.

[83] The original English text has 'his Highness the Prince Palatine'. The Latin and Spanish leave no doubt that this is an error, which we have corrected.

[84] For the sometimes positive attitude of the rabbis towards astrology, see *Shabbat* 156 a and *Moed Qatan* 28 a. We owe these references to Jacques Halbronn and thank him warmly for them.

15. You must know that all the ten tribes were not carried away at the same time. Pul, the king of Assyria (as I show in the second part of my *Conciliador*)[85] conquered and carried away the tribes of Reuben, Gad and half Manasseh, in the reign of Pekah, as you may see in I Chron. 5: 26[86] and Josephus [*Antiquities*] IX c.11.[87] Tiglath-Pileser eight years after took Ijon, Abel-neth-Maachah, Hazor, Gilead, Galilee, all the land of Naphtali, and he carried away all the captives into Assyria, in II Kings 15: 29. At last Shalmaneser, King of Assyria, nine years after, in the reign of Hoshea, the son of Elah, besieged Samaria three years; which being taken, he carried away Hoshea, with the rest of the tribes, in II Kings 17: 6. Of those, three times the prophet Isaiah speaks,[88] saying, the first captivity was gentle if you compare it with the last, which was grievous and unsufferable, when the kingdom and monarchy of Israel ceased.

16. The Ten Tribes being conquered at several times, we must think they were carried into several places. As we believe they went to the Western Indies by the strait of Anian, so we think that out of Tartary they went to China, by that famous wall in the confines of both. Our argument to prove it is taken from the authority of two Jesuits,[89] who erected their colleges in those countries.[90] Nicolas Trigault, a Dutchman, in his discourse of the Christian expedition undertaken by the Jesuits to China[91] says, we find that in former time Jews came into these kingdoms. And when that society had for some years seated itself in the Court of Pekin, a certain Jew came to Father Matteo Ricci; he was born in Kai-feng-fu, the metropolis of the province Honan, and was surnamed Ngai;[92] and now being licensed to the degree of a Doctor, he went to Pekin. But when he read in a

---

[85] *Segunda Parte del Conciliador*, p. 164.

[86] The Spanish version gives details concerning the places to which the Tribes were carried away.

[87] *The Works of Flavius Josephus, Antiquities*, ix, 11: 1.

[88] The Latin version refers to Isaiah 8: 23, the Spanish to Isaiah 8: 25, which does not exist as chapter 8 has only 23 verses, and the English translation to Isaiah 9: 1. All three references are incorrect, and we have not been able to identify the quotation.

[89] These were the two celebrated Jesuits, Matteo Ricci (1552–1610), and Alvaro Semedo (1585–1658).

[90] There are many differences, in comparison with the Spanish version, in the passage on Jews in China, but they do not affect the discussion.

[91] *De Christiana expeditione apud Sinas suscepta*, Lyon, 1616. There is a French translation of this work, *Histoire de l'expédition chrétienne au royaume de Chine de Matteo Ricci et Nicolas Trigault*, Paris 1979.

[92] On this individual and episode, see Paul Pelliots' article, 'Le juif Ngai informateur du P. Mathieu Ricci' in *Studies of the Chinese Jews*, New York, 1971, pp. 93–100.

certain book written by a Doctor of China, concerning the European affairs, that our fathers are not Saracens but know no God but the Lord of Heaven and Earth; and would persuade himself that ours did profess the Law of Moses, he went into the Church with Father Matteo Ricci. On an altar there was the effigy of the Virgin Mary, and the child Jesus, whom St John his forerunner worshipped with bended knees; now that day was the Holy-day of John the Baptist. The Jew, thinking it was the effigy of Rebecca and her two sons, Jacob and Esau, bowed also to the image, but with this apology, that he worshipped no images, but that he could not but honour those who were the parents of his nation.[93] And he, asking if the Four Evangelists on both sides of the altar were not four of the twelve sons of Jacob, the Jesuit answered, yes, thinking he had asked of the Twelve Apostles. But afterward the Jew acknowledged to the Jesuit that he was an Israelite; and he found the King's Bible and acknowledged the Hebrew letters, though he could not read them. By this occasion our people learned that ten or twelve families of Israelites were there, and had built a very neat synagogue, which cost 10,000 crowns, in which they have kept the Five Books of Moses with great veneration for 600 years. He also affirmed that in Hangchow, the metropolis of the province Chekiang, there are far more families, with a synagogue; and elsewhere that many families live without a synagogue, because that by little and little they are extinguished. He, relating many things out of the Old Testament,[94] differed by little in pronouncing those names.[95] He said that some among them were not ignorant of the Hebrew tongue, but that himself had neglected it, having studied the China tongue from childhood.[96] For which cause he was counted almost unworthy of their society by the ruler of the synagogue. But he chiefly looked after this, that he might get to be Doctor. Three years after Father Matteo Ricci sent one our our brethren to that metropolis, who found all those things true. He compared the beginnings and

[93] The original text has 'the parents of our nation', an incorrect translation of 'gentis suae parentes'.

[94] The author is reporting the Jesuits' words, otherwise he would not have used the expression *Old Testatment*: for a Jew there is only one Bible, the Hebrew Bible.

[95] In the Spanish version, Menasseh gives some examples of the Chinese Jews' pronunciation with a transcription showing that these Jews pronounced Hebrew in the manner of the Ashkenazi Jews of Central and Eastern Europe.

[96] The translator has ambiguously translated 'a puero literis chinensibus insudarat' as 'having studied the China tongue from a child'. We have clarified this in the text.

endings of the books which the Jews keep in their synagogue with our Pentateuch and saw no difference, this only that those had no pricks [points].[97] The other Jesuit is Alvaro Semedo,[98] who likewise says that there is a great number of Jews in the province of Honan in the west part of China, who know nothing of the coming and suffering of Jesus. And he from thence gathers that they are of the Ten Tribes (which opinion I also am of) because those Chinese observe many Jewish rites, which you may see in a manuscript which the noble Joachim Ficheforte[99] has. And why might not some of them sail from China to New Spain, through the strait between China and Anian and Quivira, which border upon New Spain; and thence they went to the isles of Panama, Peru, and those thereabouts. These in my judgement are those Chinese of whom Isaiah 49: 12 speaks (treating about Israel's return to his country): 'Behold these shall come from afar, and these from the North, and from the West, and these from the land of Sinim.'[100] And so Ptolemy in book VII c.3. tab.11 calls it the country of Sinim, or Sina;[101] and this is the true sense of the words. Abraham Ibn Ezra is mistaken,[102] who derives it of Sene, a bush or wood, which he places in Egypt.[103]

17. I could easily believe that the Ten Tribes as they increased in number, so they spread into more provinces before-mentioned, and into Tartary. For Abraham Ortelius in his geography of the world,[104] and map of Tartary, notes the place of the Danites, which he calls the *horda*,[105] which is the same with the Hebrew *Yerida*,

[97] At this point an important passage in the Spanish version, concerning the arrival of the Messiah, is omitted from the Latin text. Here is a translation of it: 'By means of the same messenger, the Father sent the President of the Synagogue letters written in Chinese saying that in Peking he had all the Books of the Old and New Testaments, in which were recorded all the things that the Messiah, who he believed had already come, had done. To this the Archisynagogue objected that the Messiah had not yet come.'

[98] In A. Semedo, *Relatione della grande monarchia della China*, Rome, 1643, bk. 1, ch. 30, pp. 192–3.

[99] We have found nothing on this Christian friend of Menasseh ben Israel's.

[100] In fact traditional Jewish commentators put *Sinim* in the South of Palestine.

[101] In Ptolemy's *Geography*, table 11, there is a map of Asia on which China is shown as *Sinnae*.

[102] A celebrated Spanish Jewish writer (1089–1164). His commentary of the Bible has become a classic.

[103] As a place-name this is a *hapax* in the Hebrew Bible. The Septuagint translates it as Περσα, Persia.

[104] *Theatrum Orbis Terrarum*, Antwerp, 1573.

[105] Menasseh ben Israel gives a faithful description of the Northern part of Ortelius's map. However we point out that for Ortelius *horda* meant a tribe, while Menasseh made it a geographical location.

signifying a descent. And lower, he mentions the Horda of Naphtali, possessed by Peroza in the year 476.[106] Wilhelm Schickard in his *Tarich* or series of the kings of Persia amplifies the history of this war, where from Book IV of Agathias[107] he thus says: a little after, when they were eased of that plague (i.e. 7 years drought) in the time of the Emperor Zeno, Peroza[108] made a double war with Naphtali, in which at last he was destroyed. For first of all he was brought to the straits of places unknown; who then fought for peace upon this condition (and obtained it) that he should swear that he would never after provoke them; and that he should do reverence to this conqueror in token of subjection; which afterward by the counsel of the magicians he performed craftily, for he bowed towards the eastern sun that his own people might think that he bowed rather to the sun (after his country's custom) than to honour his enemy. But he did not truly perform that first agreement, though confirmed by Letters Patent; who, because he could not digest the disgrace of bowing to his enemy, prepared a new army and went against them; but a second time he being entrapped by the badness of the country he lost his life; and many with him, in a gulf which the Naphtalites had prepared for him, having dressed it over with reeds, and some earth thrown atop; they having left in the middle some high grounds, and trees where their scouts were, that their stratagem might not be found, and that the Persians might more confidently attempt the ditch. Thus a rash king paid for his perfidy, he excelling more in daring than in counsel, as Agathias says. The patent by which peace had been agreed was hung upon a spear, and might be seen of him at a distance, that he might remember his oath, repent and desist from his enterprise; but he cared little for that. But when by his unexpected fall he saw he should die, it is said that he pulled from off his right ear a pearl of huge bigness and whiteness, and lest any after him should find it (more likely that his corpse should not be known) he threw it a great way off. The same author asks who those Naphtalites were and by many arguments he proves that they are the relics of the

---

[106] This refers to the Hephtalites, who did actually defeat Peroza, King of Persia, but in 481 and not in 476 as the writer says. See Jacob Neusner, *A History of the Jews in Babylonia*, vol. v, *Later Sasanian Times*, Leiden, 1970, p. 40. The Spanish version adds '1173 years ago'. The addition of the two dates given by Menasseh certainly confirms that he wrote *Esperança* in 1649.

[107] Agathias, *Works* in *Corpus scriptorum Byzantinorum*, Bonn, 1828, vol. 48, bk. IV, para. 27, p. 266.

[108] The original text gives 'Firuz', but refers to the king already mentioned above. We have harmonized the spelling of his name.

Jews. He says, I do wholly think that they are the relics of the Jews of
the tribe of Naphtali, whom Tiglath-Pileser the Assyrian carried
into those places (II Kings 15: 29). For (1) the name in the best
copies of Agathias, which Lewenclavius has emended,[109] is the
same fully; in other books, it wants nothing but an 'h'. Now it is
scarcely possible that in a word of so many syllables that should fall
out by chance. (2) Their countenance discovers it, for as Procopius,
book I, says, they are not black or foul in their countenance as the
Huns are among whom they live, but the only white men of that
country;[110] that it may evidently appear that they came from some
other place thither. (3) Their manners agree, for the same author
says, that they are not nomads, as the Huns who are inconstant in
their dwelling, and eat up one place after another; but they inhabit
one certain place. Besides, they observe law and equity, as the
Romans, and have policy, being well governed by their prince: both
which is rare among their neighbour nations. Also, they do not lay
abroad their dead, as the barbarians do, but they decently cover
them with earth. Lastly, the journals testify that many Jews live
there, especially in the mountains, [of those] who have searched to
the mid-land countries of East Asia (Rabbi Benjamin, f.23).[111]
From thence (the coast of Persia) is twenty-eight days' journey to the
mountains Nisebor, which are near the river Gozan. The Israelites
which come from thence into Persia say that there in the cities of
Nisebor are four tribes (Dan, Zebulun, Asher, Naphtali) of the first
captivity, which Shalmaneser the Assyrian carried thither, as in II
Kings 17: 6, he brought them to Habor and Halah, the river Gozan,
and the mountains of Media. The compass of that country is twenty
days' journey; and they possess cities, and castles upon the mountains, by one side of which runs the river Gozan; neither are they
subject to the nations but have a governor over them, by name R.
Joseph Amarkela, a Levite, and there among them some who study
wisdom. They sow and reap; yea, they wage war to the country of
Kut. In the same place Ortelius adds in the country Tabor or Tibur
(which Solinus commends in c.49)[112] there dwell a people, who,

---

[109] Jean Loewenklau (1533–93), *Zosimi Procopii Agathiae et Jornandis historiae gr. et lat.
cum notis*, Basel, 1579.

[110] Procopius, *De Bello Persico*, Rome, 1509, bk. 1, pp. 6–12.

[111] *Itinerarium D.Beniaminis cum versione et notis Constantini L'Empereur*, Leiden, 1633,
pp. 97–8, may be consulted.

[112] Fourth-century Latin writer who wrote a summary of Pliny, often quoted by Azariah
dei Rossi. We have not found the passage referred to by our rabbi.

though they have lost the holy writings, obey one king, who came into France in 1530 and spoke with Francis I, was burnt at Mantua by the command of the Emperor Charles V, because he did privately teach Judaism to Christian princes and to the Emperor himself. Botero says the same in his *Relations* of the farthest part of Tartary.[113] But both these were deceived; for Rabbi Joseph Ha-Cohen, a man writing to be believed, relates this more truly in his *Chronology*,[114] saying that the Jew who came out of that country was the brother of the king of the Israelites and was called David the Reubenite;[115] and, having seen India in his passage, he came to Portugal, where he converted the king's secretary to Judaism, who fled from there with him, taking the name Solomon Molho;[116] he in short time was so well versed in the Law, yea in the Cabbalah itself, that he made all Italy admire him. The Secretary, together with the Reubenite, endeavoured to draw the Pope, Charles V, and Francis I to Judaism. Solomon Molho was taken at Mantua and burnt alive in the year 1540. He yet was offered his life if he would turn Christian. The Reubenite was by Charles V carried prisoner into Spain, where he shortly after died. Abraham Farisol [in his] *Orhot Olam*[117] mentions the Reubenite saying, forty-five years ago David Reubeni, a prince of the Israelites, came from Tabor, a province of Tartary, into Europe, who said that two tribes are there; and other tribes a little farther, under their kings and princes, and also an unspeakable number of people. Perhaps the province Tabor is the same Habor, which is mentioned in II Kings 17:6, that the Ten Tribes were brought by Shalmaneser to Habor and Halah; now the Hebrew letters 'h' and 't' are near in fashion.[118]

Eldad HaDani, of the tribe of Dan, came out of those countries five hundred years ago (a letter from him, which we call *Sepher Eldad HaDani* is kept to this day)[119] and being examined by the Rabbis,

[113] Giovanni Botero, *Relationi Universali*, Vicenza, 1595, bk ii, pp. 120–1.

[114] See above, n. 40; fos. 206 v. to 219 v.

[115] We now have David Reuveni's actual journal available: see Adolf Neubauer, *Mediaeval Jewish Chronicles and Chronological Notes*, ii, Oxford, 1895, pp. 133–223 (in Hebrew), A. Z. Aescoly, *Sippur David Reubeni*, Jerusalem, 1940 (in Hebrew), and also I. S. Révah, 'David Rubéni exécuté en Espagne en 1538'in *REJ*, xvii (cxvii), 1958, pp. 128–35.

[116] See Joseph Shochetman and Cecil Roth, article 'Molcho Solomon (c. 1500–32)' in *Enc. Jud.*, 12:225–7.

[117] 'David, filius Salomon princeps prophetae Israelis', *Compendium viarum saeculi i. mundi*, Paris, 1601, ch. 13, pp. 54–62.

[118] The letters referred to are *ḥet* (ח) and *tav* (ת).

[119] See *Relation d'Eldad le Danite, voyageur du IXe siècle, traduite en français suivie du texte hebreu et d'une lettre chaldéenne*, by E. Carmoly, Paris, 1838, and Elkan Nathan Adler,

was found an approved man. The learned Rabbi David Kimhi, who lived 450 years since, in his *Book of Roots*[120] in the word *Segiah* says, Rabbi Jonah writes in the name of Rabbi Judah ibn Quraish that he heard Eldad the Danite say etc.[121] And so what I said is true, as appears by the testimonies produced.

18. Part of the Ten Tribes also live in Ethiopia, in the Abyssinian kingdom, as diverse Abyssinians reported at Rome. Botero in his *Relations* speaks the same thing,[122] that two potent nations live near the Nile, and that one of them is that of the Israelites, who are governed by a mighty king. A cosmographer who has added notes to Ptolemy's table,[123] says thus in his table of New Africa, that part of New Africa was unknown of old, the head of the Nile not being known, which is in the Mountains of the Moon, as the ancients call them; where there dwell a great number of Israelites, paying tribute to Prester John. Rabbi Abraham Farisol, in the book already quoted, says that in his time some who had been in those countries reported the same to Ercole, Duke of Ferrara.[124] And without question hence the Abyssinians learned circumcision, the observation of the Sabbath, and many more Jewish rites. Of these Isaiah 18: 1, 2 [and 7] seems to speak: 'Woe to the Land which under the shadow of sails doth sail beyond the rivers of Ethiopia by whom (the Prophet says) are sent ambassadors in ships of bulrushes (such as the Ethiopians use, commonly called *almadias*). Bring back a people driven out of their country and torn, and more miserable than any among us. Gifts

Jewish Travellers, A Treasury of Travelogues from 9 Centuries, New York, 1966, pp. 4–21.

120 David Kimhi, *Sefer ha-Shorashim*, Venice, 1547, col. 490. In fact the term does not exist in classical Hebrew, and is therefore a word peculiar to the Lost Tribe of the Danites.

121 As he was not a Hebrew scholar, the English translator did not understand the passage in Latin, hence the 'etc.'. It should read '. . . Eldad the Danite said, if he was busy with something, I am busy, I have segiah'. The medieval lexicographer, Jonah ibn Janah, used the same term as our adventurer. See Wilhelm Bacher, ed., *Sepher haschoraschim, Wurzelwörterbuch der hebräischen Sprache von Abulwalîd Merwân ibn Ganâh (Rabbi Jona) aus dem Arabischen ins Hebräische übersetzt von Jehuda ibn Tibbon*, Berlin, 1896, reprinted Amsterdam, 1969, p. 497.

122 G. Botero, *Relationi Universali*, bk. iii. p. 158.

123 On these 'Additions', see Azariah dei Rossi, *Meor Enayim*, edited by David Cassel, Berlin, 1867, p. 162.

124 'Et omnia illa audivi ego a viris sapientibus qui fuerunt in Calicuth. Post bienium multis diebus, duabus et nuntiarunt huc in conspectu Ducis Herculis Ferrariae hic.' Abraham Farissol, the Latin version mentioned above, n. 117, ch. 25, pp. 118–19. The 'mighty king' is probably Gideon, who fought the kings of Ethiopia in the sixteenth century. Prester John legends seem to originate in a Christian Khan of the Kerait Turks (see Godbey, pp. 389 ff) and then transferred in the 15th century to the Christian king of Ethiopia, Zara Yakub (J. Doresse, *L'Empire du Prêtre Jean*, Paris, 1957). For Jewish warrior tribes in Ethiopia, see *EJ* 6; 1143–54.

shall be brought to the Lord of Hosts, in the place where the name of the Lord of Hosts is worshipped, in Mount Zion.' The prophet Zephaniah (3: 9, 10) says the same: 'Then will I give to the people that they, speaking a pure language, may all call upon the name of God, whom they shall serve with reverence; from beyond the rivers of Ethiopia they shall bring to me for a gift *Atray [bat Pussay]*[125] the daughter of my dispersed ones' (that is the nations of Ethiopia); which agrees with that of Isaiah (66: 20): 'And your brethren (which are the Ten Tribes) shall bring gifts to the Lord.'[126]

19. And without doubt they also dwell in Media; thence they passed Euphrates, whither they were first brought as in II Kings 17: 24 and in the Book of Tobit.[127] Josephus also speaks of them in the Preface of his Book of the *War of the Jews*,[128] that the Jews did think that their brethren, who dwelt beyond Euphrates, and farther, would rebel against the Romans. Agrippa, in his oration to the people of Jerusalem, that they would not rebel against the Romans, speaks thus: 'What associates do you expect to join with you in your rebellion and war? Does not all the known world pay tribute to the Romans? Perhaps some of you hope to have help from them beyond the Euphrates.'[129] And in Book XI of his *Antiquities* (c.5), speaking of those who in the time of Ezra returned from Babylon to Jerusalem, he says: 'All Israel dwelt in Media; for two tribes only dwelt in Asia and Europe, and lived subject to the Romans; the other ten on the other side Euphrates, were there are so many that they cannot be counted.'[130] It is not therefore to be doubted, the people increasing after their first transportation, they sought out new places, which we have formerly mentioned.

---

[125] Moses Wall is not faithful to the Latin text where it reads 'Hatray bat Pussay (nationes Æthiopicas)'. On the one hand he adopts the Aramaic paraphrase and Rashi's interpretation which translates *Atray bat Pussay* as 'my worshippers, my faithful dispersed ones'. On the other he follows our rabbi, since the parenthesis referring to the nations of Ethiopia is a gloss which Menasseh introduces as the opening of the verse.

[126] The parenthesis is another gloss by Menaseh ben Israel based on various traditional commentaries.

[127] The Book of Tobit, while not forming part of the Hebrew canon, was very closely studied by writers with a tradition of Marranism and therefore familiar with the Vulgate. A good number of the events related in Tobit take place in Media, see, for example, 1: 14–15 and 14: 14.

[128] 'For the Jews hoped that all of their nation beyond Euphrates would have raised an insurrection together with them.' *The Works of Flavius Josephus, Wars*, Preface 2.

[129] Ibid., Bk. II, 16: 4.

[130] 'But then the entire body of the people of Israel remained in that country; wherefore ther are but two tribes in Asia and Europe subject to the Romans, while the ten tribes are beyond Euphrates till now, and are in immense multitude and not to be estimated by numbers.' *The Works of Flavius Josephus, Antiquities*, XI, 5: 2.

20. Lastly, all think that part of the Ten Tribes dwell beyond the river Sambatyon, or Sabbatical. Rabbi Yohanan, the author of the Jerusalem Talmud, who lived 160 years after the destruction of the Second Temple,[131] says in the tractate *Sanhedrin* [29b][132] that the Ten Tribes were carried to three places: to the Sabbatical river, to Daphne, the suburbs of Antioch, and thither where a cloud comes down and covers them. And that they shall be redeemed from those three places; for so he opens that place of Isaiah 49: 9, 'that they may say to the captives, go forth (i.e. to them who are at the Sabbatical river); to them that are in darkness, show yourselves (i.e. to them who are compassed with the cloud); and to all, they shall be refreshed in the ways' (i.e. to them who live in Daphne of Antioch, which is in Syria). Whence you may observe that the learned man l'Empereur translated it ill, 'at the sides of Antioch',[133] whereas Daphne is the proper name of a pleasant grove near Antioch. The *Seder Olam*[134] makes mention of that cloud, and calls them mountains of obscurity; and in the Babylonian Talmud *Sanhedrin* c.11.[135]

R. Jonathan ben Uziel, who lived a hundred years before the destruction of the Second Temple, on Exodus 34: 10, where the Lord says, 'I will do wonders before all thy people, such as have not been done in all the earth, or in any nation', refers all those things to the transportation of the people: 'He shall draw them to the rivers of Babylon; and shall carry them to the Sabbatical river, and shall teach them that those miracles were never performed to any nation of the known world.'[136]

Our ancient Rabbis in *Bereshit Rabbah* (no mean book) do in parashah [11][137] say that Tornophoros asking how it should appear

---

[131] The Rabbi Yohanan mentioned by our rabbi is R. Johanan ben Nappaha (*c.*180–*c.*279), see J. S. Zuri, *Rabbi Jochanan, der erste Amoräer Galiläas*, Berlin, 1918. The attribution to Johanan ben Nappaha of the Jerusalem Talmud assumed by Abraham ibn Daud and Maimonides, is rejected by Herman L. Strack in his *Introduction to the Talmud and Midrash*, New York, 1931, p. 65. The Latin text leaves out this master's very celebrated martydom, 'Rabbinus Johanan ... qui vixit annis 160 post destructionem secundi templi', although it is mentioned in the Spanish version.

[132] The pagination is that of the Krotoschin edn., 1866.

[133] In fact this refers to a translator's note, not concerning the text of the journey, but about *J. Sanh.* 29; see Benjamin of Tudela, *Itinerarium D. Beniaminis*, p. 207

[134] *Seder 'Olam Rabbah*, Constantinople. 1515; see Isaiah 49: 9.

[135] We cannot find this reference in *B. Sanh.*, ch. 11.

[136] Jonathan ben Uziel, *Targum hierosolymitanum in quinque libros legis*, Basel, 1607, fo. 29v., right-hand col.

[137] The English text, faithful to the Latin text, has 'in perasach' without giving the number of the parashah. It also distorts the spelling of Tornophorus, whom it calls

that the day which we keep is the seventh day on which God rested after the creation of the world, Rabbi Akiva (who lived fifty-two years after the destruction of the Second Temple)[138] answered by an argument taken from the stones of the Sabbatical river, which in the six days are tossed up and down with a continual motion, but do rest on the Sabbath day and move not. The same is said in the Babylonian Talmud, tractate *Sanhedrin* c.7 [65b] and in *Tanhuma* parashah c.9 [*Ki Thissa* on Exodus 33: 11–34: 35].

In *Bereshit Rabba* parashah 73[:5], Rabbi Simon says: 'The Ten Tribes were carried to the Sabbatical river but Judah and Benjamin are dispersed to all countries.' In *Midrash Rabbah*, on the last but one verse of Chapter I of the Song of Songs,[139] it is said: 'Our bed is flourishing'; by that is meant the Ten Tribes, which were carried to the Sabbatical river; and that river running all the week, causes the Ten Tribes to be shut up; for though on the seventh day the river rests, yet it is forbidden by our Law to take a journey then; and for that reason they remained miraculously as lost and concealed from us. So that of Isaiah 49: 9, 'that they say to the prisoners go forth' is interpreted of them in *Yalkut*.[140] Rabbi Akiba explains after the same manner that of Leviticus 26: 38, 'and ye shall perish among the heathen'. And that of Isaiah 27: 13, 'and they shall come who were ready to perish in Assyria'. Because they are remote from the rest, therefore another Rabbi in *Bamidbar Rabba* 16 applies to them that of Isaiah 49: 12: 'Behold them who come from far';[141] that so all those authors mention that river.

The testimony of Josephus (*Wars of the Jews* VII, ch. 5)[142] is famous for saying that the Emperor Titus passing between Arca and Raphanea, cities of King Agrippa, saw the wonderful river, which though it be swift, yet is dry on every seventh day; and that day being past, it resumes its ordinary course, as if it had no change; and always

---

[138] As with Rabbi Johanan, the Latin text omits Rabbi Akiva's martyrdom, which is noted in the Spanish version.

[139] This interpretation is not found in the *Midrash Rabbah* on the Song of Solomon 1: 16, that is para. 22. It refers, in fact, to the *Yalkut* on the Song, para. 985; see Moses David Gross, *Osar ha-Aggadah*, II, Jerusalem, 1974, p. 847.

[140] Simeon ha Darshan, *Yalqut ha-niqra Sime'oni*, Venice, 1515. See also *Midrash Rabbah* on Numbers 16:15, Warsaw edn., 1923, p. 163, and M. D. Gross, II, p. 847. Menasseh refers by mistake to Leviticus 36: 38, the text has been corrected.

[141] Reference given above, n. 136.

[142] The author mistakenly refers to ch. 24. Bk. VII has only eleven chapters.

observes this order. It is called Sabbatical, from the solemn feast of the Jews because it imitates their rest every seventh day. I know some otherwise expound those words of Josephus but they hit not his meaning, as appears by this, that he calls the river, Sabbathio or Sabbatical: which word cannot be derived but from Sabbath; and who does not see that it ceases to flow, or move, on the Sabbath day; and so Josephus must be understood according to my sense.

Pliny (*Nat. Hist.* XXXI, c.2, 18) also confirms this opinion; he says: 'In Judea a river lies dry every Sabbath.' Yet I think Pliny is deceived and ill-informed, when he says it is a river in Judea; neither is it to be found in Judea but in another place, where many Jews live.

Rabbi Solomon Jarchi [Rashi], who lived 540[143] years since, mentions that river in his Talmud commentary saying, the stones and sand of the river do continually move all the six days of the week, until the seventh.

Rabbi Samuel Jaffe in his learned book *Yefeh Toar* says the Arabians derive Sabbathion from the Sabbath, who used to add the particle '-ion' to adjectives.[144] The same says[145] that it was told him of an hour-glass filled with the sand of Sabbathion, which ran all the week till the Sabbath. And I heard the same from my father; which testimony I account as good as if I saw it myself (for fathers do not use to impose on their sons). He told me that there was an Arabian at Lisbon, who had such an hour-glass; and that every Friday at evening he would walk in the street called the new street (rua Nova) and show this glass to Jews who counterfeited Christianity and say, 'Ye Jews, shut up your shops for now the Sabbath comes.' Another worthy of credit told me of another hour-glass, which he had some years before, before the port Mysketa [the door of a mosque in

---

[143] This refers, in fact, to Rabbi Solomon ben Isaac of Troyes (1040–1105), in the text improperly surnamed Yarḥi (which means from Lunel, in Hérault). In the Latin version Menasseh does not repeat the error of the Spanish edition in which he has Rashi still alive in 1149. The text quoted, 'A river of stones which runs ceaselessly every day of the week, and stops and rests on the Sabbath', is the commentary of *Sanhedrin* 65 b.

[144] By mistake the author writes 'R. Mardochus Japhe'. It should be Samuel ben Isaac Jaffe Ashkenazi, *Yefeh-Toar, Comment. in Midrash Rabbah*, Venice, 1597–1601, I, fo. 76, right-hand col. See Meir Benayahu, 'The Funeral Oration for R. Samuel Yafeh by his son R. Isaac' in *Kobez al Yad: Minora Manuscripta Hebraica*, viii (xviii), Jerusalem, 1975, pp. 433–49 (in Hebrew).

[145] We have not found this reference. Rabbi Aaron Rothkoff in the article 'Sambatyon', *Enc. Jud.*, 14: 764, attributes the origin of the story to Menasseh ben Israel himself, no doubt basing this on this passage in the *Esperança de Israel*.

Aleppo].[146] The cadi, or judge of that place, saw him by chance passing that way, and asked him what it was. He commanded it to be taken away, rebuking the Mohammedans that by this they did confirm the Jewish sabbath. I should not speak of these glasses if the authority of such a man whom I have alleged did not move me; though I believe that God did not only work that miracle, that might keep part of the Ten Tribes there but others also as you may see in Ezra.

Rabbi Moses of Gerona [Nachmanides], a learned Cabbalist and interpreter of the Law, in parashah Haazinu [Deut. 32: 2] thinks the river Sabbathion to be the same with Gozan,[147] of *Guz*, which signifies to snatch away, because, except the seventh day, on all others, it carries with it by its swiftness the very stones. Of this there is mention in II Kings 17: 6, whither the King of Assyria led his captives; and so relates Benjamin of Tudela in his journal, that part of the Ten Tribes dwelt at the bank of the river.[148] But I know not where the river Gozan is.

In the year 5394, that is fifteen years ago, in the city Lublin, two Poles, after they had travelled long, wrote in [German][149] a book of the original of the Sabbatical river, but the Senate commanded it to be burnt at the mart of Warsaw,[150] by the persuasion of the Jesuits.

---

[146] The original text gives 'before the port Mysketa', an inaccurate translation of the Latin 'ante portam Mysketae'. It seems that the English translator had not understood the passage, which we have corrected in the text. The exact location is given in the Spanish version, 'a la puerta de una mezquita en Halepo'. Moreover, for this passage, the Spanish text refers, as the authority, to Rabbi 'Meyr Rophe' (Meir bar Hiyya Rofe) a Palestinian rabbi known for the tours of Europe he made as an emissary from the Holy Land on behalf of the community of Hebron. His father was a very learned rabbi from Safed. It was from a letter signed by him, and by Rabbi Joseph Salom of Jerusalem, that the Amsterdam community learnt in 1666 that the Messiah had appeared in the person of Shabbetai Zevi (see David Franco Mendés, *Memorias do estabelecimento e progresso dos Judeos Portuguezes e Espanhoes* . . . , p. 65). What is known of this rabbi (see Abraham Yaari, *Emissaries of the Holy Land*, Jerusalem², 1977, pp. 39, 160, 463, 464, 466, 480, 481 (in Hebrew)) does not suggest a stay in Amsterdam before 1649, so our author is the first to mention a visit to Europe by this Palestinian rabbi. Some of Meyr Rophe's letters have recently been published, see I. Tishby, 'Letters from Rabbi Meir Rophe to Rabbi Abraham Rovigo' in *Sefer ha-Yovel li-Shnéur Zalman*, Jerusalem, 1960, pp. 71–130 (in Hebrew).
[147] Moses ben Nahman, *Commentary on the Pentateuch*, edited by Chavel, Jerusalem, 1973 (in Hebrew).
[148] *Itinerarium D. Beniaminis* . . . , pp. 97–8.
[149] The translator has mistakenly rendered 'germanice' as 'Dutch'. We have corrected this.
[150] Moses Wall translates 'Werslavia' as 'Breslau'. We have corrected this. Abraham Mendel Mohr (A. M. M., fo. 19 b, see J. Zedner, *Catalogue of the Hebrew Books in the Library of the British Museum*, London, p. 558), in the additional material on the Hebrew

Abraham Farissol in his *Orhot Olam* c.24 will have this river to be in
India; he says, 'the head of the Sabbatical river is in the country of
Upper India, among the rivers of the Ganges'. And a little after:
'The Sabbatical river has its original from the other side of Calicut
(which lies far above the bound of Lamik,[151] which he places beyond
the *Sinus Barbaricus*) and it parts the Indians from the kingdom of
the Jews, which river you may certainly find there.'[152] Though he
takes Gozan for Ganges, for some nearness of writing,[153] yet it is not
to be doubted that in that place there are many Jews, witness João de
Barros in his *Decades*.[154] Eldad the Danite speaking of the four
tribes, which he places at Gozan, says, 'the Sabbatical river is among
them.'[155] Josephus says that Titus saw the Sabbathion between Arca
and Rephanea.[156] Which testimony seems to be true because it is
not to be thought that Josephus would tell a lie of him, by whom he
might be rebuked.

I think that you must look for it not far from the Caspian Sea; and I
am not alone in this opinion. Whatever it be it appears that this river
is somewhere, and that part of the Ten Tribes are hid there; and I

---

edition of the *Hope of Israel* he gave Lemberg in 1847, states that the reference is to *Gelilot
Eretz Israel, Regiones Terrae Israel* by Gershon ben Eliezer of Prague. There is no known
copy of the Lublin edition. New editions appeared at Furth in 1691 and Amsterdam in
1705, followed by translations. On this work see M. Steinschneider, *Catalogus librorum
hebraeorum in Bibliotheca Bodleiana*, col. 1011. The burnt book must have been printed
fifteen years before 1649, i.e. in 1634. Hebrew text in J. D. Eisenstein, *Ozar Massaoth . . . ,*
Tel Aviv, 1969², pp. 175–88. There is an edition of this work, with a Hebrew translation,
provided by Isaac Ben-Zvi and Gershon b. Eliezer Segal, *Gelilot Eretz Israel*, Jerusalem,
1953.

[151] Arias Montanus, in his notes on the *Itinerarium Beniamini Tudelensis*, Antwerp,
1575, p. 208, gives a lengthy commentary on the Sabbath river, saying: ' . . . Abraham
Peritsol c. 24 *Orchot Olam* situm fluminis Sabbationis plenius describit et in India quaerit.
Inter alia scribens: origo fluminis Sabbationis in regionibus Indiae istius superioris inter
flumina Gangis, et postea: Fluminis Sabbationis origo est supra Kalikout (Kalikout longe
supra terminum Lamiki, quem ultra Sinum Barbaricum locat) et distinctionem facit inter
Indos istos et regni Iudaeorum terminum: ibi illud flumen certissime invenies.' Lamik is a
corruption of Lameri or Jameri, indicated on some late sixteenth-century maps as being in
the north-west of the Bay of Bengal, south-west of Calcutta. It is the name both of a people
and a region.

[152] Abraham ben Mordecai Farissol, or Peritsol, *Iggeret 'Orchot Olam*, Ferrara, 1525,
Latin translation *Compendium Viarum Saeculi i. mundi*, Paris, 1601, pp. 123–4: 'inter
fluenta Gangis qui est lingua nostra Gozen sicut dictum illius'. Chapter 26 is mistakenly
given in the English text; we have corrected this.

[153] In Hebrew characters the two names have very similar spellings: נחן and גנגו .

[154] See Cidade edn., Lisbon, 1945, ch. 1, p. 352, and ch. 3, p. 373. We are grateful to
Jean Aubin for these references.

[155] See above n. 119.

[156] *The Works of Flavius Josephus, Wars*, VII, 5: 1.

may say with Moses in Deut. 29: 27–8: 'And the Lord cast them out of their Land in anger and in wrath; secret things belong to the Lord our God.' For it is not known when they shall return to their country; neither can it be perfectly shown where they are, God suffering it, as it is said in Deut. 32: 26: 'I determined to cast them forth unto the ends of the earth, and to make their remembrance cease from among men.' As if he should say, I will cast them out unto the furthest places of the earth that none may remember them; and therefore they are truly in Scripture called 'imprisoned' and 'lost'.

21. Neither is there weight in the argument which some have brought to me: if they be in the world, why do we not know them better? There are many things which we know, and yet know not their original; are we not to this day ignorant of the heads of the four rivers, Nile, Ganges, Euphrates, Tigris? Also there are many unknown countries. Besides, though some live in known and neighbour countries, yet they are unknown by being behind mountains. So it happened that, under the reign of Ferdinand and Isabella, some Spaniards were found out by accident at Batuecas,[157] belonging to the Duke of Alba, which place is distant but ten miles from Salamanca and near to Placencia, whither some Spaniards fled, when the Moors possessed Spain and dwelt there 800 years. If therefore a people could lie hid so long in the middle of Spain, why may we not say that those are hid, whom God will not have any perfectly to know before the end of days?

And these things we have gathered concerning the habitations of the Ten Tribes who, we believe,[158] do still keep the Jewish rites as in II Kings 17: 26 [–41] when the Israelites were carried captive by Shalmaneser, and those of Cutah came in their stead. An Israelitish priest was sent by the king to teach them, because lions infested them, for they were ignorant there was another worship used in the land; but when the priest saw that it was impossible to take that

---

[157] This is the name of a people and of a dry, wild region of the province of Salamanca, and not a particular place as the text implies. The Latin version, ' . . . invenirentur Batuecae Ducis Albae', is perfectly clear. It should be corrected to 'some Spaniards were found out by accident: the Batuecas belonging to the Duke of Alba'. Well into the sixteenth century these people were still not known to the royal authorities. On this group of people, who must have led a hidden life in a wild part of Spain, see Alonso Sánchez, *De rebus Hispaniae*, Alcalá, 1632, and the *Enciclopedia universal ilustrada europeo-americana* (Espasa Calpe), s.v.

[158] In the Spanish version Menasseh has not the slightest doubt about the ten Tribes' loyalty to their religion: 'Estos observan actualmente oy nuestra Ley divina.'

people wholly from idolatry he permitted them to worship divers gods, so that they would acknowledge one, to be the mover of all things. The same is also sufficiently proved out of all the histories which we have alleged. And our brethren do keep the law more zealously out of their land than in it, as being neither ambitious nor contentious (which has sometimes happened with the family of David) by which means they might easily err in the true religion, not acknowledge Jerusalem, and withdraw that obedience, which is due to the Lord and to his Temple.

22. We learn out of the first of Ezra (1: 5) that none of the Ten Tribes entered the Second Temple; for it is said that only some of the tribe of Judah, and some of Benjamin did return. Ezra also says the same in the first of Chronicles (5: 26),[159] that Shalmaneser carried the Ten Tribes to Hala, Habor, and Hara and to the river Gozan to this day; so that you may gather that at time they were still there. So likewise Josephus, *Antiquities* II, 5. Perhaps some will say, since Media and Persia are so near to Babylon, why did they not return to Jerusalem with the two tribes? I answer, because so few of the two neighbouring tribes did return from thence to Jerusalem, for they were well seated in Babylon; or else because they heard the Prophets say that they must not look for any redemption but that which was to be at the end of days.[160] How then can we think that they who were more remote, and also had learnt the same things of the prophets, should leave their place, perhaps to suffer new miseries and calamities? Besides, we do not read that Cyrus gave leave to any to return but only to the two tribes of Judah and Benjamin. And also it is probable (as some authors affirm) that they could not go up thence, because they had continually wars with the neighbour people.

26. Hitherto we have shown that the Ten Tribes are in divers places, as in the Western Indies, in China, in the confines of Tartary beyond the river Sabbathion, and Euphrates, in Media, in the kingdom of the Abyssinians; of all which the prophet Isaiah 11: 11 is to be understood: 'It shall come to pass in that day, that the Lord shall set

---

159 A *baraita* attributes the authorship of Chronicles to Ezra, see *Berakhot* 15 a. The critics estimate that the Book must have been written during the fourth century BC.

160 Jewish tradition maintains that the promises in the Books of the Prophets were not fulfilled by the return from the Captivity in Babylon. This question has been considered by Gerson D. Cohen in his edition, with English translation and notes, of *The Book of Tradition (Sefer ha-Qabbalah) by Abraham Ibn Daud*, London (Littman Library), 1969, pp. xxxv–xl.

his hand the second time to recover the remnant of his people, which shall be left from Assyria, from Egypt, from Pathros, from Ethiopia [Cush], from Elam, from Shinar, from Hamath, and from the islands of the sea.'[161] From which you may gather that it is meant of those places where the Ten Tribes dwell. Syria and Ethiopia shall be the two places of their general meeting, as more fully hereafter.

Pathros is not Pelusium, nor Petra, but Parthia, near to the Caspian Sea, where I think, with many others the Sabbatical river is. Although there is a Pathros in Egypt, as the learned Samuel Bochart says in his *Sacred Geography*.[162]

Cush, according to common opinion, is Ethiopia as is proved out of Jeremiah 13: 23; and in this place of Jeremiah[163] are meant the Israelites who live in the country of the Abyssinians.[164]

Elam is a province in Persia, as it appears in Daniel 8: 2 where are desert places in which perhaps the remnant of the Ten Tribes is.

Shinar is a province about Babylon, as in Genesis 10: 10 where Babel is said to be in Shinar; and in Daniel 1: 2 it is said that Nebuchadnezzar carried the holy vessels to the land of Shinar.

Hamath: there are many Hamaths mentioned in Scripture; many understand it of Antioch; but because geographers reckon up twelve places named Antioch, therefore we can affirm nothing for certain; but I think that that is meant, which is placed in Scythia. The Septuagint by Hamath understands the sun, from Hama, the sun; and they translate it 'from the rising of the sun'; and I think it no ill translation, for hereby all the Israelites who are in Greater Asia, India and China may be understood.

The islands of the Sea: so almost all translate it; but I think it is to be rendered the islands of the West, for *Yam* in holy scripture signifies the west, as in Genesis 28: 14 and in many other places; and upon this account those Israelites are implied, who are westward from the Holy Land, among whom the Americans are.

---

[161] The Spanish version gives 'las islas de Occidente'. In this Menasseh is adopting one of the meanings of the word *yam*, the West, which supports his theory about the spread of the diaspora to the New World. The Latin version and its English translation did not appreciate this variant contributed by our rabbi. This makes the point a good deal less clear in the Latin and English versions.

[162] Caen, 1646, bk. IV, ch. 27.

[163] In the Spanish version Jeremiah is replaced by Isaiah. We note that the reference is to Isaiah 20: 4.

[164] This is Menasseh ben Israel's own interpretation. Our rabbi is alluding to the Falashas.

24. The prophet adds in Isaiah 11:12: 'And he shall set up a sign for the nations, and he shall assemble the outcasts of Israel, and gather together the dispersed of Judah from the four quarters of the earth.' Where he notes two things: one, that he calls the Israelites outcasts but the Jews scattered;[165] and the reason is, because the Ten Tribes are not only far off from the Holy Land but also they live in the extremities and ends of countries; from whence the prophet calls them cast-out. But he does not say that the Israelites are to be gathered from the four quarters of the earth, because they are not so dispersed through the world, as the tribe of Judah is, which now has synagogues not only in three parts of the world, but also in America.[166] The prophet adds in v.13, 'the envy also of Ephraim shall depart, and the adversaries of Judah shall be cut off'. For then there shall be no contention between Judah and the Ten Tribes, which are comprehended under the name Ephraim, because their first king Jeroboam was of that tribe. And then, as it is in Ezekiel 37:22, 'One king shall be king over them all, and they shall be no more nations, neither shall they be divided any more into two kingdoms.' There shall be one king to them both, of the family of David. Also the Lord at that redemption will dry up the Nile, and Euphrates, and will divide it into seven streams (answerable to his drying up the Red Sea when they came out of Egypt), perhaps that the seven tribes which are in those parts may go over it; as they pass into their country, as Isaiah 27:12 says: 'And it shall be in that day, and he shall shake off from the bank of the river (some understand Euphrates) unto the river of Egypt (the Nile) and ye, O children of Israel, shall be gathered one by one', which was never done in the captivity of Babylon.

The prophet Isaiah 11:11 says 'that He will return them the second time.' Now the redemption from Babylon cannot be called such a one, because all of them were not brought back to their country. But the redemption shall be universal to all the Tribes, as it

---

165 The text distinguishes between the *nefussim* of Judah and the *nidahim* of Israel. The first root only appears in the Bible in the feminine form *nefusot* (Isaiah 11:12).

166 The American Jewish communities mentioned by Menasseh ben Israel are probably those in Dutch Brazil which had been in existence since 1630 and had, in 1641, sought the services of Isaac Aboab de Fonseca, the New World's first rabbi. It is likely that the Jewish community of Surinam in Dutch Guiana had a religious establishment from 1643, see Jacob R. Marcus, *The Colonial American Jew 1492–1776*, pp. 78 and 163. There were still groups of New Christians in the Spanish and Portuguese possessions, some of whom practised Judaism clandestinely.

was when they went out of Egypt, which redemption shall be like the first in many things, as I showed in the third part of my *Conciliador*,[167] and so it may be called the second, in reference to that first from Egypt. Whence Jeremiah (23: 7, 8) says that 'then it shall not be said: He that brought Israel out of Egypt but from the North, and from all countries whither He had driven them.' That they shall not mention their departure from Babylonia[168] for the cause fore-mentioned.

25. The same prophet, Isaiah 43: 5–7, says: 'I will bring thy seed from the East and will gather thee from the West. I will say to the North, give up; and to the South, keep not back; bring my sons from afar, and my daughters from the ends of the earth.' For Media, Persia and China lie on the East; Tartary and Scythia on the North; the kingdom of the Abyssinians on the South; Europe on the West, from the Holy Land. But when he says, 'bring ye my sons from afar', he understands America; so that in those verses he understands all those places in which the Tribes are detained. Also in Chapter 49, from verse 7 to the end of the chapter, he said that the return shall be most happy. And in 56: 8, God says: 'He that gathers the outcasts of Israel' and the prophet Jeremiah 33: 16: 'In those days shall Judah he saved and Jerusalem shall dwell safely.' It is certain, and Jerome[169] assents to all our authors, that when Judah is joined with Israel, by Israel the Ten Tribes are meant. The same adds in 31: 15, in the comforting of Rachel, who wept for the carrying away of her sons Joseph and Benjamin, the first by Shalmaneser into Assyria, the last by Nebuchadnezzar into Babylon, and says in verse 16: 'Refrain thy voice from weeping and thine eyes from tears, for thy work shall be rewarded.' And it follows in 33: 7: 'And I will cause the captivity of Judah and the captivity of Israel to return, and I will build them up as at the first.' Ezekiel says the same in 34: 13 and 37: 16[–19] under the figure of two sticks on which were written the names of Judah and Ephraim, by which he proves the gathering of the twelve tribes to be subject to Messiah, the son of David; in 37: 22[–24] he says: 'and one king shall be king to them all.' According, as

---

[167] *Tercera parte del Conciliador*, Amsterdam, 5410 (1649–50), question vi, pp. 22–4. If the author is really referring to the printed edition and not the manuscript of his *magnum opus*, and since the Jewish year 5410 began on 7 Sept. 1649, this volume probably came out during the last quarter of 1649, while the *Hope of Israel* was being written.

[168] It is not known why Moses Wall chose to translate 'ex Babilonia' as 'from Egypt'. We have amended the text in line with the Latin and Spanish versions.

[169] *Comm. in Isaiam*, Migne, *Patrologia Latina*, xxiv, 1865, p. 80.

Hosea says in chapter 2, so also says Amos 9: 14–15: 'and I will bring again the captivity of my people Israel, and they shall build the waste cities, and inhabit them; and they shall plant vineyards and drink the wine thereof; they shall make gardens and eat the fruit of them. And they shall be no more pulled up out of their Land, which I have given them, saith the Lord thy God.' So also Micah 2: 12: 'I will surely assemble, O Jacob, all of thee, I will gather the remnant of Israel, I will also place him as the flock in the sheepfold.' For that in the captivity of Babylon all were not gathered together. The prophet Zechariah 8: 7 and 10: 6 and all the rest of the prophets witness the same thing.

26. But which way that redemption shall be, no man can tell; but only so far as we may gather out of the prophets. That at that time the Ten Tribes shall come to Jerusalem under the leading of a Prince, whom some rabbis in the Talmud, and in some place of the Aramaic paraphrase, call Messiah the son of Joseph, and elsewhere Messiah the son of Ephraim; who, being slain in the last war of Gog and Magog,[170] Messiah shall show himself to be the son of David, who shall be as Ezekiel [37: 24] and Hosea [3: 5] say, 'the everlasting prince of the Twelve Tribes'.[171]

Our wise men in many places, especially in the Babylonian Talmud (*Sukkah* c.5 [52b]), make mention of that Messiah the son Ephraim; where they say that he shall die in the last war of Gog and Magog; and they so expound Zechariah 12: 10: 'And they shall look upon me whom they have pierced, and they shall mourn for him, as one mourneth for his only son.' They add also that the four captains,[172] of whom the same prophet speaks (2: [3]), are Messiah the son of David, Messiah the son of Joseph, the prophet Elijah and the high priest; which four are those dignities which shall show their power in that blessed age.

Observe that sometimes they call Messiah the son of Ephraim, sometimes of Joseph; for he shall come out of the tribe of Ephraim, and shall be captain of all the Ten Tribes, who gave their name to

---

[170] The Messiah, son of Joseph or of Ephraim, is to die fighting the enemies of God and Israel, see *Sukkah* 52 a, and *Targum* Cant. 4: 5.

[171] The many traditions about the apocalyptic war of Gog and Magog, which is supposed to precede the glorious reign of the Messiah, the son of David, are mentioned in various contradictory texts, see the article 'Gog and Magog' in *Enc. Jud.* 7: 691–3.

[172] This should be understood as 'master-smiths', the builders of the Messianic temple. On all these matters, see Gershom Scholem's classic work, *The Messianic Idea in Judaism*, New York, 1971.

Ephraim, because their first king Jeroboam was of that tribe. Not without cause do they call him the son of Joseph, for he was the true type of the house of Israel, in his imprisonment and future happiness. Add to this, that he was so long hid from his brethren that they did not know him: as in like manner the Ten Tribes are at this day, who are led captive but hereafter shall come to the top of felicity, in the same manner as Joseph did.

That Messiah of Joseph shall die in the battle of Gog and Magog, and afterwards shall rise again, that he may enjoy the dignity, not of a kingly sceptre, but the office only of a viceroy as Joseph in Egypt; for that the empire of the House of Israel fell under the reign of Hosea the son of Elah, as the prophet Amos 5: 2 says.[173] Therefore the kingdom of the Ten Tribes shall not be restored, as Ezekiel (37: [24]) says, under the reign of Messiah the son of David, who shall be everlasting; and by the death of Messiah the son of Joseph the Ten Tribes shall see, that God will not that they should have more kings than one, as it is already spoken.

27. Those tribes then shall be gathered from all quarters of the earth into countries near the Holy Land; namely into Assyria and Egypt; and thence they shall go into their country of which Isaiah 27: 13 speaks: 'And it shall be in that day, that the great trumpet[174] shall be blown, and they who lost, shall come into the land of Assyria; and they who were cast out into Egypt; and shall worship the Lord in the holy mount of Jerusalem.' As if he should say, as trumpets sound, to call an army together: so shall they come together who were dead (that is, dispersed through all Asia) into Assyria; and the outcasts (that is, which are in America) shall come by the Mediterranean Sea to Alexandria of Egypt; and in like manner those who are in Africa, when the Nile shall be dried up and Euphrates shall be divided, as we have already said. And because the gathering together of the captivity shall begin at those who are in America, therefore Isaiah [60: 9] says: 'The islands shall trust in me, and the ships of Tarshish (that is, of the ocean) first of all, that they may bring their sons from

[173] The writer bases this on David Kimhi's commentary: 'The monarchy of the House of Jehu at the death of Jeroboam, the son of Joash', and on that of Rashi: 'From the exile [of Israel] to the time of Hoshea, the son of Elah, there will be no more kings from out of the Ten Tribes'.

[174] The Spanish version, meant for a Jewish public, retains the Hebrew 'shofar', the ram's horn which is blown in serious situations and at the close of the Day of Atonement (Kippur), 'aquel dia sera tañido con Sophar grande'.

far; and, with them, their silver and gold.' They shall then come with speed from those countries, prostrating themselves at the mountain of the Lord in Jerusalem, as the prophet Hosea 11:11 says of that redemption: 'They shall come as birds out of Egypt and as doves out of Assyria.' So says Isaiah 60:8: 'Who are those who fly as a cloud, and as doves to their nest?' They which come first shall also partake of this joy, to see others come to them every moment; for which cause the prophet says [60:4]: 'Lift up thine eyes round about and behold them who gather themselves to thee.'

And because the two countries of Assyria and Egypt shall first of all kindly receive the people of Israel, and shall know the truth, first of all embracing the religion of the Jews, sacrificing and praying to God, therefore the prophet Isaiah (19:25) says: 'Blessed be Egypt, my people, and Assyria, the work of my hands; but Israel is my inheritance.' For so those words are to be understood.

All those are the sayings of the holy prophets, whence does appear the return of Israel into their country. It is given to none to know the time thereof, neither is it revealed to Rabbi Simeon bar Yohai, the author of the *Zohar*,[175] because God has reserved that mystery to himself, as Moses [Deut. 32:34] says: 'It is hid with me'; and Isaiah (63:4): 'For the day of vengeance is in my heart, and the year in which the redemption shall come.' Which the Rabbis [*Sanh.* 99a] thus interpret: 'I have revealed it to my heart and not to angels'; and elsewhere: 'If any man tell you when Messiah shall come, believe him not.' So also the angel says to Daniel [12.9]: 'All things are closed up and sealed to the time of the end.' Therefore all those who search after that time, as rabbis Saadiah, Maimonides, Nachmanides, Rashi, Abraham bar Hiyya, Abraham Zacuto, Mordecai Reato [Dato] and Isaac Abarbanel, have been mistaken;[176] for they would

---

[175] Traditionally attributed to Rabbi Simeon bar Yohai (second century), the Zohar is a mystical commentary on the Scriptures which appeared in Spain in the thirteenth century. Its real author must have been Moses de Leon (*c.*1240—1305).

[176] Saadiah Gaon (882–942) put the coming of the Messiah in 964, Maimonides (1135–1204) in 1216, Moses of Gerona, that is to say Nahmanides (1194–*c.*1270) in the course of the sixth millennium without giving an actual date, see Julius H. Greenstone, *The Messiah Idea in Jewish History*, Philadelphia, 1906, pp. 133, 150, 168. We have not found the date suggested by Rashi. For Abraham bar Hiyya (Al-Bargeloni) (1065–1136), the event was to take place about 1140, see B. Z. Dinur, *A Documentary History of the Jewish People from its Beginning to the Present*, Second Series, *Israel in the Diaspora*, vol. ii, bk. 3, Tel Aviv, 1968 [in Hebrew], p. 369. In the case of the famous Abraham ben Samuel Zacuto (1452–*c.*1515), a manuscript of uncertain attribution gives 1524 as the year of the Messiah's coming, see art. 'Zacuto Abraham ben Samuel' in *Enc. Jud.* 16:906. For

go beyond human capacity and reveal that which God concealed. And even to Daniel himself (to whom was made known the secret of the change of the Four Monarchies) it was so revealed to him that he confessed he did not understand it. Our ancients[177] did point at this from the letter 'm' [mem] in Isaiah (9:6), where he says 'of the increase of his government:' which *mem* in the Hebrew being such a *mem* as they[178] wrote only in the end of words [final *mem*], and a close letter, yet is put in the middle of a word, against common practice:[179] because the time of the Fifth Monarchy shall be hid, till the time when it shall begin.

29. Yet this I can affirm, that it shall be about the end of this age; and so the prophet speaks of that age about the end of days; and that after many labours and a long captivity. So Balaam (Numbers 24:17) prophesies: 'I see but not now; I behold but not near; a star shall come out of Jacob.' Isaiah 24:22: 'They shall be cast into prison, and they shall be visited after many days.' And Isaiah 49:14: 'And Zion said, the Lord hath forsaken me and my Lord has forgotten me.' Hosea (3:4, 5): 'The children of Israel shall be many days without a king and without a prince. . . . and after that they shall seek the Lord their God and David their king.' The king and prophet (David) complains of that delay in Psalms 44, 69, 74, 77, 83.[180] And after that, in Ps. 89:50, 51, he thus concludes: 'Remember O God, the reproach of thy servants, who suffer so many injuries of so many people . . . wherewith they have reproached the steps of thy Messiah.'[181] And yet at this day it is said that although the Messiah were lame, he might have come by this time.

Mordecai Dato (and not Reato as printed in all editions and versions of the *Hope of Israel*: the error was the author's or that of his first printer), see David Tamar, 'The Messianic expectation in Italy for the year 5335 (i.e. 1575)' in *Sefunot*, 2, 1958, pp. 66–70 (in Hebrew), and R. Bonfil, 'Una predica in volgare di Rabbi Mordekhai Dato' in *Italia, Studi e ricerche sulla cultura e sulla letteratura degli Ebrei d'Italia*, vol. i, no. 1, 1976, pp. i–xxxii. According to Isaac Abrabanel (1437–1509), the Messiah would come in 1503, see J. H. Greenstone, p. 168.

[177] Sanhedrin 94 a.

[178] The original English has 'as they write'. This is an example of a slip of the pen by a non-Jewish translator. The Latin 'ponitur' should be rendered by 'as we write' or 'as it is written'.

[179] The final form of the Hebrew consonant מ *mem* that is used here in the middle of a word.

[180] When the author speaks of the Psalmist, he means King David. However Psalm 44 is attributed to the sons of Korah; Psalm 74 is by Asaph, as well as Psalms 77 and 83.

[181] Psalm 89 is attributed to Ethan the Ezrahite.

Though we cannot exactly show the time of our redemption, yet we judge it to be near. For (1) we see many prophecies fulfilled, and others also which are subservient to a preparation for the same redemption; and it appears by this, that during that long and sore captivity, many calamities are foretold us under the Four Monarchies.[182] David says in Ps. 120: 7: 'Lord, when I speak of peace, they speak of war.' And elsewhere [Ps. 44: 23]: 'We are slain all the day for Thy name and are accounted for sheep which are slain.' In Isaiah 53: 7: 'He shall be led as a sheep to the slaughter and as a lamb before his shearers; he shall be dumb and shall not open his mouth.' O, how have we seen these things in the banishments of England, France and Spain![183] And how have they proved those crimes, which most false men have said that ours did commit! Behold they have slain them, not for wickednesses, which they did not commit, but for their riches which they had. O, how have we seen all those things done by divine providence, for those misfortunes for the most part happened on the ninth day of the month Ab, an ominous and unhappy day, on which the First and Second Temple were burnt, and the spies wept without a cause.[184]

30. What shall we say of that horrible monster,[185] the Spanish Inquisition, what cruelty has not daily been used against a company of miserable ones, innocents, old men and children, of every sex and age, who were slain, because they could not divine who was their secret accuser?[186] But let us see why in all those places (in which that

[182] The reference is to the four Empires foretold by Daniel 7: 1–26; the fifth Empire will be the Messiah's, Daniel 7: 27.

[183] The expulsion of the Jews from England (1290), from France (1306 and 1394), and Spain (1492).

[184] In fact the destruction of the First Temple (586 BC) is commemorated by the fast of 7 Av, that of the Second Temple (AD 70) took place on 10 Av. For these dates see 2 Kings 25: 8, Jeremiah 52: 12, Josephus, *Wars* VI, 4: 5, *Ta'anit* 29 a. Following the edict pronouncing their expulsion from Spain (31 Mar. 1492), the last Jews left the country on 13 July, that is 7 Av, see Y. Baer, *A History of the Jews in Christian Spain*, vol. ii, Philadelphia, 1971, p. 439. In giving the date of the event as 9 Av, Menasseh ben Israel follows a legend substantiated by Isaac Abrabanel, according to which all the Jews left Spain 'on the same day, 9 Av', see Y. Baer, ii, n. 14, pp. 511–12. The spies sent to the land of Canaan by Moses gave a pessimistic report which caused consternation among the Hebrews, see Numbers 13: 27–33 and 14: 1–14. It was the people who wept and not the spies. A day of mourning was observed for this reason: 'On 9 Av it was decreed that our ancestors would not enter the Holy Land', Mishna, *Ta'anit*, 4: 6. So 9 Av remains a day of fasting and mourning in the Jewish calendar.

[185] This is the 'fourth beast' of Daniel 7: 7 and 19.

[186] In the Spanish version, meant for an 'informed' public, Menasseh uses the word 'diminutos', a technical term of the Inquisition: it describes an accused who does not relate

Spanish tyrannical empire rules) they were slain, who would observe the law of Moses; and by how many, and how great, miracles has that law been confirmed; and what unrighteousness is there in it? We daily see examples of constancy in ours, worthy of all praise, who, for the sanctifying of God's name,[187] have been burnt alive. Truly many who are still living can witness all those things. In the year 1603 at Lisbon, Diogo da Asunção, a monk of 24, was burnt alive, who defended himself in the Inquisition against some, who would have reduced him to Christianity who was born a Christian and made a Jew: which all wonder at; the Inquisitors being grieved that they had published the reasons which he had alleged, would have recalled their sentence; but it was then too late, for it was divulged through the world, which I myself have by me.[188]

Also Don Lope de Vera y Alarcón deserves the praise of martyrdom, who being born of a noble and eminent family, and very learned in the Hebrew and Latin tongues, did embrace our religion; neither thought it sufficient to be such himself but discovered himself to many others; thereupon in the year 1644, in the twentieth of his age, he being imprisoned at Valladolid, though he lived in the dark, yet he discovered light to many; neither could the great number of Doctors, nor the greater affliction of his parents, move him from his enterprise, either by tears or promises. He circumcised himself in prison (O strange act and worthy of all praise!) and named himself believing Judah; and, at last, as a second Isaac, offered himself to the flames; contemning life, goods and honours, that he might obtain immortal life and good things that cannot perish, in the 25th year of his age.[189]

his 'Judaizing' faults accurately and completely, and who does not denounce *all his accomplices*, see I. S. Révah, 'Les Marranes', p. 43.

[187] The Hebrew *kiddush ha-Shem*, lit. Sanctification of the Divine Name, marks out the martyr.

[188] A Franciscan, born at Viana de Caminha in 1579, Frei Diogo de Asunção was only partly of Old Christian ancestry. He was convinced of the truth of the Law of Moses, and was burned alive at Lisbon on 3 Aug. 1603. The arguments he advanced against Christianity were actually published by the Holy Office and circulated among Portuguese and foreign Marranos, see C. Roth, *A History of the Marranos*, pp. 149–51 and 153.

[189] There is an extensive literature on this figure, from the years after his martyrdom onward, see C. Roth, *A History . . .*, pp. 155–7. This historian also attributes to the martyr himself a moving poem, which he has published under the title 'Le chant du cygne de Don Lope de Vera' in *REJ*, xcvii, 1934, pp. 97–113. Prof. I. S. Révah considers this poem to be the work of the Marrano writer, Antonio Enríquez Gómez, and has undertaken the preparation of a critical edition of the text, see *Annuaire de l'École Pratique des Hautes Études, IVᵉ section, 1966–7*, Paris, 1967, pp. 338–41. Without any mention of this work, Timothy

Now though those were not of the family of Israel, yet they obtained an immortal glory, which is better than this life. Also we have many examples of our own, which did equalize them, of which that is one, which is done in our time, and is worthy to be remembered. Isaac de Castro Tartas (whom I knew and spoke with) a learned young man, and versed in Greek and Latin; he being but newly come to Pernambuco, was taken by the Portuguese, and carried to Lisbon and burnt alive.[190] He was a young man of 24 years old; scorning riches and honours, which were offered to him, if he would turn Christian. They, who say he was a traitor, do lie egregiously; for he did defend that place where he was governor most valiantly, as ours do deport themselves in those fortified places which are committed to their charge. The same martyrdom was undergone at Lima by Eli Nazareno, on 23 January 1639, who after he had lived 14 whole years in prison, all which time he did eat no flesh, lest he should defile his mouth;[191] he called himself by that name after he had circumcised himself.[192] Such a martyr also, this year, was Thomas Terbiño in the city of Mexico.[193]

Oelman has offered an edition of the poem under the title 'Antonio Enríquez Gómez's Romance al divín martir Juda Creyente' in the *Journal of Jewish Studies*, xxvi, 1975, pp. 113–31. On the martyr and the poem, see Antonio Enríquez Gómez, *El siglo pithagórico y vida de Don Gregorio Guadana*, critical edn. with introduction and notes by Charles Amiel, Paris, 1977, pp. xvii–xviii.

[190] Born in SW France, Isaac de Castro Tartas was engaged in the propagation of Judaism among the New Christians of Brazil. He was taken and condemned by the Inquisition. Since his exact date of birth is not known, it is reckoned that he was burnt alive in Lisbon on 15 Dec. 1647, aged about 21. See C. Roth, *A History of the Marranos*, pp. 157–8, and by Roth, 'An elegy of João Pinto Delgado on Isaac de Castro Tartas', in *REJ*, cxxi, 1962, pp. 355–66.

[191] Jews may only eat animals which have been ritually slaughtered. In their phraseology, both the martyr under discussion and the rabbi are reflecting Daniel 1: 8–16.

[192] The reference is to Francisco Maldonado de Silva, an educated man who, while in prison, took the name of Eli the Nazarene, and wrote a number of texts extolling Judaism, as well as a letter to the synagogue at Rome. These unusual items, preserved in the papers of the trial by the Inquisition, have been published, along with some of the trial records, see Lucía García de Proodian, *Los Judíos en la America, siglo XVII*, pp. 192–3 and 340–89.

[193] Tomás Treviño de Sobremonte, *alias* Geronymo Represa, born at Medina de Río Seco in Old Castille, was one of the victims of the great *auto-da-fé* which took place in Mexico on 11 Apr. 1649. The only one to refuse the offer of being strangled before being tied to the stake, he was burnt alive. The Jesuit, Mathias de Bocanegra, in telling of this famous *auto-da-fé*, devotes four pages to him, of which these are a few lines: 'He said he was a Jew and wanted to die one, and that death had seized him just as he was completing a sixty-two hour fast ... ' The complete text in an English translation may be found in Seymour B. Liebman's excellent book, *Jews and the Inquisition of Mexico: The Great Auto de fe of 1649 as related by Mathias de Bocanegra S.J.*, Lawrence, Kan., 1974, pp. 136–40, with bibliography and sources. Menasseh notes that this martyrdom took place 'this year',

31. If the Lord fulfilled his word in calamities, he will fulfil it also in felicities. Therefore Rabbi Akiba laughed, when he saw a fox run out of the Temple being destroyed, though his companions wept; he saying, 'Now is fulfilled that prophecy of Jeremiah Lamentations 5: 18: "And the foxes shall run therein";' and he added,'and those blessings also shall follow, which the Lord has promised'.[194] We see all the curses of God come to pass, which are mentioned in Leviticus [26: 14–43] and Deuteronomy [28: 15–68]; as well as those which concern our being scattered to the ends of the earth (which is Portugal)[195] and those concerning the calamities of the Inquisition; and those of our banishments, as I have opened in my book *De termino vitae*;[196] whence it appears that all the happy prophecies shall be fulfilled. As we have perished, so also shall Bozrah (that is, Rome) perish (Isaiah 34: 6).[197]

32. Secondly, the argument, which we bring from our constancy under so many evils, cannot be eluded, that therefore God reserves us for better things. Moses (Leviticus 26: 44) says: 'Though they be in the land of their enemies, yet I will not cast them away, neither will I abhor them to destroy them utterly, and to break my covenant with them, for I am the Lord their God.' And truly these things are now fulfilled, for in this captivity and among the many reproaches which we Jews suffer, yet many of ours are honourably entertained by princes with a singular affection. So Don Isaac Abarbanel, who comes of David's line, was counsellor to the king of Spain and Portugal.[198] By this also he has got a great name for he composed the differences, which arose between the king of Portugal and the republic of Venice. And from that family of Abarbanel (which I note by the by) do proceed my children, by my wife's side.[199] And in the

which proves that he wrote the *Hope of Israel* in 1649 and that the news had already reached Amsterdam. [194] *Makkot* 24 b.

[195] The reference is to Deuteronomy 28: 64. 'To the ends of the earth' is interpreted as meaning Portugal.

[196] See the introduction, p. 35.

[197] ' . . . for the Lord hath a sacrifice in Bozrah, and a great slaughter in the land of Edom'. For the reader who might have forgotten, Menasseh ben Israel, following the medieval rabbinical reading, describes Edom in parenthesis as Rome, the chief city of Catholicism. See S. Zeitlin, 'The Origin of the Application of the Term Edom for Rome and the Roman Church', in *Jewish Quarterly Review*, 60, 1970, pp. 262–3.

[198] He was a member of one of the oldest and most celebrated Spanish families. The spellings Abarbanel, Abrabanel, and Abravanel are all used.

[199] These lines about Menasseh's wife's notable ancestry are not found in the Spanish version. Presumably his co-religionists knew all about this illustrious relationship, which he wishes to make known to his non-Jewish readers.

house of his son, Don Samuel Abarbanel[200] and of his wife
Benvenida, Doña Leonora de Toledo was brought up at Naples,
who is the daughter of Don Pedro de Toledo, the viceroy of Naples;
who afterwards was married to the most eminent Duke Cosimo de
Medici, and having obtained the dukedom of Tuscany, she
honoured Benvenida with as much honour as if she were her
mother.[201]

That peace which the Venetians made with the Emperor Sultan
Selim 75 years ago was made and ratified by a Jew, Don Solomon
Rophé, who was sent ambassador to Venice and received with great
pomp by the Venetians.[202] At Constantinople, the Ben Jaeses,
Anaucas and Soncinos are of great authority with the Turk.[203] In
Egypt, the Jews were always *sarraf-bashis* and also at this day is Don
Abraham Alhulu.[204] Who knows not that Don Joseph Nasi,
otherwise João Micas, about the 66th year of the former age
[previous century][205] was Duke of Naxos, Lord of Milos and of the
seven islands,[206] of whom see Famiano Estrada, *De Bello Belgico* (I,

---

[200] Samuel Abrabanel (1473–1547) was one of the sons of Don Isaac Abrabanel, the
well-known statesman and expounder. He was the brother of Judah Abrabanel, known as
León Hebreo, whose son, Isaac, must have been the grandfather of Rachel Abrabanel
whom Menasseh married on 6 Sept. 1623, see C. Roth, *A Life of Menasseh*, pp. 35–7. The
details probably come from family tradition.

[201] Leonor de Toledo married Cosimo de Medici in 1539.

[202] Solomon ben Nathan Ashkenazi (*c*.1520–1602), physician and diplomat, completed
the negotiations between the Sublime Porte and the Venetian Senate which resulted in the
Treaty of 1573. So it was in the next year (1649–75 = 1574), in his capacity as the Sultan's
ambassador, that he was received in Venice by the Doge. See Marco Diena, 'Rabbi
Shlomo Ashkenazi e la Republica di Venezia' in *Atti dell'Istit. Veneto di Scienze, Lettere ed
Arti*, Venice, VII, vol. ix, 1897–8, pp. 616–37.

[203] Families which played an outstanding role. For the 'Ben Iaeses', see below, n. 208.
The Soncinos were a dynasty of Hebrew printers in Italy, Turkey, and Egypt in the
fifteenth and sixteenth centuries. See Abraham Meir Habermann, art. 'Soncino' in *Enc.
Jud.* 15: 140–2. Anaucas (spelt Anacavas in the Spanish version) is perhaps a form of
Ankawa, but we do not know to whom the author is alluding.

[204] The title is that of the chief banker in Egypt, see G. Scholem, *Sabbatai Sevi, the
Mystical Messiah*, Princeton, 1973, p. 178. In the Spanish version, Menasseh makes it plain
that this office is a little less important than that of Provincial Governor. The only mention
of this figure is in the Hebrew chronicle of Joseph ben Isaac Sambari, published in A.
Neubauer, *Medieval Jewish Chronicles*, Oxford, 1887, I, p. 150 (in Hebrew).

[205] A curious translation of the doubtful Latin ' . . . anno superioris seculi praeter
propter sexagesimo sexto . . .'. It should read 'around the year 66 of the previous century'.

[206] A diplomat of Portuguese Marrano descent, Joseph Nasi, *alias* João Micas, was a
leading political figure at the court of Constantinople. Suleiman the Magnificent made
him Duke of Naxos. He held the concession of Tiberias and its environs, and embarked on
the creation of a centre of Jewish colonization there (1566). Some consider his efforts to
have been a 'pre-Zionist' enterprise. See J. Reznik, *Le Duc Joseph de Naxos: Contribution à*

5).[207] He was raised to these honours by Sultan Selim. As also by Sultan Murad, Jacob Abenaes, otherwise called Alvaro Mendes, was made governor of Tiberias; witness Botero's *Relation* (III, book 2).[208] In Barbary, the Rutes family were always governors of Fez and Taradante.[209] In 1609 Don Samuel Palache was sent ambassador to the States[-General][210] by Mulay Zidan, the king of Morocco. But he died at the Hague in 1616 and the most eminent Prince Maurice and the nobles were at his funeral.[211] In Persia who knows not of what account they are? There, thirty years since, Eleazar was second to the king and, as it were, governor. Now David Jan succeeds him, to whom others being joined they live in the Court.[212] And that must not be forgot, that when the most eminent Duke of Holstein sent Otto Bruchman ambassador to Persia in 1635, he desired commendatory letters from our Jews at Hamburg to them who (as we have already told you) live there in the Court, that they would make way there for him that was a stranger, that he might dispatch his affairs, which was also performed. By which means ours, who are in Persia, dismissed Bruchman with rich gifts and letters to the most eminent Duke of Holstein which the twelve *huja*, or princes, had subsigned. A copy of which letters the most excellent Don Benjamin

---

l'histoire juive du XVIᵉ siècle, Paris, 1936, and P. Grunebaum-Ballin, *Joseph Naci duc de Naxos*, Paris–The Hague, 1968.

[207] *De Bello Belgico*, Rome, 1632, pp. 170 ff.

[208] This in fact refers to his father, Solomon Abenaes, *alias* Álvaro Mendés, who, born at Tavira in Portugal in 1520, entered the service of the Sublime Porte, was made Duke of Mytilene by Murad III, and had the concession of Tiberias and region after Don Joseph Nasi. See Abraham Galante, *Don Salomon Aben Yaèche, duc de Métélin*, Istanbul, 1936. His son, Jacob, mentioned by Menasseh ben Israel, settled in Tiberias, but paid very little attention to its administration. See Botero, *Relationi Universali*.

[209] As Julio Caro Baroja has noted in his book *Los Judíos en la España . . .*, vol. i, p. 84, in this passage Menasseh ben Israel follows Immanuel Aboab, *Nomologia o Discursos legales*, Amsterdam, 1629, who writes on p. 306: 'Los Merinos de Africa honraron grandemente a la noble familia de los Rutes que, desde et tiempo del destierro de Portugal hasta ahora, fueron Xeques de Fez y Tarudante.'

For the Rute family in Fez in the sixteenth century, see H. Z. Hirschberg, *A History of the Jews in North Africa*, Leiden, 1974, vol. i, pp. 412–13.

[210] Of the Netherlands.

[211] Samuel Palache was also the first declared Jew in the United Provinces. It was in his house in Amsterdam that the first Jewish celebration of *Yom Kippur* was held in 1596. See David Corcos, 'Samuel Palache and his London Trial', in *Zion*, XXV, 1960, pp. 122–33 (in Hebrew with English summary), reprinted in D. Corcos, *Studies in the History of the Jews of Morocco*, Jerusalem, 1976, pp. 246–57. On his death and funeral, see David Franco Mendés, *Memorias . . .*, in *Studia Rosenthaliana*, pp. 30–1.

[212] We have found nothing on these two individuals.

Mussafia, one familiar with the prince, helped me to.[213] Also
Claude Duret in his *Thrésor de l'histoire des Langues* (p. 302) says that
there are an almost infinite number of Jews in Asia, especially in
India, and that the king of Cochin is their great favourer.[214] Yea,
Linschoten says (where he treats of Cochin) that they have synagogues there, and that some of them are of the king's council.[215] At
Prague, Mordecai Meisel had arms given him by the Emperor
Matthias, who also knighted him.[216] Which honour Jacob Bassevi
also had under the reign of Ferdinand;[217] and many other families
are graced with other honours. And in this very captivity[218] (who
could think it) they are so wealthy that (God's providence favouring
them) they may challenge to themselves a place among the most
noble.

33. Who can enumerate the number of ours who are renowned by fame
and learning? The learned Rabbi Moses bar Maimon[219] was
physician to Saladin, the king of Egypt; Moses Hamon to the
emperor, Sultan Bajazet[220]; Elijah Montalto to the most eminent
queen of France, Marie de Medici; and was also her counsellor.[221]

---

[213] Benjamin ben Immanuel Mussafia (1606–75) had been physician to Christian IV of
Denmark before settling in Amsterdam in 1648. See Itzhak Alfassi, art. 'Mussafia
Benjamin ben Immanuel' in *Enc. Jud.* 12.717. We have found no trace of these letters.

[214] *Thrésor de l'histoire des langues de cest univers*, Yverdon, 1511; on Claude Duret, see
Myriam Yardeni, 'Science et décadence au temps de la Renaissance: Claude Duret' in
Revue d'histoire moderne et contemporaine, Apr.–June, 1977.

[215] Jan Huygen van Linschoten, *II pars Indiae Orientalis . . .* , Frankfurt, 1599, ch. 45, p.
109.

[216] Mordecai Meisel was a prominent member of the community in Prague, where he
built a synagogue which still bears his name, see S. W. Baron, *A Social and Religious History
of the Jews*, vol. xiv, pp. 164–6 and notes pp. 365–6.

[217] Jacob Bassevi of Treuenberg (1570–1634). See Ruth Kestenberg-Gladstein, art.
'Bassevi of Treuenberg, Jacob' in *Enc. Jud.* 4: 316–17.

[218] The author is here referring to the situation of exile, experienced by the Jews since
the destruction of the First Temple.

[219] This is Maimonides, who was a physician but also the supreme philosopher of
medieval Judaism with his *Guide of the Perplexed*. He was one of the first codifiers of Jewish
Law with his *Mishneh Torah*. All encyclopaedias and bibliographies refer to the many
works devoted to him. See G. Vajda, *Introduction à la pensée juive du Moyen Age*, Paris,
1976², pp. 129–51, and bibliographical supplement ch. VII, sect. 2.

[220] Moses Hamon (*c.*1490–*c.*1554) was in fact physician to Selim I and Suleiman the
Magnificent. See Simon Marcus, art. 'Hamon' in *Enc. Jud.* 7: 1248–9.

[221] It is not known why the Latin version mistakenly attributes the name Louise to
Queen Marie de Medici, 'Serenissimae Galliarum Reginae Ludovicae de Medicis'. The
mistake is reproduced by the English translator, who writes 'Loysia de Medici'. We have
made the correction. There are many partial studies of Elijah Montalto, but no
comprehensive work. See however Harry Friedenwald, *The Jews and Medicine. Essays*, vol.
ii, New York, 1967, pp. 468–96, and J. M. Pelorson, 'Le Docteur Carlos Garcia et la

At Padua, Elijah of Crete[222] read philosophy; and Rabbi Abraham de Balmes,[223] Hebrew Grammar. And how much honour had Elijah the Grammarian[224] at Rome? And almost all the Princes of Italy honoured with all kind of honour Abraham Colorni; as appears by a letter written to him by Tommaso Garzoni in his work *La Piazza Universale*.[225] Pico della Mirandola (who used to say that he had but small understanding, who only looked after his own things, and not after other men's) and others had Hebrew teachers.[226] David de Pomis dedicated his book to Pope Sixtus V, who lovingly and courteously received both the author and work.[227] So at this day we see many desirous to learn the Hebrew tongue of our men. Hence may be seen that God has not left us;[228] for if one persecutes us, another receives us civilly and courteously; and if this prince treats us ill, another treats us well; if one banishes us out of his country, another invites us by a thousand privileges; as divers princes of Italy have done, the most eminent King of Denmark[229] and the mighty

colonie hispano-portugaise de Paris (1613–19)' in *Bulletin hispanique*, vol. 51, nos. 3–4, Bordeaux, July–Dec. 1969. For his tomb in the Ouderkerk cemetery, see L. Alvares-Vega, *Het Beth Haim van Ouderkerk*, p. 27.

[222] Better known as Elijah del Medigo, he translated many Greek philosophical works for the benefit of Italian intellectuals, among whom was Pico della Mirandola. See C. Roth, *The Jews in the Renaissance*, New York, 1965², pp. 74–5, 112–13.

[223] Abraham de Balmes was one of the most popular authors of medical books in the sixteenth century. Physician to Cardinal Grimani in Venice, he translated Arabic medical treatises into Latin.

[224] Elijah Levita was one of the founders of modern Hebrew grammar. He had many Christian pupils, and his fame was such that Francis I offered him a chair at the Collège de France. See Gerard E. Weil's admirable book, *Elie Lévita, Humaniste et massorète (1459–1569)*, Leiden, 1963.

[225] *La piazza universale di tutte le professioni del mondo*, Venice, 1587. See the last sonnet and the letter addressed to Abraham Colorni at the end of the unpaginated dedicatory epistle. Colorni was a famous Mantuan engineer and inventor in the service of Alfonso II of Este and Ferrara. See Giuseppe Lare, *Abramo Colorni*, Ferrara, 1891.

[226] The great Pico della Mirandola was the father of the Christian Kabbalah, see Francois Secret, *Les Kabbalistes chrétiens de la Renaissance*, Paris, 1964, pp. 24–43.

[227] In addition to *Zemah David*, the Plant of David, the encyclopaedic dictionary in Hebrew, Latin, and Italian referred to by our rabbi, Venice, 1587, he published in 1588 an apologia for Jewish medicine entitled *De Medico Hebraeo Ennaratio Apologetica*. See C. Roth, *The Jews in the Renaissance*, pp. 223–5.

[228] The Hebrew translator (Lemberg edition, 1847, fo. 14 v.) sees here an implied quotation from Genesis 49: 18, 'I have waited for thy salvation, O Lord.' The terms used in the Spanish version seem to refer rather to Genesis 49: 10, 'The sceptre shall not depart from Judah, nor a lawgiver from between his feet.' This verse, according to the traditional Jewish interpretation, promises that the Jewish people will always have their *own authorities* until the Messiah comes, these authorities being their rabbis and scribes.

[229] Having allowed the Jews various privileges at Glückstadt, Christian IV of Denmark wrote a letter on 25 November 1622 to the leaders of the Portuguese community in

Duke of Savoy in Nice.[230] And do we not see that those republics do flourish and much increase in trade, which admit the Israelites?[231]

34. Moses says in his last song [Deut. 32: 42–4] that God would revenge the blood of his people who are scattered. And Jeremiah 2: 3 says: 'Israel is the Lord's holy thing, the first fruit of his increase; all who devour him shall be found guilty; evil shall come upon them, saith the Lord.' And that the histories of divers times, even from Nebuchadnezzar, do testify. Have not the monarchies of great princes been destroyed? Consider with me the miserable ends of Antiochus, of Pompey, of Sisebut, of Philip the king of France, of Alfonso the son of João II.[232] And we may remember how King Sebastian with his fourth generation,[233] and with all his nobles, was slain in a battle of Africa, in that same place in which he had caused the Jews to be banished.[234] Ferdinand and Isabella were the great

Amsterdam saying, among other things: 'Our gracious will is to witness to you by these presents that, if any one or more of your Nation is, or are, moved to come and settle in our said city, they should send one or two persons from among them to examine the condition of the place and report to you about it, having no doubt that you will be sufficiently satisfied.' Letter published in *Privilèges dont les Juifs portugais jouissent en France depuis 1550*, Paris, 1777, pp. vi–vii. The Danish charters are preseved in the Archives of the Portuguese Community of Amsterdam in the Amsterdam Municipal Archives, PA. 334. 89.

[230] In 1648 the Duke of Savoy attempted to create a free port at Villefranche and to attract Marranos to it, see C. Roth, *History of the Jews of Italy*, Philadelphia, 1946, p. 350.

[231] This argument was developed by our rabbi in his pamphlet, *How profitable the nation of the Iewes are*. See the introduction, p. 57.

[232] Antiochus IV Epiphanes began the religious persecution of Jews in 167 BC. His death, after appalling suffering, is described in 2 Maccabees 9: 5–28. Pompey, who took Jerusalem in 63 BC, was assassinated in Egypt after his defeat by the armies of Caesar at Pharsalus (48 BC). Sisebut, a Visigoth king of Spain (612–21), had a policy of forced conversion of Jews. According to the Portuguese Jewish chronicler, Samuel Usque, he was poisoned and replaced by a king who favoured the Jews (see *Samuel Usque's Consolation for the Tribulations of Israel*, translated by Martin A. Cohen, Philadelphia, 1965, p. 228). Philip the Fair, who expelled the Jews from France, died as the result of a terrible hunting accident. See Jean Favier, *Philippe le Bel*, Paris, Fayard, 1978, pp. 530–1. João II seized Jewish children from their parents and deported them to São Tomé in 1493: his son died falling from his horse during the celebrations to mark his marriage to the daughter of the King of Castille, *Usque*, p. 229. Our rabbi is again following the *Nomologia* of Immanuel Aboab, p. 307 (see above, n. 209).

[233] Poor translation attributable to the Latin text. It should read 'to the fourth generation'.

[234] King Sebastian's death at the battle of Alcazarquivir in Morocco on 4 Aug. 1578 is well known, see however G. Vajda, *Un Recueil de textes historiques judéo-marocains*, Paris, 1951, pp. 15–16. The historical allusion is difficult to understand. It must be made clear that our author is summarizing Immanuel Aboab, who writes, p. 308: 'Permitió el Señor que, a la quarta generación viniesse quasi toda la nobleza de Portugal y su Rey Don Sebastián a África para ser en destruidos, y captivos en el mismo lugar, adonde sus abuelos

persecutors of our nation, but how did both he and she die?[235] As for his son-in-law, his own subjects did persecute him;[236] and his only son died (leaving no issue) on his wedding day, being seventeen years old. His daughter, being heir of the kingdom, and of her father's hatred, would not marry Manuel, king of Portugal, unless he would compel us to be banished[237] and change our religion. But she died in childbirth of her son [at] Saragossa, and also her son, before he was a year and a half old;[238] and the succession was devolved upon the kingdom of Spain.[239] It is not long since that the Spaniards exercised upon us at Mantua whatever cruelties they could invent;[240] what shall we say of what at Madrid in the year 1632 was done by the Inquisition, the king and princes of the kingdom concurring;[241] but in the very same month died the Infante Car-

indigna e cruelmente mandaron los affligidos Israelitas.' Actually seven or eight Jews, who had resisted the forced conversion carried out in Lisbon in October 1497 by King Manoel the Fortunate, were cast on to the African coast, see Meyer Kayserling, *História dos Judeus em Portugal*, Portuguese trans. by G. Borchardt da Silva and A. Novinsky, Sao Paulo, 1971, p. 117.

Did our rabbi know that King Sebastian had sworn, on pain of death, to baptize the Jews of such Maghreb cities as he might conquer? Did he know that the Jews instituted a special *purim* to commemorate his defeat? See Moses Ginsburger, 'Deux pourim locaux' in *Hebrew Union College Annual*, x, 1935, pp. 445–50.

235 'The queen, Isabella the accursed lady, was overtaken by a bitter fate: half her body was eaten away by a malignant sore, called cancer, of which she died. God is just!' Joseph ha-Cohen, *La Vallée des Pleurs, Chronique des souffrances d'Israël*, trans. Julien See, Paris, 1881, p. 102. Isabella the Catholic and Ferdinand of Aragon had expelled the Jews from Spain on 31 Mar. 1492. Ferdinand was actually attacked by his son-in-law, Philip I, husband of his daughter, Doña Juana.

236 Incorrect translation of '. . . ille, quam gener, propriique subjecti persequebantur'. It should read '. . . and he, persecuted by his son-in-law and his own subjects'.

237 The idea of banishment has been inserted by the English translator and makes no sense. Why indeed would they be converted and immediately banished? The Latin and Spanish versions allow this to be corrected. It should read '. . . before we had been exiled or forced to embrace her religion'. The Infante Don Juan, who had married Margaret of Austria, daughter of the Emperor Maximilian, died in 1497. The Infanta Isabella made it a condition of her second marriage to King Manuel of Portugal that he would expel the Jews from his kingdom. Her son was called Don Miguel.

238 We have corrected the translation which had 'half a year old' for 'sesquiannum'.

239 As well as making a serious omission, Moses Wall wrongly translates the phrase '. . . successio per masculos in regno Hispaniae desiit'. It should read 'the succession, through the male line, died out in the Kingdom of Spain'.

240 The Jews of Mantua suffered greatly as a result of the sack of the town on 18 July 1630: modern historians blame the Germans rather than the Spaniards. See S. Simonsohn, *History of the Jews in the Duchy of Mantua*, Jerusalem, 1964 [in Hebrew], vol. i, pp. 38–42; English trans., Jerusalem, 1978, pp. 53–5.

241 On the great *auto-da-fé* in Madrid on 4 July 1632, see Yosef Hayim Yerushalmi, *From Spanish Court to Italian Ghetto*, pp. 105–21.

los[242] and their kingdom declined. What wonder is it if God has chastised divers kingdoms by sundry ways: but of this I treat further in my History of the Jews.[243] Let us conclude therefore that good, which God has promised, will shortly come, since we see that we have suffered those evils which he has threatened us with, by the prophets.

35. The shortness of time (when we believe our redemption shall appear) is confirmed by this, that the Lord has promised that he will gather the two tribes, Judah and Benjamin, out of the four quarters of the world, calling them *Nephussim*.[244] Whence you may gather that for the fulfilling of that, they must be scattered through all the corners of the world; as Daniel (12: 7) says: 'And when the scattering of the holy people shall have an end, all those things shall be fulfilled.' And this appears now to be done, when our synagogues are found in America.[245]

36. To these let us add that which the same prophet speaks (Daniel 12: 4), 'that knowledge shall be increased'; for then the prophecies shall be better understood, the meaning of which we can scarce attain to, till they be fulfilled. So after the Ottoman race began to flourish, we understood the prophecy of the two legs of the image of Nebuchadnezzar, which is to be overthrown by the Fifth Monarchy, which shall be in the world. So Jeremiah, after he had handled in chapter 30 the redemption of Israel and Judah, and of the war of Gog and Magog (of which Daniel also speaks in chapter 12), when he treats of the sceptre of the Messiah, the son of David, of the ruin of the nations, of the restoration of Judah, of holy Jerusalem, and of the third Temple, adds in 30: 24: 'The fierce anger of the Lord shall not return, till he hath executed it, and till he hath performed the intents of his heart; in the latter days, ye shall understand it.' Whence follows what we have said, that the time of redemption is at hand. And because Jeremiah in that chapter makes an abridgement of all things that shall be, therefore it is said in verse 2: 'Write all the words which I have spoken to thee in a book.' By this means making the prophecy clearer, by relating it in a clear style, whatever the prophets had foretold; imitating Moses, the last words of whose

---

[242] The unbalanced Prince Carlos was incarcerated on the orders of his father, Philip II; it has sometimes been alleged that Philip II himself put him to death.

[243] Nothing remains of this *History* in preparation, to which Menasseh ben Israel often refers. See C. Roth, *A Life of Menasseh ben Israel*, p. 304. See also n. 5, above.

[244] Hebrew: dispersed. See above n. 165.   [245] See above n. 166.

song are, 'Sing, O ye nations, with his people' (Deut. 32: 43). Also the last words which he spoke, after he had blessed the tribes are these: 'Happy art thou, O Israel, who is like to thee, O people? Saved by the Lord, who is the shield of thy help, and the sword of thy excellency; and thine enemies shall be found liars to thee, and thou shalt tread upon their high places' [Deut. 33: 29]. Whence it appears that God will revenge the blood of Israel, which had been shed. Joel ([4:]19) confirms the same: Egypt shall be a desolation and Edom shall be a filthy desert, for the violence and injury offered to the Jews and because they have shed innocent blood in their land. And as they shall be punished by the just judgement of God who wish us evil; so also God will give blessings upon those who favour us. And those are the trees of the field which then shall rejoice [Isaiah 55: 11]. So God said to Abraham (Genesis 12: 3): 'I will bless them who bless thee and curse them that curse thee.'

37. These are the things which I could gather concerning this matter, which has not been heretofore handled; whence these consequences may be deduced:

1. That the Western Indies were anciently inhabited by a part of the Ten Tribes, which passed thither out of Tartary, by the strait of Anian.[246]

2. That the tribes are not in any one place, but in many; because the prophets have foretold their return shall be into their country out of divers places; Isaiah especially says it shall be out of eight.

3. That they did not return to the Second Temple.

4. That at this day they keep the Jewish religion.

5. That the prophecies concerning their return to their country are of necessity to be fulfilled.

6. That from all coasts of the world they shall meet in those two places, Assyria and Egypt [Isaiah 27: 13]; God preparing an easy, pleasant way and abounding with all things, as Isaiah (49: 11) says, and thence they shall fly to Jerusalem as birds to their nests [Isaiah 60: 8].

7. That their kingdom shall be no more divided; but the Twelve Tribes shall be joined under one prince, that is under Messiah the son of David; and that they shall never be driven out of their land.

[246] At this point the Spanish text reiterates the nub of Menasseh's argument, that is that through Divine Providence some of the Ten Tribes are still living today in America, hidden in unknown regions.

CONCLUSION

38. I return to the relation of our Montezinos, which I prefer before the opinions of all others as most true. That Peru should be derived from the name Ophir, as Guillaume Postel,[247] Goropius [in his work] on Ortelius,[248] Bozius in his *De Signis Ecclesiae* (Book III, chapter 3),[249] Marinus in his *Arca Noe*,[250] Father Sá in his *Regum* (Book III),[251] Pomarius in his *Lexicon*,[252] and Possevin in his *Bibliotheca* (Book II)[253] think, cannot be proved. As Pineda has well observed in *Job* (chap. 28, p. 500),[254] for we have said out of Garcilaso de la Vega, that that name was unknown to them of Peru.[255] Ophir then is the Eastern Indies, if we believe Josephus (*Antiquities* VIII, chap. 6) and Acosta in his *Historia . . . de las Indias* (Book I),[256] whence Solomon fetched gold and precious stones. But what Gomara in part I of his history of the Indies (fo. 120)[257] and Zarate in his *Prohemio . . . Historia . . . de Peru*[258] would have, that ours did pass over that famous and much praised (by Plato in *Critias* and *Timaeus*)[259] Island of Atlantis, and so went to the neighbouring

[247] François Secret, whom we have consulted on this point and to whom we are most grateful, thinks that the reference to Postel has less to do with the etymological link between Peru and Ophir than with the history of the Ten Tribes, as has already been observed by Basnage, *Histoire des Juifs*, Rotterdam, 1706, vol. iv, pp. 952–9: 'Menasseh is not alone in this thought. Postel had it before him.' Guillaume Postel's theories may be found set out in *De la république des Turcs*, Poitiers, 1650 (pt. 2, Histoire et considérations de l'origine et coutumes des Tartares, Persiens, etc., pp. 23 ff.) and in *De Universitate Liber*, Paris, 1563 (alterius partis, pp. 38–9). Both Postel and Menasseh refer to the Zohar.

[248] Jean van Gorp, *Hispanica* in *Opera*, Antwerp, 1580, bk. 7, p. 112. Note that the references concerning Marinus, Sá, Pomarius, and Possevinus are taken straight from G. García, *Origen de los Indios*, bk. 1, ch. 1, para. 1, pp. 32–3.

[249] *De Signis Ecclesiae Dei*, Cologne, 1593, ch. 3, p. 748. The Latin version refers incorrectly to bk. II.

[250] *Arca Noe Thesaurus Linguae Sanctae Novus*, Venice, 1593, letter *aleph*, p. 43.

[251] *Notationes in Totam Scripturam Sacram*, Antwerp, 1598. In III Regum, ch. 9, p. 78.

[252] We have not found the book in question.

[253] *Bibliotheca Selecta de Ratione Studiorum*, Venice, 1603. The Spanish edition gives ch. 5, and the English version ch. 8, however we have not been able to find the information concerning the origin of the name Peru referred to by Menasseh ben Israel.

[254] *Commentaria in Job . . .*, Cologne, 1603, ch. 28, pp. 419–20.

[255] *Primera parte de los comentarios reales . . .*, bk. I, ch. 4 and 5, 'Los Indios naturales del Pirú, ni usan, ni saben tal nombre de su tierra'.

[256] *Historia natural y moral de las Indias*, see bk. I ch. 14.

[257] López de Gomara, *Primera y segunda parte de la historia general de las Indias*, pp. 291–2.

[258] A. de Zarate, *Declaración de la dificultad que algunos tienen en averiguar por donde pudieron pasar al Perú las gentes que primeramente lo poblaron*, in *Historia del descubrimiento y conquista del Perú*, Antwerp, 1555, Al lector, an unpaginated introduction.

[259] Plato, *Timaeus*, 26 a, and *Critias*, 108 e–109 a.

Leeward Islands, and thence to the mainland, and at last to the kingdom of Peru and New Spain; it is deservedly exploded as fabulous, and Acosta laughs at it, in book I, chap. 12, of his History of the Indies.[260] But Marsiglio Ficino in his commentary on the *Timaeus* (chap. 4) and *Critias*,[261] that he might defend Plato (and his disciples Porphyry, Origen, and Proclus who follow him), thinks all that which is in *Critias* and *Timaeus* is to be understood allegorically. And who will believe Lescarbot, who says that they are Canaanites, who fled thither for fear of Joshua?[262] For I cannot be persuaded that they sought out countries so far remote. They, who will have them of Peru to have come out of Norway or Spain, may be confuted by their very form, manners, and the unlikeness of their languages. But that is more false that they are Israelites, who have forgotten circumcision and their rites. For they are of a comely body and of a good wit, as says Doctor Juan de Huarte in his book which is called *Examen de Ingenios* (chap. 12).[263] But contrarily all men know that the Indians are deformed, dull, and altogether rude. And we have abundantly shown with how great study and zeal the Israelites have kept their language and religion out of their country.

39. Montezinos then speaks most likely; that, as other people forced the Israelites to betake them to the mountains,[264] so America being first of all inhabited by the persecuting Tartars, they were driven to the Cordilleras mountains, where at last they were hidden, as God would have it. Truly, comparing the Israelites themselves, or their laws, with other people, I see not anything that comes nearer truth. Perhaps America was of old contiguous to Asia on the north side. It does not seem to me such an absurdity to say that the Israelites went out of Tartary into America by land;[265] and afterwards that God, to

---

[260] *Historia natural y moral de las Indias*; Menasseh ben Israel refers by mistake to ch. 22.

[261] *Commentarii in Parmenidem Sophistum, Timaeum . . .*, Florence, 1496, vol. ii, ch. 4, fo. 1 v.

[262] Marc Lescarbot, *Histoire de la Nouvelle France*, Paris, 1617, ch. 3, pp. 19–20.

[263] *Examen de ingenios para las sciencias*, Valencia, 1580. Our rabbi refers by mistake to ch. 14.

[264] Strangely, the Latin edition does not, at this point, mention the example given by Menasseh ben Israel in the Spanish version to back up Montezinos's account, namely that 'in olden times the Britons had to regroup in the Welsh mountains as a result of the warfare inflicted on them by the Saxons'. This would have interested an English reader.

[265] Moses Wall has reproduced blindly the error in the Latin text, 'Forte etiam olim America Asiae non contigua fuit parte septentrionali. Non absurdum adeo videtur mihi statuere Israelitas terrestri itinere ex Tartaria Americam petiisse . . .' in which the two phrases are contradictory. We have corrected this in the text. The Spanish version, however, is perfectly clear.

preserve his, among other miracles, also wrought this, to make that a sea where now is the strait of Anian. Yea, that might be done without a miracle, by accident, as we know, that more than once the sea by a violent storm has carried away the land and made islands. Xenophon in his *Aequivocis* mentions the inundations of Egypt which happened in the days of Prometheus and Hercules.[266] Also Berosius (in Book V)[267] and Diodorus (Book V)[268] mention the inundation of Attica in which Athens stands. Pliny (Book II, chap. 85 and XIII, chap. 11),[269] Strabo (Books I and XII)[270] and Plutarch in his *Life of Alexander*[271] relate the drowning of the Isle of Pharos; of which Lucan speaks so elegantly in his last book.[272] Besides, who knows not how many, and how great, cities have at divers times been almost wholly ruined by several earthquakes? Tacitus[273] writes that under Tiberius twelve cities have been by this means ruined. Orosius (Book VII, chap. 4)[274] and Dio Cassius (Book 57)[275] affirm the same, though they differ about the time. Tacitus (Book XIV)[276] and Eusebius in his *Chronicle*[277] relate the destruction of that famous and rich city of Laodicea—Origen in vol. 28 on *John*[278] and Baronius in vol. II, year 340, of *Annales Ecclésiastiques*[279] speak of other earthquakes which have destroyed divers and very many men

---

[266] See Myrsilius Lesbius, *Fragmenta Vetustissimorum Autorum . . .* , Basel, 1530, p. 47.

[267] Berosus Babilonicus, *De his quae pracesesserunt Inundationem Terrarum*, Paris, 1510, see ch. *Xenophon, De Equivocis Temporum*, fo. 21.

[268] Diodorus, *Natural History*, Paris, 1737. The reference should be to bk. V, p. 287, and not to bk. VI as given by Menasseh ben Israel.

[269] Pliny the Elder, *Historia Naturalis*, bk. II, ch. 85, and bk. XII, ch. 21; the reference to XIII: 11 is incorrect.

[270] Strabo, *Geography*, bk. I, first pt.

[271] Plutarch, *Lives*, bk. IX, Alexander, Caesar.

[272] Lucan, *Bell. Civ.*, bk. X, ll. 509–11.

[273] Menasseh ben Israel incorrectly refers to Suetonius. See Tacitus, *Annals*, Tiberius, bk. II, ch. 47.

[274] Orosius, *Adversus Paganos Historiarum*, Mainz, 1615, bk. VII, ch. 4, p. 518. See also bk. VII, ch. 12, p. 535.

[275] In his *History of Rome*, Dio Cassius certainly alludes to a cataclysm, but he puts it in the reign of Trajan, which would explain the discrepancy in the dates noted by Menasseh ben Israel. The reference is taken, along with all the references in this passage, from G. García, *Origen de los Indios*, bk. IV, ch. 12, p. 385. It is clearly inaccurate as the work does not contain 57 books. See Dio, bk. lxviii, ch. 24.   [276] *Annals*, bk. XIV, ch. 27.

[277] Eusebius Pamphili, Bishop of Caesarea, *Chronicorum Historiae*, in *Patrologia Graeca* (Migne), XIX, p. 543.

[278] We have consulted Pierre Nautin, to whom our thanks, who considers that 'the text cited by Menasseh ben Israel could be the following passage from Origen's commentary on St Matthew's Gospel, *comm. ser.* 39 in Migne, *Patrol, gr.*, XIII, 1354 B'.

[279] Cesar Baronius, *Annales ecclésiastiques . . .* , Paris, 1616, year 340, p. 764.

and cities. And Father Alonso Venero in his *Manual de los Tiempos*[280] relates that the same happened in our days. He says that in the year 1638, a great earthquake happened in the Terceira Islands, but especially in San Miguel, where the governor dwells; for that unheard of shaking of the earth and houses struck so great terror into the inhabitants that all fled out of their houses and lived in the fields; a little after, two miles from there, they say the sea vomit up abundance of fiery matter, which made a very thick smoke, which covered the very clouds; and it cast up many great stones which seemed like rocks; part whereof falling down again made an island in the sea which was half a mile over, and 60 fathoms high, and 150 fathoms deep. That hot exhalation, which that fiery mountain sent forth, pierced the very waters and stifled so many fishes that two ships of the Indies could not carry them. The same island two years after was swallowed up again of the sea.

40. He that seriously weighs those things, may (I think) well gather that the sea of the strait of Anian was an inundation. By affirming which, this doubt may be answered: namely, that after the universal flood, mankind increased again, and all beasts, which had been preserved in the Ark. But how could so many kinds of beasts (which come by propagation and are not bred out of the earth)[281] be found in those countries? Some did swim thither, some were brought thither by some huntsmen, some were brought out of the earth, as Augustine thinks happened in the first creation.[282] But what land beast can swim over so great a sea? And would huntsmen carry lions thither, and other such kind of beasts, often times to the great hazard of their lives? And if God would have created those beasts out of the earth, he would not have commanded Noah to have kept them in the Ark. I am fully persuaded that those that are found there passed that way into America; unless any thinks that the New World is joined to the old on some other side, as Herrera believes (*Decadas III*, Book II, chap. 10).[283]

---

[280] Alonso Venero, *Enchiridion o manual de los tiempos*, Alcala, 1640, pp. 339 and 339 v.

[281] Menasseh is alluding to the theory according to which there are two kinds of animals. Some are perfect and breed, others are imperfect and born from the earth. See St Augustine, *The City of God*, bk. 16, ch. 7.

[282] This is the Bishop of Hippo, whom Menasseh ben Israel is reluctant to call St Augustine. See *The City of God*, bk. 16, ch. 7. St Augustine did not, of course, make any allusion to the stocking of the New World with animals!

[283] Antonio de Herrera, *Historia general de los hechos de los castellanos en las islas y tierra firme del mar Oceano*, Madrid, 1601.

41 As for the other things in the relation of our Montezinos, they say nothing which savours of falsehood. For their saying the *Shema* [Deut. 6: 4], truly it is the custom of our people in what part soever of the world they live; and it is the abridgement of the confession and religion of the Jews.[284] The revelation of the magicians whom they call Mohanes agrees with those things which in 4 Esdras you may see concerning the miracles which God wrought for the Israelites, as they passed over Euphrates,[285] concerning those conditions of not revealing secrets to any but such a one as has seen 300 moons (which make twenty-five years); it appears to be true, by what the famous De Laet tells in many parts of America, that the Indians compute their years by moons.[286] That a secret must be told in the field, does that not argue a Jewish custom, which the ancients have observed in Jacob, who being about to depart from Laban, called his wives into the field?[287]

I now conclude this discourse, in which this only was in my intention, that I might briefly and correspondingly declare mine, and the Rabbi's opinion concerning those things which I have handled. I hope that this my endeavour will not be unacceptable, being desired by many men famous both for birth and for learning; nor unprofitable, having therein explained the relation of Montezinos, with what brevity I could. The name of God be blessed for ever. Amen.[288]

---

[284] For the Jewish profession of faith (Deuteronomy 6: 4), see above n. 14.

[285] 'Fecit enim eis tunc Altissimus signa et statuit venas fluminis usque quo transirent', 4 Esdras 13: 44 (Vulgate).

[286] J. de Laet, *Histoire du Nouveau Monde ou description des Indes occidentales*, Leiden, 1640, bk. XI, p. 407.

[287] Genesis 31: 4, cf. Berakhot 8 b and Rashi, s.l., 'as the saying goes "walls have ears"'.

[288] In the Spanish version, Menasseh ben Israel divided his text into 72 chapters, and ended with the following statement: 'I have written this book as briefly as possible in seventy-two chapters, thus reflecting the seventy-two names of the Lord, may He be Blessed now and for ever.' It would seem that this phrasing, which was based on the formula 'The Holy name of the Lord is made of seventy-two names', was intended for a knowledgeable Jewish public. On the formula, see G. Scholem, *Les Origines de la Kabbale*, Paris, 1966, pp. 88, 112, 160; G. Vajda, *Le Commentaire d'Ezra de Gerone sur le Cantique des Cantiques*, Paris, 1969, p. 368. The essential source is the *Sefer ha-Bahir*, ed. R. Margulies, Jerusalem, 1951, nos. 63, 76–9. We owe this information to Georges Vajda and take this opportunity of thanking him warmly. In fact we do not know whether Menasseh ben Israel took this number from a written source or oral teaching: for, although the *Sefer ha-Bahir* was written during the seventeenth century at the latest, it was not published until 1651 in Amsterdam. We note, however, that this calculation is primarily made up of the letters of each of the verses of Exodus 14: 19, 20, and 21, see Abraham ibn Ezra's commentary; also the commentaries of Rashi and the Tosafists on the seventy-two names of God in *Sukkah* 45 a.

A Note on Moses Wall

RICHARD H. POPKIN

PRACTICALLY nothing is known about Moses Wall. In the literature it is mentioned that he was a friend of John Milton and the translator of Menasseh ben Israel's *The Hope of Israel*. His only published writing, besides the translation, is an essay appended to the Menasseh text entitled 'Considerations upon the point of the Conversion of the Jews', and an answer to a critic, Sir Edward Spencer, also added to the translation. All that is known about his relations with Milton comes from a letter he wrote to Milton on 26 May 1659, answering a letter from the poet. This letter indicates that they had been friends for quite a long time, and that both were very discouraged by the political and theological developments at the end of the Commonwealth.

In addition to these known items, there are several unpublished letters of Moses Wall to Samuel Hartlib, in the rich collection of Hartlib materials at Sheffield University, and some discussions about Wall in the correspondence of Hartlib and Vice-Chancellor John Worthington of Cambridge published in the nineteenth century. When all this is put together, it is not enough to enable us to construct a biographical sketch of the man, but it does allow one to see him first as an ardent millenarian, full of great expectations, then withdrawing from the centre of political and theological activity, engaging in experiments in animal husbandry, in science and in linguistics, while seeing all his hopes dashed by the events going on in England and Continental Europe.

The letters in the Hartlib collection begin in 1652, after the publication of the editions of *The Hope of Israel* (which is not mentioned in any of the letters). In a letter dated 3 April 1655 Wall explained to Hartlib, one of the central figures in the millenarian world of the time, that he, Wall, had been looking 'after Apocalypticall works & ye appearings of God' for twenty to thirty years. He had generally accepted Joseph Mede's theory for calculating when the events predicted in the books of Daniel and Revelation would occur. Mede's *Clavis Apocalyptica* had been published in 1627 and 1632, which would more or less coincide with Wall's statement of when he became interested in these matters. Hartlib was corresponding with Mede in the 1630s and disseminating his views to various millenarians like John Dury.

Mede died in 1638 and left a large legacy of unpublished tracts and letters on matters crucial to understanding the millenarian expectations. He also left a group of students, convinced of his views, who played important roles in the dramatic events of the Puritan era. Among his students were John Milton, Henry More, John Worthington (editor of Mede's works), and Isaac Barrow, the teacher of Newton. We cannot tell if Wall was a direct student, or learnt the views second-hand from books and friends. Wall's indications of erudition would suggest that he had received some university education.

One of Mede's views, which circulated in a letter to the Revd William Twisse, procurator of the Westminster Assembly, was on a topic of great concern to Wall, namely how and when the conversion of the Jews would occur. Wall refers to it in his answer to his critic, Edward Spencer. In a discussion of the text of 1 Tim. 1: 16 Mede had said that the Jews would be converted not by men, but by God, and it would take place miraculously and by a type, as happened in the case of St Paul. Hence, Wall claimed he was not trying to convert the Jews by translating Menasseh's work. 'I believe the maine of their conversion will be from Heaven, and extraordinary; though the *Gentiles* by provoking them to emulation, and also by their gifts and graces, may some way be auxiliary to them.'

Wall did not explain, in the material we have, why he was chosen as the translator. No doubt the arrangements were made by Hartlib and John Dury, who was in close contact with Menasseh ben Israel at the time. Wall indicated he did not have any direct relations with Menasseh, but had learned from 'those who are acquainted with him, that he is a very ingenuous and civill man'.

The surviving correspondence of Wall with Hartlib begins with a letter by Wall from Greenwich on 18 June 1652. Wall had sent Hartlib a manuscript copy of the 'Narrative of the Jews Councill near Buda', an important millenarian work that was not published until the following year. This purports to be an eyewitness account of a council of three hundred rabbis that took place in 1650 to discuss, after the terrible pogroms of 1648–9, whether the Messiah had, in fact, come, and the Jews were being punished for not accepting this. The rabbis, in the account, were about to convert, when they were repelled by Roman Catholic superstition. And the story ends with a rabbi explaining that they wished an English Protestant minister had been there. Then presumably they would have been converted by the pure Christianity of the English Puritans.

This report was published in 1653, attributed to an unidentifiable Samuel Brett. It was reprinted many times in the seventeenth, eighteenth, and nineteenth centuries, but Menasseh ben Israel told the hopeful English Millenarians in 1656 that the great council had never taken place. It is interesting that Wall had access to a manuscript in 1652. He told Hartlib that he did not know whether the story was true, but he fervently hoped so and was looking for the beginnings of the Jews turning to Christ. He had hoped that something would have happened in 1650 (when *The Hope of Israel* was published). That would have involved the conversion of the Jews and the world's great restoration. Now that 1652 was half over, Wall was still confident that it would happen, '& it shall be gods work, & not mans'.

In letters in 1654 and 1655, Wall gave his opinion to Hartlib about various millenarian tracts, and expressed his conviction that the world would soon be transformed. However, by May 1655 he was expressing concern that nothing of the expected apocalyptic scenario had occurred. 'Well, Sir, 1655 year is passant, & yet what hath God wrough[t]?' There is only one more letter, in 1655, in June, in the series, so we have no indication of whether Wall was involved with Menasseh's visit to England and with the negotiations over readmitting the Jews. The next letter, dated from Causham, in the country, on 4 January 1658, indicates that Wall had withdrawn from the theological–political arena and had begun to be disillusioned. The letter begins 'That you have not heard from me of late years, is not from want of respect to you.' Wall then explained that now that he was living in the country, 'where I retire to my own thoughts, without mixing with the Court, or City vanitys, I have some changes in my apprehensions.' The first change was his realization that the Court was changed into a commonwealth in name only, and the government was just as corrupt as ever. Next he saw that an empty form of religion had been set up to oppose the spirit of God. More good people had been persecuted during the Commonwealth than in the days of kings and queens. Useless wars are being fought. So, Wall had devoted himself to agrarian pursuits, and sent Hartlib 'a bird of my own breeding'.

The next letter, dated five days later, 9 January 1658/9 goes further into Wall's disillusionment.

In my last letters to you, I wrote to you some of my thoughts. I shall now open myself somewhat further. That that doth and hath afflicted my spirit in these late months and years, is thus, to consider the dark & dismall world in wch we live, the greatest evill of which (and that that is the root of all others) is, God's withdrawing himself from us. In the time of the wars against the late King, I thought I saw God clearly; God was among us, he showed himself plainly, he roused up himself like a mighty gyant, and was ready to give us most of himself, and to open his bosome to receive us; but upon this unhappy grasping of power into the hands of the late usurper, god withdrew and hid himself, and the body of the Nation proved apostaticall.

Wall realized he had been mistaken to support the Revolution. When he lived near Whitehall he was carried away with fervour. But when he retreated to the country, he could see how bad Cromwell really was, and how un-Christian the society had become. After bemoaning the situation, Wall commented on a paper Hartlib had sent him about the number 666. 'I have perused; but confess myself at a loss in apocalyptical prophecyes; for many hopes from thence have been given us, but every vision faileth. With all of our hopes, darkness is still upon us.' Wall was no longer interested in hearing about foreign wars, or what was going on in the world.

In the next letter, twelve days later, Wall spent the first page and a half discussing his agricultural experiments, especially concerning clover grass, and then briefly dealt with educational reform. He was in favour of having five or six universities in England, patterned after Leiden. At the end he indicated he still hoped, in spite of how dismal things were, that God was about to do great things.

Three days later, 24 January 1658, Wall wrote again, after receiving a letter from Hartlib. This time Wall indicated his disdain for theology and philosophy derived from the 'putrid fountains of the Schoolman'. He preferred the practical theology that was conducive to the bettering of man that he found in the Quaker writers, Burrough and Howgill, though he had not joined the group. He found them better than all that there was in the Councils, Schoolmen, Fathers, and commentators put together. He then discussed telescopes and Pococke's work on Arabic history. This is followed by an intriguing discussion of the theory of universal language propounded by Sir Edmund Stafford, an Englishman who had lived in Paris and had left a manuscript including a universal language consisting of thirty-two words that can be used for communication by people of different nations, plus quick ways of learning languages. He followed this with hopes that with Cromwell dead, divine providence might improve things.

The next letter of 6 February 1658/9 by Wall again discussed experiments with clover and his inability to get his telescope functioning. It was eighteen feet long, but he was unable to reassemble it since he had moved to the country. He hoped Hartlib could tell him what to do. He then told Hartlib he had promised not to make copies of Sir Edmund Stafford's work on universal language, when he made a transcription from Sir Henry Vane's copy. Wall ended his letter with the hope that God is hastening a new heaven and a new earth. However he was concerned that God was about to cause a great catastrophe, with a glorious issue. He hoped that God would undo the damage Cromwell had caused England.

This series of letters stops at this point. The next bit of information we have about Moses Wall is in his letter to John Milton a couple of months later, on 26 May 1659. Wall had worried about what Milton thought in these dark times. Milton's latest book reassured him that they shared a dismal view of what had happened. They had both hoped for liberty, both spiritual and civil, and saw forces dragging them back to Egypt. After moaning about how bad things had become, Wall said, 'We have waited for Liberty, but it must be Gods work and not Mans.' He hoped, in spite of all, the better world Milton, Dury, and Wall struggled for would be achieved. In the letter Wall exhibited his learning in Latin, Greek, and Hebrew.

The last letter we have of Wall's is to Hartlib in late 1660. Wall was sending Hartlib a turkey. He had last seen Hartlib when he was physically very ill. Wall was concerned about how Hartlib was 'in these gloomy and mysterious times' and what he thought God was doing 'so far as you think it safe for you to write'. This would indicate that one or both of them was being watched by the authorities as the Restoration began. Wall then discussed a Dutchman who had visited him, and told Hartlib how he had been forced out of his house by Lord Cravin. He hoped Hartlib's son could help. The letter ends on the sad words, 'I pray god direct us in this dark and distracted world.'

The last information about Moses Wall appears in some letters between Hartlib and Worthington in the second half of 1661. Worthington was trying to locate Wall to borrow a book about the Temple in Jerusalem, which he thought was by Leo of Modena. He asked Hartlib if Wall lived in London and Hartlib replied he was sure he would have seen Wall if he was in London. He expected to see him around Michaelmas. Worthington told Hartlib he had seen Leo of Modena's work in Dr Ralph Cudworth's study, and Cudworth told him it was Wall's copy. Hartlib reported, in the last mention of Wall, that he had not returned to London as of 19 November 1661.

From this scanty information, we can gain a vague picture of

Menasseh's translator. He seems to have been a bit younger than Hartlib, a millenarian follower of Joseph Mede, probably with university training. From the people he knew one would guess that he was a Cambridge man. He shared Hartlib's agrarian, as well as his scientific interests. Wall was a very enthusiastic millenarian around 1650, and was excited about the forthcoming conversion of the Jews. He became disturbed that nothing cosmic had happened by 1655. He seems to have been disillusioned early with Cromwell's Protectorate, and moved away from the scenes of action, to ruminate in the country. As the Commonwealth disintegrated, Wall sought some clues about God's plans, and feared that God was disappearing from human history. He sought encouragement from either Hartlib or Milton as the Commonwealth was succeeded by the restored monarchy.

Hartlib died in 1662. So far we have found no clue as to what happened to Wall, and how long he lived. His only published work is the translation of *The Hope of Israel*, with its accompanying essay on the conversion of the Jews, and his answer to Sir Edward Spencer. This was probably the high point of Wall's millenarian convictions and expectations. The picture that emerges from his known correspondence shows a more and more disillusioned millenarian, finding the whole episode of the Puritan Revolution a corrupt disaster, followed by the grim Restoration. Just a trace of his previous convictions still remained, a hope that his friends Hartlib or Milton might help him find God's plan. He still expected the Apocalypse, but was no longer sure when and where it might occur.

The letters of Wall in the Hartlib papers provide many clues about whom Wall knew. Perhaps, following these leads we may be able to find more solid facts about him and his career and learn how he became Menasseh's translator.

Bibliography

Abravanel, Isaac ben Judah, *Mashmiya Yeshuah*, Salonika, 1526 (= Amsterdam, 1644).

———*Mayané ha-Yeshuah*, Ferrara, 1551.

———*Yeshu'ot Meshiho*, Karlsruhe, 1828.

Abenatar Melo, D., *Los CL psalmos de David en lengua española en varias rimas . . .*, Frankfurt, 1626.

Adler, E. N., *About Hebrew Manuscripts*, Oxford, 1905.

Aescoly, A. Z., *Jewish Messianic Movements. Sources and Documents on Messianism in Jewish History from the Bar-Kokhba Revolt until Recent Times*, Jerusalem, 1956 (in Hebrew), (only vol. i publ.).

Alem, J.-P., *L'Espionnage à travers les âges*, Paris, 1977.

Alvares-Vega, L., *Het Beth Haim van Ouderkerk, Beelden van een Portugees-Joodse begraafplaats. The Beth Haim of Ouderkerk aan de Amstel. Images of a Portuguese Jewish Cemetery in Holland*, Assen, Amsterdam, 1975.

Amador de los Rios, J., *Études historiques, politiques et littéraires sur les Juifs d'Espagne*, Paris, 1861.

Ancona, J. d', 'De Komst der Marranen in Noord-Nederland. De Portugeze gemeenten te Amsterdam tot de vereeniging (1639)' in *Geschiedenis der Joden in Nederland*, i, Amsterdam, 1940.

Arckenholtz, J., *Mémoires pour servir à l'histoire de Christine reine de Suède*, Amsterdam, 1751.

Aron, M., *Histoire de l'excommunication juive*, Nîmes, 1882.

Avermaete, R., *Rembrandt et son temps*, Paris, 1952.

Azariah de Rossi, *Liber Meor Enajim iuxta editionem principem Mantuanam editus. Accedunt Liber Mazref le Kesef et carmina liturgica ejusdem auctoris*, ed. David Cassel, Berlin, 1867.

Azevedo, J. Lúcio de, *História dos Cristãos Novos Portugueses*, Lisbon, 1921, 2nd edn., 1975.

———Review of J. S. da Silva Rosa, *Geschiedenis der Portugeesche Joden te Amsterdam*, in *Lusitania*, iii, Apr. 1926, no. 9, pp. 430–7.

Baer, Y., *A History of the Jews in Christian Spain*, Philadelphia, 1971.

Barbour, V., *Capitalism in Amsterdam in the Seventeenth Century*, Baltimore, 1950.

Barnett, R. D. (ed.), *The Sephardi Heritage*, London, 1971.

Baron, S. W., *A Social and Religious History of the Jews*, New York–London–Philadelphia, 16 vols., 1952–76.

Bartolocci de Celleno, G., *Bibliotheca Magna Rabbinica*, Rome, 1675–93.

172 *Bibliography*

Basnage de Beauval, J.-C., *Histoire des Juifs depuis Jésus Christ jusqu'à présent*, The Hague, 1716.
Bass, Shabbetai, *Sifte Yeshenim*, Amsterdam, 1680.
Bayle, P., *Dictionnaire historique et critique*, Paris, 1820.
Beinart, H., *Marranos on Trial by the Inquisition*, Tel Aviv, 1965 (in Hebrew).
Belinfante, J. C. E., *Joods Historisch Museum, Jewish Historical Museum*, Haarlem, 1978.
Belmonte, Moseh, *Paraphrasis Caldaica en los Cantares de Selomoh*, Amsterdam, 1644.
Benayahu, M., 'The Funeral Oration for R. Samuel Yafeh by his Son R. Isaac', in *Kobez al Yad. Minora Manuscripta Hebraica*, iii (18), Jerusalem, 1975, pp. 433–49.
Besso, H. V., *Dramatic Literature of the Sephardic Jews at Amsterdam in the XVIIth and XVIIIth Centuries*, Nogent-le-Rotrou, 1947 (= *Bulletin Hispanique*, nos. 39 and 41).
Beverovicius, I., *Epistola quaestio de vitae termino fatali an mobili cum doctorum responsis*, Dordrecht, 1634.
Birmingham, S., *The Grandees: America's Sephardic Elite*, New York–London, 1971.
Blok, F. F., 'Some humanists of the Jerusalem of the West' in *Humanists and Humanism in Amsterdam. Catalogue of an exhibition in the Tippenhuis, Amsterdam, 20–25 Aug. 1973*, Amsterdam, 1973.
——'Caspar Barlaeus en den Joden. De geschiedenis van een Epigram' in *Nederlands Archief voor Kerkgeschiedenis*, lviii, 1976–7, no. 1, pp. 85–108 and pp. 179–209.
Bloom, H. I., *The Economic Activities of the Jews of Amsterdam in the Seventeenth and Eighteenth Centuries*, Williamsport (Pa.), 1937.
Bok, W. (ed.), *Bibliographie sur le judaïsme et les Juifs et sur les relations entre Juifs et non-Juifs* (Andrée Notre), Brussels, 1971 (= *Social Compass*, xviii, 1971–3, pp. 445–523).
Brun, J., *La Véritable religion des Hollandais*, Amsterdam, 1675.
Capp, B. S., *The Fifth Monarchy Men*, London, 1972.
Cardoso de Bethencourt, 'Lettre de Menasseh ben Israël à Issac Vossius 1651–1655', in *REJ*, xlix, pp. 98–109.
Caro Baroja, J., *Los Judíos en la España moderna y contemporánea*, Madrid, 1961.
Casaril, G., *Rabbi Siméon Bar Yochaï et la cabbale*, Paris, 1961.
Castro, A., *Réalité de l'Espagne. Histoire et valeurs*, Paris, 1963.
Catalogus van de Bibliotheek der Vereniging Het Spinozahuis te Rijnsburg, Leyden, 1965.
Menasseh ben Israel 1604–1657. Catalogus van de Tentoonstelling georganiseerd door het genootschap voor de Joodse wetenschap en het Joods Historich Museum, Amsterdam, 1957.
Catalogus van de tentoonstelling in de Bibliotheek van Ets Haim Gehouden van 21 t. en

m. 31 maart 1977 ter herinnering aan het verschijnen 350 jaar te voren van het eerste door Menasseh ben Israel te Amsterdam Gedrukte Hebreeuse boek, Amsterdam, 1977.

Caumont, A., *Étude sur la vie et les travaux de Grotius ou le Droit naturel et le Droit international*, Paris, 1862.

Cazaux, Y., *La Naissance des Pays-Bas*, Paris, 1983.

Chaunu, P., *Conquête et exploitation des Nouveaux Mondes* (XVIᵉ siècle), Paris, 1977².

——*La Violence de Dieu*, Paris, 1978.

Cohen, G. D., *Messianic Postures of Ashkenazim and Sephardim* (*Prior to Sabbethai Zevi*), New York, 1967 (= Leo Baeck Memorial Lecture 9).

Costa, Uriel da, *Exemplar humanae vitae*, trans. A. B. Duff and P. Kaan, Paris, 1926.

Dahl, F., *Amsterdam, Earliest Newspaper Centre of Western Europe: New Contributions to the History of the first Dutch and French Corantos*, The Hague, 1939.

Dehergne, J. and Leslie, D. D., *Juifs de Chine à travers la correspondance inédite des jésuites du dix-huitième siècle*, Paris–Rome, 1980.

Descartes, *Œuvres et Lettres*, Paris, Bibliothèque de la Pléiade, 1953.

Desmarets, S., *Chiliasmus enervatus ad D. P. Serarium*, Groningen, 1664.

Dieno, M., 'Rabbi Shlomo Ashkenazi e la Repubblica di Venezia' in *Atti dell'Istituto Veneto di Scienze, Lettere ed Arti*, ser. vii, vol. ix, 1897–8, pp. 616–37.

Dury, J., *An epistolicall discourse of Mʳ John Dury to Mʳ Thorowgood concerning his conjecture that the Americans are descended from the Israelites. With the history of a Portugall Iew Antonie Monterinos attested by Manasseh ben Israel to the same effect*, St. James, 27 Jan. 1649, in Thorowgood, T. *Jews in America . . .*, London, 1650.

Eisenberg, J., *Une histoire des Juifs*, Paris 1970.

Emmanuel, I. S. and S., *History of the Jews of the Netherlands Antilles*, Cincinnati, 1970.

Epstein, M., Prolegomenon to Godbey, J. H., *The Lost Tribes . . .*, New York, 1974.

——'New Light on the Ten Lost Tribes' in *Proceedings of the Sixth World Congress of Jewish Studies* (*Jerusalem, 1973*), ii, Jerusalem, 1975, pp. 21–30.

Eusden, J. D., *Puritans, Lawyers and Politics in Early Seventeenth Century England*, New Haven, Yale University Press, 1958.

Evans, A., *Light for the Jews or the means to convert them in answer to a book of theirs called the Hope of Israel written and printed by Manasseh ben Israel, chief agent for the Jews here*, London, 1656.

F. W. R., 'The Return of the Jews' in *South Place Magazine*, xi, no. 3, London, Dec. 1905, pp. 33–43.

Farinelli, A., *Marrano* (*storia di un vituperio*), Geneva, 1925.

Farrar, Abraham, *Declaração das seiscentas e treze Encommendanças da nossa Santa Ley*, Amsterdam, 1627.

Faucher, M., *Aguirre ou la fièvre de l'indépendance. Relation véridique de l'expédition de l'Omagua et de l'El Dorado (1560–1561) de Francisco Vazquez*. Traduction, présentation et notes, Paris, 1979.

Felgenhauer, P., *Bonum nuncium Israeli*, Amsterdam, 1655.

Franco Mendés, David, *Memorias do estabelecimento e progresso dos Judeos Portuguezes e Espanhoes nesta famosa citade de Amsterdam*. A Portuguese Chronicle of the History of the Sephardim in Amsterdam up to 1772 by . . . (*Studia Rosenthaliana*, ix, 1975, no. 2).

Fuks, L., and Fuks-Mansfeld, R. G., *Hebrew and Judaic Manuscripts in Amsterdam Public Collections. I. Catalogue of the Manuscripts of the Bibliotheca Rosenthaliana, University Library of Amsterdam; II. Catalogue of the Manuscripts of Ets Haim-Livraria Montezinos Sephardic Community of Amsterdam*, Leiden, 1973–5.

—— ——'Menasseh ben Israel as a Bookseller in the Light of New Data' in *Quaerendo*, xi, no. 1, Amsterdam, 1981, pp. 34–45.

—— ——*Hebrew Typography in the Northern Netherlands 1585–1815*, Leiden, 1984.

Fuks-Mansfeld, R. G., 'Sources for the History of the Jews in the Netherlands' in *Fourth Congress of Jewish Studies, Abstracts of Papers. Medieval and Modern Jewish History*, Jerusalem, 1965, pp. 23–4.

Gabriel ben Josue, *La Porte de la Pénitence*, Paris, 1879.

García, G., *Origen de los Indios de el Nuevo Mundo e Indias Occidentales*, Valencia, 1607.

García de Proodian, L., *Los judíos en América. Sus actividades en los Virreinatos de Nueva Castilla y Nueva Granada, Siglo XVII*, Madrid, 1966.

Gebhardt, C., *Die Schriften des Uriel da Costa*, Amsterdam–Heidelberg–London, 1922.

Geyl, Peter, *The Netherlands in the XVIIth Century 1609–1648*, London, 1961–4.

Ginsburger, M., 'Deux pourim locaux', in *Hebrew Union College Annual*, x, 1935, pp. 445–50.

Glaser, L., *Indians or Jews?*, Los Angeles, 1973.

Godbey, A. H., *The Lost Tribes. A Myth. Suggestions towards Rewriting Hebrew History*, New York, 1974.

Gollancz, H., 'A Contribution to the History of the Readmission of the Jews' in *Transactions of the Jewish Historical Society of England*, vi, 1908–1910, Edinburgh–London, 1912, pp. 189–204.

Graetz, H., *History of the Jews*, 1882–97.

Greenstone, J. H., *The Messiah Idea in Jewish History*, Philadelphia, 1906.

Granada, L. de, *Quarta parte de la introducción del symbolo de la fe*, Madrid, 1730.

Grotius, H., *Remonstrantie nopende de ordre dije in de landen van Hollandt ende Westvrieslandt dijent gestelt op de Joden*, pub. by J. Meijer, Amsterdam, 1949.

Gross, B., *Le Messianisme juif*, Paris, 1969.

Grunebaum-Ballin, P., *Joseph Naci duc de Naxos*, Paris–The Hague, 1968.

Hannover, N. N., *Le fond de l'Abîme*, Introduction, traduction et notes par J.-P.Osier, Paris, 1982.

Herrero García, M., *Ideas de los Españoles del siglo XVII*, Madrid, 1966.

Hill, Christopher, *Puritanism and Revolution*, London, 1958.

——*Antichrist in Seventeenth Century England*, London, 1971.

——*The World Turned Upside Down: Radical Ideas during the English Revolution*, London, 1972.

——*Change and Continuity in Seventeenth Century England*, London, 1974.

Huddleston, L. E., *Origins of the American Indians, European concepts*, Austin–London, 1967.

Huet, *Huetiana ou pensées diverses de M. . . .*, *Evesque d'Avranches*, Paris, 1722.

Hulsius, A., *Theologiae Iudaicae*, Breda, 1653.

Jennet, J., *Histoire de la République des Provinces-Unies des Païs-Bas depuis son établissement jusques à la mort de Guillaume III*, The Hague, 1704.

Joly, M., *Voyage fait à Munster en Westphalie et autres lieux voisins en 1646 et 1647*, Paris, 1670.

Kant, I., *Anthropologie*, Paris, 1964.

Kaplan, Y., 'The Attitude of the leadership of the Portuguese Community in Amsterdam to the Sabbatian Movement 1665–1671' in *Zion*, xxxix, 1974, nos. 3–4 (in Hebrew), pp. 198–216.

——*From Christianity to Judaism. The Life and Works of Isaac Orobio de Castro* (in Hebrew), Jerusalem, 1982; English translation in Littman Library, Oxford (in press).

——'The Social Functions of the *Herem* in the Portuguese Jewish Community of Amsterdam in the Seventeenth Century' in *Dutch Jewish History*, Jerusalem, 1984, pp. 111–55.

——'La communauté juive d' Amsterdam au XVIIᵉ siècle entre tradition et changement' (in Hebrew) in *Proceedings of the Israel National Academy*, vii, no. 6, Jerusalem, 1986, pp. 161–81.

Karpe, S., *Étude sur les origines et la nature du Zohar*, Paris, 1901.

Katz, D., *Philosemitism and the Readmission of the Jews to England 1603–1655*, Oxford, 1982.

Katz, J., 'A State within State. The History of an Antisemitic Slogan' in *The Israeli Academy of Sciences and Humanities, Proceedings*, iv (3), Jerusalem, 1969.

Kaufmann, D., 'David Carcassoni et le rachat par la communauté de Constantinople des juifs faits prisonniers durant la persécution de Chmielnicki' in *REJ*, xxv, 1892, pp. 202–16.

Kayserling, M., *Menasse ben Israel, sein Leben und Werken*, Berlin, 1861.

——*Biblioteca Española-Portugueza-Judaica*, Strasburg, 1861; reimpr. enlarged by Y. H. Yerushalmi, New York, 1971.

——'Une histoire de la littérature juive de Daniel Lévi de Barrios' in *Revue des Études Juives*, xviii, 1889, pp. 276–90.

Kessous, J., 'La "Chronique" de Joseph ha-Cohen', in *Archives juives*, xiii, 1977, pp. 44–53, 56–75.

Koen, E. M., 'Notarial Records Relating to the Portuguese Jews in Amsterdam up to 1639' in *Studia Rosenthaliana*, xi, 1977, no. 1, pp. 216–27, and no. 2, pp. 212–31.

Kolakowski, L., *Chrétiens sans Église. La conscience religieuse et le lien confessionnel au XVIIᵉ siècle*, Paris, 1965.

Korn, B. W., art. 'Philadelphia' in *Encyclopaedia Judaica*, 13, cols. 368–76.

Labrousse, E., *L'Entrée de Saturne au Lion*, The Hague, 1974.

La Peyrère, I. de, *Du rappel des Juifs*, n.p., 1643.

——*Praeadamitae sive exercitatio super versibus duodecimo decimotertio et decimoquarto capitis quinti Epistolae D. Pauli ad Romanos quibus inducuntur primi homines ante Adamum conditi*, n.p., 1655.

Leibniz, G. W., *Théodicée*, Paris, 1900.

León Templo, Juda, *Retrato del Templo de Selomoh*, Middleburg, 1642.

L'Estrange, H., *Americans no Iewes or the improbabilities that the Americans are of that race*, London, 1651.

Lévi de Montezinos, E., 'The Narrative of Aharon Levi, alias Antonio de Montezinos' in *The American Sephardi*, vii–viii, 1975, pp. 63–83.

Lévinas, E., *Difficile liberté. Essais sur le judaïsme*, Paris, 1963.

Levy, S., 'John Dury and the English Jewry' in *The Jewish Historical Society of England, Transactions*, iv, London, 1971.

Liebman, S. B., *Jews and the Inquisition of Mexico: The Great Auto de Je of 1649 as related by Mathias de Bocanegra S. J.*, Lawrence, Kan., 1974.

——*The Inquisitors and the Jews in the New World, Summary of procesos, 1500–1810 and Bibliographical Guide*, Coral Gables, Fla., 1976.

Lipkind, G., art. 'Dury, John', *Jewish Encyclopedia*, v, p. 19.

Lutaud, O., *Les Niveleurs, Cromwell et la république*, Paris, 1967.

——*Winstanley, socialisme et christianisme sous Cromwell*, Paris, 1976.

Luzzato, L., 'Un ambassadore ebreo nel 1574 (Salomone Askenazi)' in *Il Vessillo Israelitico*, xli, 1893, pp. 245–6.

Magnus, K., *Jewish Portraits*, London, 1905.

Maimonides, *The Guide for the Perplexed*, trans. M. Friedländer, 2nd edn., London, 1942.

Marcus, J. R., *The Colonial American Jew 1492–1776*, Detroit, 1970.

Maton, R., *Israel's Redemption redeemed or the Jewes generall and miraculous conversion to the faith of the Gospel, on purpose to satisfye all gain sayers and in particular Mʳ Alexander Petrie Minister of the Scottish Church in Rotterdam*, London, 1646.

Méchoulan, H., 'L'Altérité juive dans la pensée espagnole 1550–1650' in *Studia Rosenthaliana*, viii, 1974, no. 1, pp. 31–58 and no. 2, pp. 171–202.

——'Nouveaux éléments dans la controverse des statuts de pureté de sang en Espagne au XVIIe siècle' in *Studia Rosenthaliana*, 1976, no. 2, pp. 142–50.

——'Morteira et Spinoza au carrefour du socinianisme' in *REJ*, cxxxv, 1976, fasc. 1–3, pp. 51–65.

——'Spinoza face à quelques textes d'origine marrane' in *Raison présente*, no. 43, 1977, pp. 13–24.

——'Quelques remarques sur le chapitre III du *T.T.P.*' in *Revue Internationale de Philosophie*, nos. 119–20, 1977, pp. 198–216.

——'Menasseh ben Israël et l'expérience de l'exil', in *Philosophes ibéro-américains en exil*, Toulouse, 1977, pp. 71–8.

——'A propos de la visite de Frédéric-Henri, prince d'Orange, à la synagogue, une lettre inédite de Menasseh ben Israël à David de Wilhem suivie de la traduction française du discours de bienvenue' in *Lias*, v, 1978, no. 1, pp. 81–6.

——'Lorsque Saumaise consultait Menasseh ben Israël: deux lettres inédites du rabbin d'Amsterdam à l'humaniste de Leyde' in *Studia Rosenthaliana*, xiii, 1979, pp. 1–17.

——'Le problème du latin chez Menasseh ben Israël et quelques implications religieuses et politiques à propos d'une lettre inédite à Beverovicius', in *Studia Rosenthaliana*, xiv, 1980, no. 2, pp. 1–6.

——'Revélation, rationalité et prophétie. Quelques remarques sur le livre de Daniel' in *Raison Présente. Revue des Sciences philosophiques et théologiques*, 64, no. 3, Paris, July 1980, pp. 363–71.

——'Le herem à Amsterdam et "l'excommunication" de Spinoza' in *Cahiers Spinoza*, no. 3, winter 1979–80, pp. 117–134.

——'Philosémitisme et politique' in *Les Nouveaux Cahiers*, Paris, spring 1980, pp. 19–29.

——'Juif Hébreux et pharisiens dans le *Traité théologico-politique*' in *Spinoza nel 350° anniversario della nascita*, Urbino, 1982, pp. 439–60.

——'Menasseh ben Israël au centre des rapports judéo-chrétiens en Hollande au XVIIe siècle dans une lettre inédite d'Isaac Coymans à André Colvius' in *Studia Rosenthaliana*, xvi, no. 1, March 1982, pp. 21–4.

Meinsma, K. O., *Spinoza et son cercle*, Paris, 1983.

Melkman, J., 'Moshe Zacuto's Play Yesod ʿOlam' in *Studia Rosenthaliana*, i, 1967, no. 2, pp. 1–26.

Menasseh ben Israel, *De Creatione problemata XXX*, Amsterdam, 1635.

——*De termino vitae: libri tres*, Amsterdam, 1639.

——*Conciliador o de la conveniencia de los Lugares de la S. Escriptura que repugnantes entre si parecen.* pt. 1, Frankfurt, 1632; pt. 2, Amsterdam, 1641; pt. 3, Amsterdam, 1650; pt. 4, Amsterdam, 1651.

——*De la resurrección de los muertos, libros III en los quales se prueva la inmortalidad del alma y resurrección de los muertos*, Amsterdam, 1636.

——*Gratulacão de Menasseh ben Israel em nome de sua Nacão ao celcissimo Principe de Orange Frederique Henrique no sua vinda a nossa synagoga*, delivered at Amsterdam, 1642.

——*De la fragilidad humana y inclinación del hombre al pecado*, Amsterdam, 1642.

——*Piedra gloriosa o de la estatua de Nebuchadnesar*, Amsterdam, 1655.

——*Esperança de Israel*, Amsterdam, 1650.

——*Nišmat Ḥayim. De Immortalitate animae libri quatuor*, Amsterdam, 1652.

——*To his highnesse the Lord Protector of the Commonwealth of England, Scotland and Ireland. The humble Adresses of . . ., a divine and Doctor of Physics, in behalfe of the Jewish Nation*, London, 1655, repr. H. T. Dwight, Melbourne, 1868.

——*Vindiciae Judaeorum*, London, 1656.

Mendes dos Remedios, J., *Os Judeus portugueses em Amsterdam*, Coimbra, 1911.

Milton, J., *The Works of John Milton*, New York, 1936, vol. xii, pp. 333–36.

Misrahi, R., 'Le droit et la liberté politique chez Spinoza', in *Mélanges de Philosophie et de Littérature Juives*, i–ii, 1956–7, pp. 153–69.

Montezinos, A., alias Aaron Lévi, 'En Équateur chez les Indiens Juifs (1641)'. Introduction by G. Nahon, transl. and study by Charlotte Sémach, in *Les Nouveaux Cahiers*, 39, 1973, pp. 37–45.

Morais, H., *The Jews of Philadelphia, their history from the earliest settlement to the present times; a record of events and institutions and of leading members of the Jewish community in every sphere of activity*, Philadelphia, 1894.

Morteira, Saül Lévi, *Tratado de la verdad de le Ley de Moseh y Providencia de Dios con su pueblo*, Amsterdam, n.d.

Mugnier-Pollet, L., *La Philosophie politique de Spinoza*, Paris, 1976.

Nahon, G., Review of Katz, J., 'A State within a State. The History of an Antisemitic Slogan', Jerusalem, 1969, in *REJ*, cxxix, 1970, pp. 324–6.

——Review of Beinart, H., *Marranos on Trial by the Inquisition*, Tel Aviv, 1965, in *REJ*, cxxxix, 1970, pp. 286–99.

——'Les Sephardim, les Marranes, les inquisitions péninsulaires et leurs archives dans les travaux récents de I. S. Révah', in *REJ*, cxxxii, 1973, pp. 5–48.

——Review of Baron, S. W., *A Social and Religious History of the Jews*, xiv, New York, Philadelphia, 1973, in *REJ*, cxxxiv, 1975, nos. 1–2, pp. 184–94.

——'Les rapports des communautés judéo-portugaises de France avec celle d'Amsterdam au xviie et au xviiie siècles', in *Studia Rosenthaliana*, x, 1976, no. 1, pp. 37–78, and no. 2, pp. 175–88.

——'Les Marranes espagnols et portugais et les communautés juives issues du marranisme dans l'historiographie récente (1960–1975)', in *REJ*, cxxxvi, 1977, nos. 3–4, pp. 297–367.

——'Amsterdam métropole occidentale des Séfarades au XVIIᵉ siècle' in *Cahiers Spinoza*, no. 3, winter 1979–80, pp. 15–50.

——'La communauté polonaise face aux assauts des Cosaques en 1648 d'après *Yewen Mesulah* de Nathan ben Moïse Hannover (Venise 1653)' in *École Pratique des Hautes Études, section Sciences religieuses; Annuaire*. Résumés des conférences et travaux, Paris, vol. xc, 1981–2, pp. 261–4.

Namenyi, E., 'L'Esnoga d'Amsterdam (1675–1750)', in *Revue de la Pensée Juive*, ii, 1950, no. 5, pp. 74–85.

Nehama, J., *Dictionnaire du Judéo-espagnol*, Madrid, 1977.

Néher, A., *Jewish Thought and the Scientific Revolution of the Sixteenth Century: David Gans*, Littman Library, Oxford, 1986.

Netanyahu, B., *Don Isaac Abravanel, Statesman & Philosopher*, Philadelphia, 1968.

——*The Marranos of Spain from the Late XIVth to the Early XVIth Century according to Contemporary Hebrew Sources*, New York, 1973.

——'Did the Toledans in 1492 rely on a Real Royal Privilege?', in *American Academy for Jewish Research, Proceedings*, xliv, Jerusalem, 1977, pp. 93–125.

Nicholas, E., *Apology for the noble nation of the Jews*, London, 1648.

Odos, J.-P., *Recherches sur la vie et l'œuvre d'Isaac de La Peyrère (1595?–1676)*, thesis, Grenoble, 1974.

Oelman, T., 'António Enríquez Gómez's Romance al divín mártir Juda Creyente', in *Journal of Jewish Studies*, xxvi, 1975, nos. 1–2.

Offenberg, A. K., 'Bibliography of the works of Jacob Jehudah Leon (Templo)', in *Studia Rosenthaliana*, xii, nos. 1–2, July 1978, pp. 111–32.

Osier, J.-P., *D'Uriel da Costa à Spinoza*, Paris, 1983.

Paquot, J. N., *Mémoires pour servir à l'histoire littéraire des Provinces-Unies des Pays-Bas . . .*, Louvain, 1763.

Paul, R. S., *The Lord Protector: Religion and Politics in the life of Oliver Cromwell*, London, 1955.

Pelorson, J. M., 'Le Docteur Carlos Garcia et la colonie hispano-portugaise de Paris (1613–1619)', in *Bulletin hispanique*, 51, nos. 3–4, Bordeaux, July–Dec. 1969.

Perelman, Ch., *L'Empire rhétorique*, Paris, 1977.

Pereyra, A. I., *La Certeza del camino*, Amsterdam, 1666.

——*Espejo de la vanidad del mundo*, Amsterdam, 1671.

Phelan, J. L., *The Kingdom of Quito in the Seventeenth Century: Bureaucratic Politics in the Spanish Empire*, London, 1967.

Philosophes ibériques et ibéro-américains en exil, Toulouse, Publications of the University of Toulouse-Le Mirail, 1977.

Pieterse, W. Ch., *Inventaris van de Archieven der Portugees-Israelietische gemeente te Amsterdam 1614–1870*, Amsterdam, 1964.

——*350 jaar dotar. Gedenkschrift samengesteld door . . . ter gelengenheid van het 350-jarig bestaan in opdracht van de vereniging, Santa Companhia de dotar*

Orphas e Donzellas te Amsterdam, Amsterdam, 1965.

——*Daniel Levi de Barrios als geschiedschrijver van de Portugees-Israeliëtische gemeente te Amsterdam in zijn*, 'Triunpho del govierno popular', Amsterdam, 1968.

——*Livro de Bet Haim do Kahal Kados de Bet Yahacob*, Assen, 1970.

Pina, P. de, *Diálogo de los Montes*, Amsterdam, 1767.

Poliakov, L., *History of Anti-Semitism 1*, London (Littman Library), 1974.

Pollack, M., *Mandarins, Jews and Missionaries. The Jewish Experience in the Chinese Empire*, Philadelphia, 1980.

Popkin, R. H., 'Menasseh ben Israel and Isaac La Peyrère', in *Studia Rosenthaliana*, viii, no. 1, Jan. 1974, pp. 59–63.

Proceedings of the Symposium on Menasseh ben Israel, Tel-Aviv–Jerusalem, 1985, The Van Leer Foundation, to be published.

Puente Ojea, G., *Ideología e Historia : la formación del cristianismo como fenómeno ideológico*, Madrid, 1976.

Révah, I. S., 'Menasseh ben Israel et Ropicanefma de João de Barros', in *Revista de Filologia*, vol. 4, t. I–II, Rio de Janeiro, 1958, pp. 25–7.

——*Spinoza et le Dr. Juan de Prado*, Paris–The Hague, 1959.

——'Les Marranes', in *REJ*, cxviii, 1959–60, pp. 29–77.

——'Le premier règlement imprimé de la "Santa Companhia de dotar orfans e donzelas pobres"', in *Boletim internacional de bibliografia luso-brasileira*, iv, Lisbon, 1963, pp. 650–91.

——'Aux origines de la rupture spinozienne: Nouveaux documents sur l'incroyance dans la communauté judéo-portugaise d'Amsterdam à l'époque de l'excommunication de Spinoza', in *REJ*, cxxiii, nos. 3–4, July–Dec. 1964, pp. 359–83.

——'Langues et littérature du Midi de la France et de la Péninsule ibérique', in *École Pratique des Hautes Études, IVᵉ section, Annuaire 1966–1967*, Paris, 1967, pp. 338–41.

——'Fragments retrouvés de quelques éditions amstellodamoises de la version espagnole du rituel juif', in *Studia Rosenthaliana*, ii, 1968, no. 1, pp. 108–10.

——'Les Marranes portugais et l'Inquisition au xviᵉ siècle', in *The Sephardi Heritage*, ed. R. D. Barnett, London, 1971, pp. 479–526.

Reyner, W., 'Babylons ruining earthquake and the Restauration of Zion' (London, 1644), in *Fast Sermons to Parliament*, vol. 12, July–Sept, 1644, London, 1671.

Reznik, J., *Le duc Joseph de Naxos: contribution à l'histoire juive du XVIᵉ siècle*, Paris, 1936.

Rivkin, E., 'The Utilisation of Non-Jewish Sources for the Reconstruction of Jewish History', in *The Jewish Quarterly Review*, xlviii, 1957–8, pp. 183–203.

Rodríguez de Castro, J., *Biblioteca española de los escritores rabinos españoles*, Madrid, 1781, repr. Hildesheim–New York, 1977.

Rogers, P. G., *The Fifth Monarchy Men*, OUP, 1966.

Roth, C., art. 'Templo, Jacob, Judah (Aryeh) Leon', in *Encyclopaedia Judaica*, 15, cols. 998–9.

——*A Life of Menasseh ben Israel, Rabbi, Printer and Diplomat*, Philadelphia, 1934.

——'The Resettlement of the Jews in England', in *Three Centuries of Anglo-Jewish History*, London, 1964, pp. 3–25.

——'The Role of Spanish in the Marrano Diaspora', in *Studies in Book and Booklore. Essays in Jewish Bibliography and Allied Subjects*, n.p., 1972.

——*A History of the Marranos*, New York, 1974[4].

Rougemont, D. de, *L'Avenir est notre affaire*, Paris, 1977.

Sadler, J., *Rights of the Kingdom*, London, 1649.

Salomon, H. P., *Portrait of a New Christian, Fernão Alvares Melo*, Paris, 1982.

——*Os primeiros portugueses de Amsterdão. Documentos do Arquivo Nacional da Torre do Tombo 1595–1606*. Introdução, leitura, notas e cartas genealógicas, Braga, 1983.

——'The Portuguese Background of Menasseh ben Israel's Parents as Revealed through the Inquisitorial Archives at Lisbon', in *Studia Rosenthaliana*, xvii, 1983, no. 2, pp. 105–46.

Salvador, J., *Histoire des Institutions de Moïse et du peuple hébreu*, Paris, 1862.

Sarachek, J., *The Doctrine of Messiah in Medieval Jewish Literature*, New York, 1932.

Saraiva, A. J., *Inquisição e Cristãos Novos*, Oporto, 1969.

——'Antonio Vieira, Menasseh ben Israël et le cinquième empire', in *Studia Rosenthaliana*, vi, 1972, no. 1, pp. 25–57.

Sayous, A. E., *Le Rôle d'Amsterdam dans l'histoire du capitalisme commercial et financier*, Paris, 1939.

Schenk, W., *The Concern for Social Justice in the Puritan Revolution*, London, 1948.

Schmidt, E., *L'Histoire des Juifs à Anvers (Antwerpen)*, n.p., n.d. (Antwerp, 1969).

Schneider, W., *Adam Boreel*, Giessen, 1911.

Schoeps, H. J., *Philosemitismus im Barock*, Tübingen, 1952.

Scholem, G., *The Messianic Idea in Judaism*, London, 1971.

Schorsch, I., 'From Messianism to Realpolitik: Menasseh ben Israel and the Readmission of the Jews to England', in *Proceedings of the American Academy for Jewish Research*, 45, 1978, pp. 187–208.

Scult, M., *Millenial Expectations and Jewish Liberties: A Study of the Efforts to Convert the Jews in Britain up to the Mid-Nineteenth Century*, Leiden, 1978.

Séché, A., *Histoire de la Nation Juive des origines à nos jours*, Paris, 1944.

Serrurier, P., *Assertion du règne de Mille ans ou de la prospérité de l'Église du Christ en la terre pour servir de réponse au traité de M. Moïse Amyraut sur ce même sujet*, Amsterdam, 1657.

Sicroff, A. A., *Les Controverses des statuts de pureté de sang en Espagne du XVe au XVIIe siècle*, Paris, 1960.

Silva Rosa, J. S. da, *Geschiedenis der Portugeesche Joden te Amsterdam 1593–1925*, Amsterdam, 1925.

Silver, A. H., *A History of Messianic Speculation in Israel from the First through the Seventeenth Century*, New York, 1927.

Slotki, J. J., *Menasseh ben Israel, his Life and Times*, London, 1964.

Sokolow, N., *History of Zionism, 1600–1918*, London, 1919, reprint with a new Introduction by Arthur Hertzberg, New York, 1969.

Sorbière, S., *Soberiana ou bons mots, rencontres agréables, pensées judicieuses et observations curieuses de M . . .*, Paris, 1694.

Spencer, Sir E., *An Epistle to the learned Manasse ben Israel . . .*, London, 1650.

Spinoza, *Œuvres complètes*, Paris, Bibliothèque de La Pléiade, 1954.

Spinoza, Troisième Centenaire de la mort du philosophe, Institut Néerlandais, Paris, 1977.

Spizel, Th., *Elevatio Relationis Montezinianae de repertis in America Tribubus Israeliticis*, Basle, 1661.

Steinschneider, M., *Catalogus librorum hebraeorum in Bibliotheca Bodleiana*, Berlin, 1852–1860, repr. Hildesheim, 1964.

Stern, A., 'Menasseh ben Israël et Cromwell', in *REJ*, vi, 1883, pp. 96–111.

Swetschinski, D., 'The Portuguese Jews of Seventeenth Century Amsterdam Cultural Continuity and Adaptation', in *Essays in Modern Jewish History*, New York, 1982.

Teensma, B. N., 'De Levengeschiedenis van Abraham Perengrino alias Manuel Cardoso Macedo', in *Studia Rosenthaliana*, x, 1976, no. 1, pp. 1–36.

Thorowgood, T., *Iewes in America of probabilities that the Americans are of that race with the removall of some contrary reasonings and earnest desires for effectual endeavours to make them christians*, London, 1650.

Thurloe, J., *A Collection of the State Papers of John Thurloe Esq.*, London, 1742.

Tishby, I., 'Lettres de Rabbi Méir Rofé à Rabbi Abraham Rovigo', in *Sefer ha-Yovel li-Shnéur Zalman*, Jerusalem, 1960 (in Hebrew), pp. 71–130.

Toon, P., *Puritans, the Millennium and the Future of Israel: Puritain Eschatology*, Cambridge, 1970.

Touati, Ch., 'L'excommunication de Spinoza', compte-rendu de conférence, in *Annuaire de l'École Pratique des Hautes Études*, V^e section Sciences religieuses, 80–1, Paris, 1974, pp. 221–3.

——*La Pensée philosophique et théologique de Gersonide*, Paris, 1973.

Uri ben Aron ha-Levi, *Narracão da vinda dos Judeus espanhoes a Amsterdam*, Amsterdam, 1711.

Vajda, G., *Un recueil de textes historiques judéo-marocains*, Paris, Larose, 1951.

La Vie en Hollande au XVIIe siècle, tableaux, dessins, estampes, argenterie, monnaies, médailles et autres témoignages. Exposition organisée par l'Institut néerlandais, Paris, 1967.

Vignols, L., 'Le commerce hollandais et les congrégations juives à la fin du xviiᵉ siècle', in *Revue Historique*, XVᵗʰ year, 44, 1890, p. 330.

Vulliaud, P., *Spinoza d'après les livres de sa bibliothèque*, Paris, 1934.

——*La Fin du monde*, Paris, 1952.

Wall, E. van der, 'Petrus Serrarius (1600–1669) et l'interprétation de l'Ecriture', in *Cahiers Spinoza* no. 5, pp. 187–217, 1984.

——'Three letters by Menasseh ben Israel to John Durie. Philo-judaism and the "Spes Israelis"', in *Nederlands Archief voor Kerkgeschiedenis*, 65, pp. 46–63, 1985.

Wehr, G., and Deghaye, P., *J. Böhme*, Paris, 1977.

Weil, G. E., *Élie Levita, humaniste et massorète (1469–1569)*, Leiden, 1963.

Weill, G., 'Charles Netter ou les oranges de Jaffa', in *Les Nouveaux Cahiers*, no. 21, Summer 1970, pp. 1–36.

Wilson, Charles H., *The Dutch Republic and the Civilization of the Seventeenth Century*, London, 1968.

Wistnitzer, A., 'The Merger agreement and Regulations of Congregation Talmud Tora of Amsterdam 1638–1639', in *Historia Judaica*, xx, 1958, pp. 109–32.

Witsius, H., *Aegyptiaca . . .*, Amsterdam, 1683.

Wolf, L., *Menasseh ben Israel's Mission to Oliver Cromwell*, London, 1901.

Worthington, J., *The Diary and Correspondence of John Worthington*, edited by James Crossley, Cheltham Society, vols. xiii and xxxvi.

Yerushalmi, Y. H., *From Spanish Court to Italian Ghetto: Isaac Cardoso. A Study in Seventeenth Century Marranism and Jewish Apologetics*, New York–London, 1971.

Zac, S., 'Spinoza et l'État des Hébreux', in *Speculum Spinozanum 1677–1977*, London, 1978, pp. 543–71.

Zacuto, M., *Yesod Olam*, Berlin, 1874 and Livorno, 1874 (in Hebrew).

Zumthor, P., *La Vie quotidienne en Hollande au temps de Rembrandt*, Paris, 1960.

MANUSCRIPT SOURCES

Bibliotheek der Rijksuniversiteit te Leiden, MS Br. F. II, ep. 801.

Bibliotheek der Universiteit te Amsterdam, Catalogue.

Correspondence and Papers of Samuel Hartlib, 1600–1662, Manuscript Collection of the University of Sheffield, 34/4/1–30. All citations from the Hartlib manuscripts are made with the kind permission of Lord Delamere.

Déclaration royale relative aux Juifs portugais de Bayonne, Archives nationales, E 3706¹², no. 198.

Inquisition Document concerning Antonio de Montezinos, Archivo Histórico Nacional, Madrid, Section Inquisición, libro 102, fol.158–9.

Libro dos Acuerdos A, Archives municipales d'Amsterdam, PA 334.19.

Pinto, M. de, (tr.), *Espérance d'Israël, œuvre composée avec une grande curiosité par*

Menasseh ben Israël, teologien et Philosopho (sìc) *hebreu, laquelle traite du dispersement des dix tribeus et leur reduction à la patrie. Dediée aux Seigneurs Parnasim de la Congregation de T, T, d'Amsterdam.*

——The Hague, 5484–1724 (Fuks, L., and Fuks-Mansfeld, R. G., *Hebrew and Judaic Manuscripts in Amsterdam Public Collections*, vol. I, no. 631, p. 279).

Library of the University of Amsterdam, *Catalogue des manuscrits de l'Église remontrante*, vii, 1923, no. 40, pp. 94–6.

Royal Library of the University of Leiden, MS Br. F. II, ep. 801.

Index of Place and Proper Names

N.B. Place names are italicized.

Printed and bound by CPI Group (UK) Ltd, Croydon, CR0 4YY

13/04/2025

14656581-0002